MIND-BODY COMMUNICATION IN HYPNOSIS

THE SEMINARS, WORKSHOPS, AND LECTURES OF MILTON H. ERICKSON

Volume III

Edited by
Ernest L. Rossi
Margaret O. Ryan

IRVINGTON PUBLISHERS, INC.
NEW YORK

ISBN 0-8290-1805-0

Typography by Dimensional Graphics, Roselle, New Jersey

Printed in the United States of America

CONTENTS

PREFATORY NOTES

Regarding References

Because of the informal nature of the material presented in this series, the editors have used footnotes placed at the end of the book. However, Part III of this volume utilizes the standard APA format for referencing because of the comprehensive research orientation of the material.

Regarding the Index

While the editors continue to disavow any effort to systematize Erickson's material in these volumes, we have made a careful effort to catalogue the subject matter in two ways. First we have provided frequent headings which appear on every page or two to focus attention on the major theme that Erickson is presenting. *These headings are the editors' efforts to catalogue—not Erickson's.* The contents in these headings are then used to select key subject words for the index. *The index is thus the key to the subject matter in these volumes*, and can serve as a reference tool for future scholars.

Regarding the Typesetting

To indicate Erickson's frequent shifts of attention during demonstrations from subjects to audience and back to subjects, all verbatim trance material spoken directly to subjects is in bold face type. His shifts of focus back to the audience are indicated by additional spacing and regular (Roman) type. It should be noted, however, that although addressing the audience, many of Erickson's remarks are being directed to the subjects as forms of indirect suggestions. Lastly, any added commentary by the editors (indented from ongoing text) was written after Erickson's death and without the benefit of prior discussion with him.

LIST OF TABLES

INTRODUCTION

This volume on mind-body communication in hypnosis contains much of the source material wherein Milton H. Erickson first expressed his original views on psychosomatic medicine and healing. It will be of vital interest to students, therapists, and practitioners of therapeutic hypnosis who want to integrate Erickson's approaches with the current breakthroughs that are taking place in psychoneuroimmunology and the new mind-body methods of holistic healing.

The issues dealt with in this volume are fundamental. Many laboratory researchers believe we are in the midst of a profound revolution that is resolving the mind-body problem. The Cartesian dualism that has separated mind and body in philosophy, psychology, and medicine for the past 400 years is dissolving. Recent well-designed research experiments are demonstrating the psychobiological pathways by which mind modulates the biochemistry of the body. We are learning how the languages of mind (thought, imagery, emotion, and sensation) are communicating with the languages of the body (hormones, messenger molecules, information substances).

The rapidity with which this new research is providing a scientifically valid basis for constructing new belief systems about our potentials for self-generated health and healing has taken most practitioners by surprise. Patients are coming to therapists with higher levels of expectation about the possibilities of mind-body healing; therapists are sometimes at a loss as to how they can support and facilitate the realization of these possibilities.

It is precisely in this area of practical hypnotherapeutic methodology that Erickson offers a useful guide. Part One of this volume, "The Hypnotic Alteration of Physiological Functioning,"* illustrates a wide range of his approaches to mind-body communication and healing. In this presentation, Erickson begins by distinguishing between the normal and hypnotic ranges of control over a number of psychophysiological processes regulated by the autonomic nervous system, such as blood flow and pupil dilation. He goes on to illustrate how therapeutic hypnosis can affect endocrinal and hormonal processes that regulate menstrual functioning and breast development. He demonstrates how the most effective approach is not by direct suggestion but, rather, by utilizing the patient's personal psycho-dynamics and emotional needs. The hypnotic alteration of physiological functions thus proceeds along a holistic pathway that recognizes how symptoms and illnesses can be important aspects of a person's overall psychological development. This is most vividly exemplified in the case of a teenager who may have been on the brink of schizophrenia. Her presenting problem was her concern about her complete lack of breast development. Hormonal injections had failed to induce any biological development, but Erickson's balanced approach of utilizing the girl's general emotional situation was effective in facilitating both her physical and psychological growth. Erickson discusses how these approaches can be effective in an extraordinary range of applications with individuals, children, couples, and families.

In 1961 Erickson presented the lecture and demonstration in Part Two that we have entitled, "Symptom-Based Approaches in Mind-Body Problems." In this presentation, one immediately senses a significant advance in Erickson's maturing views of therapeutic hypnosis as the communication of ideas that can help people utilize their own mind-body processes for healing. He discusses a wide array of problems, ranging from asthma and migraine head-

---

*An hour-and-a-half audio cassette of a portion of this 1952 presentation accompanies the volume. Much of the material given in this tape served as a basis of his 1977 paper, "Control of Physiological Functions by Hypnosis."

aches to polio, and he illustrates how the clinician can explore the functional dynamics of a symptom. He discusses some of the ways in which he engages the patient's own unconscious processes to facilitate symptom resolution, as opposed to relying upon a preconceived theory of how the therapy should proceed. In a variety of ways, Erickson demonstrates how he helps patients explore and "play" with their symptomatology as a prelude to transforming and resolving it. There can be no better training for the hypnotherapist than to learn how to facilitate these very flexible and perpetually creative processes of mind-body communication and healing. Erickson emphasized the need for research into the physiological basis of therapeutic hypnosis with these words (Erickson, 1980a, pp. 322-323):

> *Hypnosis is a state of awareness in which you offer communication with understandings and ideas to a patient and then you let them use those ideas and understandings in accord with their own unique repertory of body learnings, their physiological learnings.* Once you get them started, they can then proceed to utilize a wealth of other experiences. I do not know how that patient got rid of a migraine headache that she had on the right side repeatedly over a period of 11 years, but she did lose it right there in the office. She proceeded to develop a left-sided headache, which I was able to hypnotically suggest away. The left-sided migraine, as the right-sided one, was willingly given up by some utilization of body learnings. I don't know what they were. I don't know if she dissociated from her headache, or whether she just displaced the headache, or reinterpreted the headache, or just forgot the headache, or whether she suppressed the pain impulse that gave her a perception of headache. I know only that I presented ideas intended to stimulate the patient to behave in accord with actual body learnings over a long period of time.
> .... It is more productive scientifically to wonder what the processes are that constituted that experience. I fully recog-

nize that you and I cannot apply the most useful concepts nor give the right terms as yet. We haven't examined the items of behavior most meaningfully, perhaps not defined these items of behavior in the most useful language.

Erickson recognized that his time was not yet ripe for a psychophysiological understanding of therapeutic hypnosis because we simply did not have enough knowledge about basic biology. In Part Three of this volume, I propose that we are rapidly accumulating this needed knowledge; indeed, the time may be at hand for making a fresh effort to conceptualize the psychobiology of therapeutic hypnosis. Recent research into the mind modulation of the autonomic, endocrine, and immune systems provides the basis for understanding many of the seemingly impossible results of hypnotherapy. The scientific validation of these new channels of mind-body communication is reviewed, and a *state-dependent memory and learning theory of therapeutic hypnosis* is outlined as a means of integrating these newly recognized patterns of information flow.

Paradoxically, this new research is providing a scientific basis for the ancient dreams and practices of alchemists, shamans, and spiritual healers of all times and cultures. It validates the view that psyche, mind, and brain are pervasively integrated in modulting body processes in health and illness. The "miracle cures," spontaneous remissions of lethal diseases, and placebo effects that seemed inexplicable to the scientific mind only a few years ago can now be understood as manifestations of mind-body information systems that extend far beyond the limitations formerly placed on the central nervous system. Part Three of this volume was thus written as a state-of-the-art exploration of the therapeutic possibilities that may be on our near horizon. It is hoped that the reader will receive it in this spirit, and perhaps take some further steps to facilitate its actualization.

Ernest Lawrence Rossi
Malibu, 1986

x

PART I

HYPNOTIC ALTERATIONS OF
PHYSIOLOGICAL FUNCTIONING*

Hypnotic Control of Physiological Functions

Hypnotic Techniques as a Function of
Patient-Therapist Psychodynamics

My topic for this afternoon is the control of physiological functions by hypnosis. I am also listed for a later discussion of hypnotic approaches to therapy. Actually in any approach to physiological control one also makes use of therapeutic approaches. I am not going to try to make a differentiation between the two topics, or give you a pat lecture on either. Both topics involve a question of techniques, and both are concerned with the adequate and desirable functioning of the individual as a personality. Therefore, while the two presentations will be distinctly separate, they will also overlap—although I shall try to place emphasis accordingly.

First of all, it must be borne in mind that one's appreciation for and understanding of the normal or the usual is requisite for any understanding of the abnormal or the unusual, just as a knowledge of normal physiology constitutes a background for a knowledge

*Hypnosis seminars conducted in Los Angeles, California, in 1952. Audio cassette of this transcript accompanies the volume.

1

and understanding of pathological conditions. Similarly, a knowledge of the approach to an understanding of normal physiology constitutes a means of approaching an understanding of abnormal physiology. And any approach to either must be based upon a knowledge of techniques, perhaps fundamental in character, but varying according to the conditions. I want to amplify that point. When I say that techniques vary according to conditions, I mean that you vary them according to the personality of the individual, according to the psychological situation at that particular time, and according to the psychological situation of the hypnotist as well as of the patient or the subject. One simply cannot handle these matters without having an understanding of both at the time.

Now since I'm a psychiatrist as well as a psychologist—but I'm primarily engaged in psychiatric practice—I shall rely mostly upon my experience as a psychiatrist.

I am going to try to avoid any reference to my previous publications as much as possible. They are easily available to you and it would only use up your time to keep referring to them; however, I shall make reference to them occasionally.

Nonhypnotic Alterations in Physiological Functions

Voluntary Control of Vasomotor, Pupillary, and Capillary Fluctuations

I shall begin by considering the matter of controlling physiological functions. I don't think this type of problem should be taken too lightly. In the laboratory I've seen a hypnotized subject with his hands in the plethysmogragh [a device for measuring blood flow] respond excellently to my instruction, "Make your right hand smaller and your left hand larger." Indeed, the blood vessels shrunk in one hand and dilated in the other. Now, that seemed to be an excellent demonstration of the possibility of bringing about physiological changes by hypnotic measures. But when I actually questioned the subject, his reaction—his explanation—was, "I can do that without being in a trance"; and he very neatly and carefully proceeded to demonstrate the same phenomenon. What was his way of [achieving these physiological alterations]? The man had a very, very vivid imagination. He would think about holding ice and getting his hand very, very cold; and he would think about immersing the other hand in very warm water. Natually he got his vasomotor dilation, and the hypnosis had nothing to do with it!

I've also seen subjects who could dilate the pupil of one eye and contract the pupil in the other eye while looking at the same light in the hypnotic trance state. My question, however, was: "Can you do that whenever you want to?" Then I would have others investigate (but not tell them my suspicions), thus removing my presence [and ensuring the most objective results possible]. Surely enough, there are people who can look at a light and dilate one pupil while contracting the other—not a hypnotic phenomenon, just simply a matter of personal, voluntary control of a physiological function.

Take these anesthesias that you can develop in hypnosis. I've seen people [develop them just as adequately] in the ordinary waking state. When I was working my way through college, I met a workman who would offer to stick pins through his skin for a package of cigarettes. I had enough knowledge of psychology at that time to know about capillary contractions with pain reactions. And this workman would stick the pins through the skin of his legs, his cheeks, and so on, with absolutely no pain reaction. He didn't need hypnosis to do it. So I'm always exceedingly suspicious [of jumping to the conclusion that hypnosis is the cause of this or that phenomenon].

I remember one carefully controlled experiment about inducing blisters on the arm. The experiment was carried out by a friend of mine in the army who wrote me about it in great detail. He explained that he had kept his subject under absolute observation for 24 hours, and the subject had produced a blister on the exact area of his arm that had been marked with a pencil. Now my first question was: Was the subject kept under observation for 24 hours? He was, so then I got extremely specific about it. How many times a day did the man go to the lavatory? Who went with him and who watched him? Surely enough, the man had had some cigarettes concealed which he merely lit in the lavatory, thereby producing his blister. But it certainly wasn't hypnotic in orgin. Twenty-four-hour observation means *24 hours* per day, to be scientifically accurate.

Normal and Hypnotic Psychophysiological Responses

Voluntary Physiological Alterations in Perspiration, Pulse Rate, and Blood Pressure

Another issue is the question of defining normal physiological reactions. What do you know about them? How readily can you decide what is normal and what is induced? I think one of the best approaches to this problem can be illustrated by the following example.

Perspiring is a very common phenomenon. You can have a nice cool room, and you can talk to your subject about various topics without him showing any signs of perspiration. Last week one of my patients commented on how cool my office was, and how comfortable he felt sitting in it. We talked about various other subjects, but my idea in talking to him was to see if I could induce a sudden flow of perspiration. I really wanted to see if I could do that.

Now he was sitting in the chair, comfortable and at ease—decidedly at ease. We were talking about his hometown, the people he knew there, and so on. Casually I threw in a question about his wife's relative. Immediately he yanked out his handkerchief and started wiping the perspiration off his face. I had gotten the name of that relative from a letter his wife had written to me. The man wiped his brow again and said, "What happened—has the cooler been turned off? This room is awfully warm." And I said, "It's probably some reaction you're having—just never mind."

And on we went, discussing a trip that relative had made. Then I mentioned that I had heard his name mentioned at luncheon to-day—Dr. S. So I mentioned "Louisville, Kentucky," and Dr. S was there. Immediately my patient started perspiring again. He wondered why. Well I knew why: his wife's letter had provided the explanation that clarified to me why my patient should perspire at the mere mention of Louisville, Kentucky, and at the mere mention of his wife's relative. Now I think that sort of [indirect] physiological control is much more reliable than when you try to have somebody [directly] increase his heartbeat or his blood pressure, or something of that sort.

One of my subjects could increase his pulse rate by 10 points when in a trance if you asked him to. But he also could do the very same thing in the ordinary waking state at the request of a friend of mine whom he didn't know was a friend of mine. And indeed, he increased it 20 points, with a range of error between 1 and 3 points. He could also increase his blood pressure, and hypnosis had nothing to do with it. How did he do it? He fantasized walking up a certain hill and that would raise his pulse rate a certain amount; then he would fantasize running up that same hill—and he would really fantasize it very vividly—and that would raise his pulse rate as much as 20 points.

This same subject could raise his blood pressure by another very simple mechanism: that of contracting his abdominal muscles, and you weren't able to notice it under his clothes. It was beautifully done, and he himself was not aware that he was doing it. Now I put this subject in a hospital bed to check on that blood pressure, and I had a nurse check on his abdominal musculature at the same time [that I was taking his blood pressure]. He thought the nurse was just giving him a massage or something of that sort, but she was actually testing his muscles. He had a skin condition and that was perfectly proper. He really could raise his blood pressure by the very simple measure of contracting his abdominal musculature, [and hypnosis had nothing to do with it].

As you know, patients get terribly tense in insurance examinations; their muscles tighten up and their blood pressure goes up. So you take the blood pressure in the beginning of the examination, and then you take it again when the examination is finished—and you find that it has dropped 20 points, even 40 points, because the tension has gone. So *any physiological manifestation that you can perform in the ordinary waking state I do not think should be credited to hypnotic suggestion.* I have had subjects who could raise their blood pressure, increase their rate of perspiration, things of that sort, simply by thinking about things that made them angry. Watching Lester Beck's film this afternoon, I thought about subjects who had made use of similar situation by deliberately recalling a past traumatic experience: suddenly they broke out in a cold sweat; suddenly they had altered their blood pressure. And that *isn't* hypnotic suggestion; that is normal physiological behavior.

Indirect Methods in Hypnotic Research

Accepting and Utilizing a Spontaneous Stocking Anesthesia in Broken Feet

I think the most valid changes in physiological functions are those that are brought about by unconscious processes. Mentioning "Louisville, Kentucky" to my patient was a much more valid measure of producing a physiological change than any direct effort. In fact, *it is my feeling that one should resort to indirect methods in hypnotic reasearch as much as possible in order to prevent the subject from cooperating with you intentionally and complaisantly; in order to prevent him from giving you the desired results. The results you really want are those that come about as a genuine response to suggestion, not because your subject helps you along.*[2]

I'd like to illustrate this point. A brilliant GI student was failing badly in all of his courses. To join a beer party one evening, he rather recklessly leapt down a flight of stairs. Two weeks later he came to the Veterans Administration Hospital, with which I was associated, for an examination. He complained that he tired much too easily and that he was worried about his heart. Well, my examination soon disclosed that he had a stocking anesthesia—a complete numbness of both feet. I examined his feet and made my own diagnosis: he had fractured bones in both of them. I promptly had another physician examine him, who also reached the same conclusion: fractured bones. We contacted the X-ray technician and explained to him what we wanted done. Meanwhile I gave the

6

student a very, very nice talk about his skin condition—about the swelling of the skin on his feet, and I told him that I was going to have the X-ray technician give him a skin treatment. The technician cooperated very, very nicely, and we got an X-ray which verified the fracture of the bones in his feet. So there was no doubt about it. But that stocking anesthesia was a very important matter. [How did it come about so spontaneously?]

In investigating the patient's past history, we discovered that he would have a personality collapse if he cut his finger, if he nicked himself shaving—why, he was practically laid up for a day or so from a little razor nick. He was the type of person who just simply collapsed at the slightest physical injury. His discharge from the army had been a medical one, based on that. And yet this same man had been walking around with badly fractured bones in his feet for two weeks. How? He unconsciously produced certain changes in himself that enabled him to continue to attend his classes.

Now what I did was to put him in a trance and give him a long and deceptive story about his skin disease, my worry about it, and the treatment for it: medicated gauze protected by a cast with iron supports in it so that he could walk around. And so he attended his classes and got along just fine. [What was I doing?] I was accepting his particular physiological condition. I wasn't trying to correct it, but instead I was giving him a type of invalidism from which he wouldn't have to collapse. In the trance state I gave him an overwhelming urge to want to enjoy his skin condition and the numbness in his feet, and to preserve that enjoyment until the medicated gauze had healed everything completely. I did that so that as new sensations of healing developed in his feet, he would not have to drop out of school and become an irascible invalid. Now, if I had told him that he had broken bones in his feet, he would have been thoroughly incapacitated in bed. As it was, he made A's in all of his courses—as he should have done, for he was a brilliant chap.

Eds: There is an inconsistency between the presentation of this case, in which Erickson does not tell the GI he has fractured bones, and his later published summary in which he

7

says the GI was informed about the fractures.[3] The editors suspect that the earlier and more detailed presentation in this 1952 version is probably the more correct one. Sometimes Erickson would alter a case to use it as a vehicle for indirect suggestions to a particular audience, but we cannot determine if that is true for either of these versions.

Dreams Facilitating Comfortable Menstruation

Utilizing Time Distortion and Hypnotic Amnesia to Correct a Painful Menstrual Syndrome

Now another example is a patient in her thirties who had an irregular menstrual cycle. Each period resulted in severe headaches, vomiting, gastrointestinal disturbances, and actual invalidism for five days—she had no invalidism the first day, and no invalidism the last day. She wanted medical help but she did not want psychotherapy.

She consented to go into a trance to please me, and I was perfectly willing to be pleased. I carefully induced a deep trance and instructed her that on any Saturday night she chose she would have a dream in which time would be telescoped. I explained that in this dream she would experience a whole week's menstrual invalidism; that is, the dream would seem to last five whole days, during which time she would be invalided—she would dream that she was vomiting, had diarrhea and cramps, and everything else that went with her past history. And yet she would sleep soundly and awaken the next morning rested, refreshed, and energetic. I concluded by suggesting an amnesia for the entire dream experience, and by suggesting that the dream experience itself would result in a satisfactory menstrual period later.

Two weeks later she was surprised to find herself mentruating without any difficulty, without any invalidism, without pain or discomfort. She came to me and asked me what I had done—what had happened—for she had a lifelong experience of painful menstruation. And here she was feeling like a queen, perfectly comfortable, perfectly at ease. Why *didn't* she have cramps, she asked me. What was wrong?? Now in the trance state she knew exactly what I had done, but consciously she had no awareness whatsoever of it. Since our session—and that was several years ago—she has had no painful menstrual periods whatsoever. Everything has gone along perfectly all right. She's regular in her menstruation; there is no pain, no difficulty, no distress. I think that this example readily comes under the heading of the control of physiological functioning, but it is an indirect measure. The history certainly warrants the belief that if I hadn't used an indirect measure, her pattern of painful menstruation would have continued.

Hypnotic Facilitation of Breast Development

Enhancing Blood Flow and Feminine Identification in a Possible Case of Latent Schizophrenia: Utilizing Ideosensory ("that tremendous surging feeling") and Ideomotor (touching her hand to her shoulder) Processes

A third example is that of a normal 18-year-old girl who was very, very distressed over the fact that she had not shown any evidence of breast development.[3] Her father was a physician, and at the age of 12 he had loaded her up with every kind of hormone possible. Yet there was no breast development of any sort; still none by 13, or 14, or 15. He finally quit the treatments and just gave up hope. By the age of 18, the girl was making an extremely schizoid adjustment, withdrawing completely. She had an extremely disagreeable, unpleasant mother, and she just hated her mother thoroughly. So her doctor-father sent her to me, asking me, "What can you do to keep my daughter from becoming schizophrenic?"

Well, it took me about an hour to get the girl to tell me herself that she had no breast development whatsoever. She did agree, however, to go into a trance, and so I spent a couple more hours putting her into a deep trance very cautiously, very gently, very indirectly. Then while she was in a deep trance state I explained to her how ignorant a man is about what a breast feels like; that he can't have any idea of how it feels to grow a breast; that he can't

9

know what a breast feels like during a menstrual period; that he cannot really know what a woman's nipple feels like during menstruation. And I spent a good deal of time presenting that sort of idea to her very repetitiously.

Next I explained in a similarly repetitious manner that since she was a girl, somehow or other she must have the right nerves, the right blood vessels with which to grow breasts. I brought out anatomy pictures to show how vascular distribution differs in the chest of the male from that of the female; and I went all through that in a most thorough way. I impressed upon her that she did have a background for breast development, and that what I wanted of her was a complete amnesia for everything I had said to her in the trance state. But when she was alone in the privacy of her room— especially at night where her mother would not annoy her, because her mother was very rigid about sleeping in a certain part of the house—she would someway, somehow, get a *tremendous surging feeling in the breast area; and suddenly, somehow, her rudimentary nipples would feel warm, and she would have the feeling that something was happening.* I told her very honestly that I didn't know what that feeling was, but that *she* could find out; and that she could get *that tremendous surging feeling,* that growing feeling or whatever it was, and then drift off to sleep very comfortably.

The other point I added was to tell her that I could put my hand on my shoulder; but when you ask a woman to do it—and I exaggerated [the motion]—she does it *this* way [Erickson apparently demonstrates the way in which a woman's arm must bend around the breasts in order to reach the shoulder]. I told her that she would have a tremendous unconscious need to put her hand on her shoulder in that fashion. Yet she would not be aware of that need. During the course of the day, evening, wherever she was—if she happened to get a mosquito bite up here, or an itch—she would unconsciously raise her elbow [in this new manner]. During the course of the next few weeks, she would have a thorough conviction that she was growing breasts—*really growing breasts.*

I saw her once a week. We usually talked it over; and usually I put her in a trance and said: "We've discussed this matter before; and I'm just reminding you that we've discussed it. Why should we talk about it any more? I just want you to know that we've really discussed it, and that you're really going to carry out *all* my instructions—even though I don't really know what I've instructed you to do."

I saw her once a week for two months, at which time she had very well developed breasts. In the trance state she told me that she had them, and wanted to know if I wished to examine them to see if they were real. I told her no, it wasn't necessary, because she could do all of that examining, and that she could be much more critical of her breasts than I would be. Her breasts belonged to her, and she should reserve for herself the right to criticize them.

As I said, I stopped seeing her at the end of two months. At the end of three months, she came back and said: "Dr. Erickson, I came to see you a while ago. I was awfully withdrawn. I liked to sit in the corner, hide behind the piano, and I avoid all company. I just wanted to report to you that I don't do that any more. I'm dating regularly." Her father, the medical man, came to me and said, "What hormones did you use?" I told him I was a variation of the Christian Scientist—that I heal from a distance! [Laughter]

Now just exactly what did I do to that girl? I think that I brought about a change in physiological functioning; I certainly produced tremendous changes in her. She's got decidedly well-developed breasts; she's very proud of herself; her schizoid state has been corrected; and I have her father's statement that he himself has examined those breasts and they are perfectly good breasts. And, besides, I have the word of a number of young men who said they were perfectly good breasts!

How much did raising the elbow in that fashion contribute to her breast development? How much did that idea of a surging feeling in the chest wall contribute? There was nothing more vague, really, [than the ideas I presented to her]. Yet she'd had hormone therapy discontinued several years before; she had menstruated regularly since the age of 13; but she just hadn't developed breasts. And that was all there was to it. But in two months' time she did develop breasts. I think it's fairly reasonable to assume that my suggestions brought about in her a control of her physiological functioning.

Eds: In this case Erickson facilitated what today we would call a new "state-dependent memory and learning system": a *physiological process* (increased blood flow) was associated with a *psychological process* (a new self-awareness and feminine identification) in a manner that lead to breast development. See Part IV of this volume for more details about this psychophysiological approach to hypnotherapy.

An Emotional Double Bind

Utilizing the Patient's Personality to Facilitate Consummation of a Marriage: Erickson's "Mistake": The Defensive Use of Menstruation

Now another case that I will cite is the following. A young man married an exceedingly attractive girl. The man's weight at the time of the wedding was 170 pounds. Nine months later he came into see me weighing 120 pounds. He said that he couldn't stand it any longer and he wanted to have a psychiatric interview with me. I interviewed him, and his story was very simple. It was to this effect:

"Every time I try to consummate my marriage, my bride goes into a hysterical panic. It's just driving me crazy—I can't take it much longer. I lie awake nights wondering how to please her, and every night she promises me, and every night she goes into a hysterical panic."

I told him to bring his wife into see me, and for her to bring every bit of information possible about her menstrual cycle. The astonishing thing was that she had started to menstruate at the age of 11, and she had kept a diary recording each period thereafter—for all those years. According to that diary, she menstruated regularly every 33rd day, and she usually began to menstruate between ten and eleven o'clock in the morning. Now when you look through a diary of that sort, you wonder about its owner's personality. Then you can understand more about her panic reactions, more about how she must have felt when her husband wanted to consummate the marriage, and so on.

I had an interview with her husband, and then I had an interview with her in which I made a rather serious mistake. I discussed sex relations with her, and I really laid down the law to her thoroughly: it was to be an evening of fun. Then I got the two of them together, and I really laid down the law to them: they were to consummate their marriage that night, as soon as they got home, 17 days before the wife's next period. They lived two miles from my office. Halfway home the woman started to menstruate! [Laughter] Now that sort of reaction is not too uncommon medically—an unexpected early menstruation to avoid the consummation of a marriage, the failure of menstruation because of a desired pregnancy, and so on. But here was this girl with a long history of exceedingly regular menstrual periods—verified by that diary which she had kept—beginning her menstrual period that night at about eight o'clock, 17 days ahead of time.

She had a normal period. When she came back at the end of the period, I apologized very greatly for my error, my mistake, my failure, really, to understand. I was right in apologizing, because I had failed to understand. I now told her that she and her husband should consummate their marriage, but that they could do it on Saturday night or Sunday night, or Monday or Tuesday or Wednesday or Thursday. I would prefer *Friday* or Saturday or Sunday or Monday, but *I would prefer Friday*. I went through that routine several times to drive home a point that she couldn't possibly recognize consciously.

> Eds: This is an example of the type of emotional bind Erickson used therapeutically long before Bateson, Jackson, Haley, and Weakland coined the term "double bind."[4]

Of course, nothing happened Saturday night or Sunday night or Monday, Tuesday, or Wednesday nights. But, you know, that's getting awfully close to Friday night, and she had already demonstrated that I couldn't dictate anything to her. And when I said I preferred Friday, and nothing had happened by Wednesday night—well, she had no choice because I'd also mentioned Saturday and Sunday, too. So she fixed me! They consummated their marriage, have two nice children, and are happily married.

Later her husband told me, "When nothing happened Saturday, Monday, Tuesday, Wednesday, I was beginning to get sick of you and to think that I'd better see another psychiatrist who might do some good. But Thursday night I got taken by surprise!'' [Laughter] Now one can make the various ribald comments here [laughter], but my technique led to a happy marriage, to regular sex relations, and to *enjoyment* of those sex relations—because *she* had taken the initiative. [What had the problem been?] She had placed so much emphasis on sex since the age of 11 that she had kept a monthly record of her menstrual periods. There again, I think that I interfered with or altered or changed physiological functioning.

Now I want to stress that particular emphasis I placed upon *my* preference for Friday night. I had no right to express any preference whatsoever. With patients in hypnotherapy as well as with subjects in experimental work, you have no right to express a preference. It is always a cooperative venture of some sort, and the personality of the subject or the patient is the issue of primary importance. It is not what the therapist or hypnotist thinks or does or feels, but what he can do to enable the subject or patient to accomplish certain goals. It is a matter of the personality involved, and the willingness of the hypnotist and the therapist to let the subject's personality play a significant role.

Controlling the Knee Jerk Reflex

Depotentiating Hypnotic Anesthesia via Summation of Nerve Impulses

Another item in the control of physiological functioning concerns the knee jerk. A lot of people can inhibit the knee jerk; we know that they can do it physiologically, and we know that they can do a beautiful job of it. You can take a naive person who has never studied physiology, yet he can control the knee jerk so that he doesn't exhibit it. But there is one thing the naive person doesn't know, and that is the item of summation of nerve impulses.

I remember taking one of my hypnotic subjects to see a professor of physiology. I told the professor, "I've produced an anesthesia of this subject's legs." Rather, I should say that I brought the physiologist in to see my subject, because my subject couldn't walk!

The physiologist said, "The knee jerk is a spinal reflex and therefore you cannot interfere with it."

So a very careful examinaiton was carried out and verified by a second physiology professor, and so on.

Then the knee jerk itself was tested: there was no contraction of the muscles and no apparent inhibition. So the physiologist said, "Well, apparently there is an inhibition of nerve impulses. But there is one other test that should be attempted." And so we investigated the phenomenon of summation. If the physiologist timed the blows just right—13 or 14 rapid blows properly timed— a knee jerk resulted; otherwise there was no knee jerk. In other words, the synapses had been separated in some way so that an anesthesia was produced and you could test it in various ways without his awareness of it. [Hypnotic anesthesia could render a normal knee jerk ineffective; but with enough stimulation the summation of nerve impulses was sufficient to render the anesthesia ineffective.]

Hypnotic Deafness[5]

Selective Interference with Contextual Cues: Robert Erickson's Exploration of the Taste of Potatoes via Contextual Sensory and Kinesthetic Cues

Now I know that Sears has done work on anesthesia and the psychogalvonometer.[6] And yet what do you do in order to test at a psychological level? When you want to produce a psychological deafness that is real, you render a subject hypnotically deaf. But the way you test for it isn't by having the subject show you that he doesn't hear anything; instead you test for any response to sounds that are unexpected. For example, as you ride on a bus and look at the people sitting in the seats ahead of you, you notice that so-and-so doesn't turn his head at the honk of a horn. Why not? And then you notice he still doesn't turn his head at the sound of another car horn. And at that point you begin to question his ability to hear.

Now in psychological deafness hypnotically induced, I think

one of the neatest and meanest tricks of all is to render the person hypnotically deaf and then tell him a whole series of riddles and stories and jokes. And when your hand is this way, palm up, he can hear you; when the palm is down he can't hear you. And you've told him a whole series of things, [some of which he hears and some of which he doesn't hear, all depending upon the position of your palm, which is a non-auditory cue for turning hypnotic deafness on and off].

Take Norman Meyer's reasoning experiments, for example. Once you get insight into a problem, what can you do about it? Two strings are suspended from the ceiling; you've got a board and a short string [and you want to tie all three strings together]. You take hold of your short string and you try to tie the two strings hanging from the ceiling together. But there's nothing you can do because when you walk the full length of this string, you can't reach that string. What has the board got to do with it? Nothing at all—until finally you reason it out: "I tie this monkey wrench to this string, start it swinging, and then I can walk over and catch it and tie the two strings together." A whole series of that sort of problem.

I've done something similar with psychological deafness. You read the subject a series of 500 items; part of the time your palm is up and part of the time it is down. Now just try to sort out that kind of problem in your memory, and you're awfully at a loss. And then you test the subject indirectly for the items you listed when your palm was like this: he remembers the items when your palm was like that, but he can't remember when it was like this. Think of how very, very difficult it would be for any one of you, listening to two people sitting here conversing, to be asked afterwards to report on it: "What did so-and-so say; did he, or was it he, or he, or he?" Very, very confusing, and yet your hypnotically deaf person actually can do it. Selective deafness? Yes. But is it because we select out the things that we're not going to hear, or is it because hearing depends upon certain other cues?

I think one of the best examples I can give in answer to the question is that of my son, Robert. A few years ago Robert was served a new dish of potatoes. He took a mouthful, tasted it, was uncertain. He closed his eyes and took another mouthful, was still uncertain; and so he did this [Erickson apparently demonstrates], tasted it, and was still uncertain. Now he got up off the chair, stood up, and tasted it; then he sat down on the floor and tasted it. And it was good, just as he'd suspected in the first place—but he wasn't sure right away.

In considering psychological deafness hypnotically induced, how many different kinds of cues enter into this matter of hearing? When a speaker speaks in too low a tone of voice, what is the tendency but to close the eyes and listen so as not to be distracted; so as to give full attention to listening. What does hypnotic deafness do? It interferes with certain other functions and cues that enter into the hearing process.[7]

Treating Delayed Menstruation Indirectly

Structuring a Reverse Set; Evoking Somatic Memories to
Facilitate Menstruation; the Ideodynamic Response

Another item is the matter of delayed menstruation. In one week I had two cases come into me involving delayed menstruation. Both patients were frightfully worried about it, distressed terribly, and they wanted to be certain that everything was all right.

Hypnotically, what did I do? I avoided the question entirely. I think I should have, because I wanted to relieve the minds of those two women. So I suggested that it would be very, very nice if they went to a swimming party next Saturday. I really built up that swimming party into a gala event, a wonderful experience. I did everything in the world I could think of to draw together all of their happy childhood memories about swimming, all the happy times they had ever had swimming. They definitely were to go to a certain swimming pool in Phoenix, and they were to go swimming and really recapture all the joys of their youth, their girlhood, young womanhood, and so on. I built that up very, very carefully and extensively—and then I put into their minds *the fear that they might menstruate that night!* [Laughter] Now that may seem like a mean trick, but what was my problem? That of correcting a rather serious fear. The result was that both girls menstruated—and before Saturday, too. They missed that swimming experience![8]

Another technique I've used with this same problem is the following. A woman comes to me fearful because she has missed her period, and she has never missed a period in her life. I get a very careful history: she is as regular as clockwork. Then I have her sit there in the chair while I raise the question, "Have you got a Kotex with you? Would you mind putting it on—just in case?" And then I have her sit down again, and I have her explain to me in tremendous detail all the sensations she has ever had in relation to menstruating. She tells me how her breasts feel, how her nipples feel, about the ache in her shoulders, about the feeling of congestion in her back—innumerable things peculiar to each individual woman. And I've had more than one woman start menstruating right there and then in the office. But why? Because I built up that complete story of what menstruation feels like so strongly that their bodies have to respond in that particular way.

> Eds: This is a classic example of an *ideodynamic response:* by verbal associations, an idea evokes a dynamic psycho-physiological response of the endocrine system which regulates menstruation.

Treating Phobias

Resolving a Phobic Fainting Response by Redirecting Attention and by the Therapeutic Implantation of an Obsessive-Compulsive Idea

I want to cite another example. A young man, thirty years old, came to me as a patient. But he didn't want to be my patient because he said he didn't want it known or even suspected that he was seeing a psychiatrist. In his work he had to enter a certain tall building, and he had to take the elevator up to the seventh floor. It was a rapidly moving elevator, and his friends would get on that elevator [with no problems], but my patient [had a big problem]: either he fainted when he entered the building, or he fainted when he stood in front of the elevator, or he fainted when he got in the elevator. It was a very distressing problem for him; he didn't like it, and could I do something about it.

What I did was relatively simple. Since he was an excellent hypnotic subject, I agreed that I wouldn't be a psychiatrist—I'd just be an ordinary hypnotist. I put him in a trance, and in the trance state I had him describe to me, *not* the feeling of the elevator going up, but all the feelings he has when the elevator comes *down*. His history had disclosed that he never fainted when the elevator came *down;* at that point he was just so relieved and so comfortable, and thank goodness he was going to get out of that building. And so he described the feelings and sensations to me over and over again: that tremendous feeling of going *down*, those somatic sensations as he experienced going down; that relief, that need to grab onto his hat in case there was a woman in the elevator—things of that sort. And then I gave him, you might say, an obsessive-compulsive idea to the effect that the next time he entered that building, *it would be impossible for him to think of anything else except those peculiar, pleasant, comfortable feelings of going down in the elevator.*

He hasn't fainted since. Why should he? I soon found out the cause of his fainting—because he then decided that it was perfectly all right to be a patient—and it related to tremendous conflicts in his home. I don't know whether you would put fainting under the heading of the control of physiological functioning, but I think it belongs there because it is a failure of function in a certain sense of the word.

Treating Phobias

Resolving a Phobic Fainting Response: Life Review via Time Distortion, and an Indirect Posthypnotic Suggestion to Alter Vasomotor Behavior: "I Should Have Done Something"

Not long ago a dentist called me in extreme distress. It seemed he had the perfect assistant. And I think that when a dentist hires the perfect assistant, he's really found something! But she had one fault: every time she saw a bloody tooth, she fell flat on her face in a faint. Now the dentist was getting tired of picking her up off the floor [laughter] and reviving her, so the question was, "Can you do something for this girl?" I told him that I was perfectly willing to do so—at least I was perfectly willing to *try* to do so—and therefore, what could I do?

The girl came to my office and said, "You're a psychiatrist, you're a hypnotist. I want it distinctly understood that I do not want psychiatric treatment, I want hypnotic treatment. I want to gain control of myself so that I don't fall down flat on my face every time I see a bloody dish or a bloody tooth, or something of that sort. Several times I've gotten a nosebleed [from fainting the first time], and then fainted *again* as a consequence!"

Actually, what did I do for the girl? And really, this example should come into my next lecture because it concerns *a technique, a therapeutic approach.*

> Eds: Erickson's spontaneous equating of the words *technique* and *therapeutic approach* at this point represents a critical shift in the history of hypnosis. Here he intimates the move from the older authoritarian view wherein hypnotic suggestion was conceived of as a *technique* by which to insert something into the subject's mind, to the more current *permissive approaches* of evoking, facilitating, or reframing therapeutic associations. By the time the Erickson-Rossi volumes were published in the 1970's, the term *therapeutic approaches* was used almost exclusively.

I merely had the girl describe her problem, and then I told her to go into a deep trance. She went into a very nice, satisfactory, deep somnambulistic trance—an absolutely delightful trance. I told her that I was tired, and would she mind if I smoked a cigarette. She agreeably told me to go ahead and smoke. I told her that as I was smoking my cigarette, I wanted her to review everything in her life that had been traumatic or in any way connected with blood or fear or fainting; and review it in her mind; and review it without having any awareness of what she was reviewing. That is, all of the material would flash through her mind like a thought can flash through the mind. You see somebody on the street: "Wait a minute—what was that I was going to say?" That sort of reaction.

She agreed, and so for the next 20 seconds I smoked a cigarette and she did her reviewing. Then I awakened her and we chatted about the dentist, about this and that, about Phoenix in general. We concluded our chat, and I told her my bill. She said, "Well, you haven't done anything for me—don't you think that's pretty steep?" I agreed with her that it was. Really, *I should have done something for her.* There was no question about it: if I charge such a fee, *I should have done something for her.* And we went round and round on that point: *I really should have done something for her.* Of course, she didn't realize that I was giving her a posthypnotic suggestion [that *I really had done something for her*]! So she left the office rather discontented with me. But she hasn't fainted since.

The next morning the dentist handed her a tray filled with bloodied teeth. She took it, dumped out the teeth, washed out the tray, brought it back to him and said, "Sir, I didn't faint—what's the matter with me!" And he said, "I don't know, that's right—[you didn't faint]."

Now what did I accomplish? Physiologically speaking, in that brief period of time (which I'll take up in my next lecture), I induced a rapid process of thinking concerning blood, trauma, injury—all those things, and had them flash through her mind while I apparently smoked a cigarette. Then I interrupted her review and concluded by emphasizing that, considering my fee, *I really should have done something for her.* * Now that was the point that really convinced her: *I should have.* And so she walked out in 10 minutes' time. About nine minutes of it were spent in inducing a deep trance and taking history; about 10 to 20 seconds were spent letting her review things in distorted time; and the remaining few minutes were spent awakening her and discussing my fee and reiterating that *I should have done something for her.* What could

---

Editors' Note: Actually, Erickson's fees throughout his career were usually somewhat lower than the prevailing rate for psychiatrists (or therapists in general) in private practice.

the girl do except alter her vasomotor behavior? How I did it, I don't know—and neither does she. We're all very ignorant on that subject!

Hypnotic Alterations in Visual and Auditory Processes

Research in Unilateral Visual and Auditory Changes; Indirect Hypnotic Induction of Bilateral Blindness or Deafness via Behavioral Cues and the Structuring of Altered Ideomotor Associations

One of the areas of physiological control that I am tremendously interested in is the matter of unilateral visual changes, unilateral auditory changes. I haven't done any work in that area yet—I haven't had the apparatus to do so. But I think achieving such a response would constitute one of the most interesting and startling discoveries in the field. There is the simple technique of using a stethoscope where one side of it is plugged up—but the subject doesn't know it is plugged up, and so you really go to town on him inducing hypnotic deafness in one ear. Another example: There is an apparatus at the University of Michigan that I was going to use where, by use of mirrors, what you think you are seeing with your right eye, you are really seeing with your left eye. That would be a wonderful thing to do, and I hope that somebody someday does more work in this area.

Now in regard to this matter of inducing bilateral blindness: I don't think you ought to proceed by telling the subject, "You are getting blinder by the moment." I don't think that is the right way to proceed because it isn't quite fair. I picked up that manner of technique in the book on experimental hypnosis that LeCron is publishing shortly.[9]

In producing physiological changes, one ought to go about it with the realization that those physiological changes occur in a total body and in relationship to a total psychological picture that

22

exists at the time. I don't like to tell a person that he's becoming blind, that he's not going to be able to see, because he can cooperate with me too easily and too readily; and I'm not going to get a valid picture. I can tell a person to become deaf, and he can cooperate with me and simply ignore sounds.

What I try to do is to build up the picture first: How does a blind man walk? How does a deaf man sit in a chair—just *how?* And you go into those matters in great detail, because a deaf man sits differently than a man who has full control of his hearing. And so you very carefully build up that certain muscular rigidity, that certain lack of response to extraneous sounds. You build that up and build that up, and then you call attention to the fact that we hear sounds that are close to us with a certain quality; we hear more distant sounds with another quality; and remote sounds with still another quality. You get that idea across to the subject very carefully until he begins to appreciate that deafness is not just a closing down. It is a matter of circumscribing, bit by bit, until finally the subject begins to look at your face and study your lips: "You spoke, didn't you—I didn't quite hear you—do you mind speaking louder?" So you take a deep breath, and you speak a little *softer.* And then he looks at you and says, "You'll have to speak louder." And you shift your attitude, your position, and you lean forward. The first thing the subject knows is that he himself is convinced, and then he starts to lean forward and to cup his ear. But why shouldn't he? You want psychological deafness; you want it to be very genuine.

In the matter of blindness you use the same sort of technique. I don't think a direct technique is very satisfactory because a subject can fake it so well. What you want to do instead is to give a reaction that the light is failing; then you look pleased because it's come back on again; and you just give that suggestion by your total behavior. You test out the switch on the wall to see if the light is really on, and you go through all manner of suggestive behavior. Next you raise the question of how the subject might react if he were blind. For example, what sort of groping movements would I make if I were blind and reaching for this notebook? I can't do it very well because I'm not blind—I haven't learned. But the serious-minded subject can take that as a very definite project. And the first thing he knows he has built up a generalized pattern of [blind] behavior.

Learning to Recognize Minimal Cues

The Role of Ancillary Body and Behavior Processes in the Control of Physiological Functioning: Problems with Experimental Design

Now how much do your eye movements, your foot movements, your shoulder movements, your head posture, and the way you bend your neck enter into your vision and your hearing and your speech? You walk behind somebody who is wearing a brand new suit. You wonder who it is until the person starts talking to somebody in front of him, and you recognize his characteristic head movements—not because you heard his voice, but because you recognized certain characteristic head movements that in the past you learned to relate to that person but you never differentiated from his voice.

You can use soundproof rooms to experiment with this sort of thing. When I was instructing at the Menninger Clinic this question was raised [and we decided to do an experiment]. A number of people whom I knew were brought into a soundproof room. They were dressed quite differently, were very carefully disguised; their heads were tightly draped so that I couldn't see the color of their hair or get a profile of any sort; and they were cautioned to keep their hands at their sides. Then I had them start talking, and all I did was watch for characteristic head movements while they talked. And I successfully identified each person from my soundproof room.

How many investigators are aware of these subtle aspects? Most just take these matters for granted. But I think that in the hypnotic control of physiological functioning, it is tremendously important to pay attention to all the little things that enter into it. To think that speech comes just from the mouth—it doesn't come just from the mouth; the neck is involved, respiration is involved, shoulder movements are involved, tension in the hands is involved. Everything is involved, and once you understand that pattern of inter-relationship you can learn a great deal more. But I think it's awfully wrong experimentally to isolate physiological functioning, as so many psychologists do, as a single unitary phenomenon. You are dealing with a human being who is a physical creature, who is a psychological creature, who is actually a personality— and a personality who is responding to you and to the room you are in. Lecturing in a totally dark room is one thing; lecturing in a room with windows is an entirely different thing. Your behavior is going to be entirely different, no matter how interested you are in giving that lecture to the group. When I try to induce physiological changes, I try to start at the beginning—that is, as far as I personally can understand the beginnings of those things. I try to build up and build up new patterns in such a general fashion that my subject or my patient can translate them into his own experiential life.

Hypnotic Anesthesia and Analgesia for Childbirth

Utilizing the Patient's Experiential and Physiological Background; Utilizing Dissociation and the Redirection of Attention to Differentiate between Desired Sensations and Undesired Pain

One of the physiological functions that I neglected to mention is that of anesthesia. I know there are dentists present, and I've had a little experience of anesthesia with dentists, and some with child-birth situations. Now how do you go about it? I've had quite a number of women experiment with [hypnotically induced] anesthesia for childbirth, and together with their obstetricians they reached the conclusion that it was a total failure, a total loss. And yet when I reviewed the case, there was plenty of reason why it should have been a total failure, a total loss.

How do you build up a hypnotic anesthesia? Well, how aware is the average person of the way his shoes feel right now? When you stop to consider that question, you suddenly become aware of the shoes on your feet; you become aware of your collar, the way you are sitting on the chair, and so on. And in inducing an anesthesia, my feeling is that you build it up from the total personality and experiential background of the patient.

I remember one case in particular. Rhea came to me on December 18th, and she was going to have her baby on January 18th (she said it would be on January 12th, but her obstetrician said January 18th—and he was right). Rhea said to me, "I can come to see you only three times, and I want to have a painless childbirth, and what can you do about it?" The first thing I did was to spend over an hour getting her to define to me what she meant by a painless childbirth. Did it mean all loss of feeling? No. She wanted to know what it was like to give birth to a baby. She didn't want any pain, but she did want certain feelings. So I defined the word *anesthesia* and the word *analgesia* for her until I was sure that she understood my definitions. Now we were on safer ground, and we could really discuss analgesia and what it meant, and anesthesia and what it really meant. When are you anesthetic and when are you analgesic?

Next I went into her personal background for examples of each. Had she ever sat on a rough bench in a bathing suit and never noticed the roughness? Yes, she had. Why hadn't she noticed it? And why didn't she notice the feeling of her shoes, and now she is suddenly aware of that feeling. I asked her about the ring on her finger, and she became very acutely aware of the ring on her finger and the sensations thereof. So I very carefully laid down *a pattern of past experiences by which she could recognize the possibility of not noticing things and yet of having those things still take place.*

> Eds: "Not noticing things and yet having those things still take place" is a form of mental dissociation that is a classic approach to facilitating hypnotic anesthesia or analgesia.[10]

I went into the actual process of childbirth: muscle contractions, abdominal muscle contractions, a peristalsis—all of those matters. Did she need to feel pain with abdominal muscle contractions? Did she need to feel pain with peristalsis? I proceeded along those lines until Rhea was thoroughly informed. Then I suggested to her that while she sat in this chair she could look over at that

26

chair. Remember, she was in a deep trance. [Momentary break in tape]

... And [this] enables them to put into operation their own physiological processes. For me to tell a woman, "I want you to have a painless childbirth"—what do I know about childbirth in the first place! What do I know about anybody else's sense of pain? I don't know anything. I know about my own sense of pain—at least I think I do—but somebody else's sense of pain is another matter. How does my patient react to pain? How does she react to the absence of pain when she thinks she should have it? How is she going to take it when she thinks she should have it and she hasn't got it? These are extremely important psychological questions in regard to anesthesia. One of the reasons anesthesia so often fails is because the patient has the feeling that "I *ought* to feel pain under these circumstances," and he or she proceeds to feel it. So you get a reaction to the question, "How will you feel in its absence?", and you build up the proper attitude.

Hypnotic Pain Relief

An Example of the Indirect Utilization Approach: Reframing
Pain into Meaningful Experience

Now Rhea said, "Well, if I don't have pain—if I have analgesia rather than anesthesia—that means I still will be able to feel the baby's head moving down. What am I going to be thinking about when I feel that movement? And if the baby's head moves down, that means a dilatation of the birth canal, and I wonder what that would feel like. It won't be painful, anymore than opening my hand feels painful. I know I'm opening my hand; I enlarge my buckle cavity; it doesn't hurt, yet I can feel it happening."

I built up Rhea's anesthesia entirely on those grounds, and I built it up while she explained to me and helped me explain to *that girl sitting over there* who was also decidedly pregnant, that that was the way she, too, should feel. [And what is the name of that girl sitting over there?] Her name is Rhea.

Next I asked her about the episiotomy. For those of you who are not acquainted with that word, it means a certain surgical procedure of cutting the perineum [to facilitate the birth process]. And how should that girl over there feel when the episiotomy is performed? Well, if you cut flesh there ought to be a sound—that's right, and what kind of a sound? When the needle is inserted, ought you not feel it going through the skin and through the tissues? But can you not feel it going through without experiencing pain?

Rhea delivered her baby, and she kept up an interested commentary for her obstetrician: "You just started the episiotomy, and I heard you start it. Judging from the sound, I would say it must have been about an inch long, but I'm not sure.

She counted the stitches for him with the greatest of interest. She told him, "You know, the baby's head is in a new position now. Do you suppose that means it has left the uterus and entered the vaginal canal? It's really in a new position; I can feel it there."

She was perfectly happy, perfectly contented. She had a nice sense of feeling, I could say the same way that my fingers are on my palm, and I'm approaching my middle finger, my third finger, and now they are on it—that sort of reaction, but no pain. I built up her response from the idea of anesthesia, the idea of analgesia. What was her particular interest? What did she want, and how did she want it? She could have exactly what she wanted. In other words, I redirected her attention to all the elements I could possibly think of in that situation.

> Eds: It cannot be emphasized too strongly how this section illustrates the essence of Erickson's indirect utilization approach to hypnotic suggestion. Erickson utilized Rhea's interests and motivations to redirect, restructure, or reframe her attention to all the real events of childbirth in which she was interested. She can then focus on having an informative and comfortable experience rather than being aware of the pain, which is irrelevant and of no interest to her. This indirect approach is in contrast to the older direct approach of simply suggesting, "You will have no pain." Erickson's approach facilitates creative, experiential alternatives to the more mundane, chaotic, and "disorganized" experience of

pain by reframing it into meaningful and desirable experience.

QUESTIONS AND ANSWERS*

Delayed Trance Ratification

Q. [Questioner from audience] How long a discussion did you have with the fainting dental assistant about how you really should have done something for her?

A. [Answer given by Erickson] Oh, I think somewhere around ten minutes' time, during which I helped her belabor me for my fee and *I really should have done something!* [Laughter]

Q. You didn't back down?

A. No, I *should have* done something.

Q. I mean, you didn't back down on changing your fee, or anything like that?

A. No.

Q. Did you agree with her—did you knock down the fee?

A. No, I didn't. I charged the regulation fee, and I agreed with her that *I should have done something!*

Q. What we'd all like to know is this: is she still mad about the fee, or what? [Laughter]

---

*Editors' Note: Because of the poor auditory quality of this Question and Answer section, the following material is a highly edited version of the original and conveys only the major substance of Erickson's remarks.

A. The next day at work, after not falling flat on her face, she called me up and said, "You *did* do something for me!" [Laughter] And I said, "That's right, I did. Aren't you glad? Will you call me up tomorrow and tell me how glad you are?" And she said, "I'll call you up anytime you want me to and tell you how glad I am!"

Hypnotic Deafness

Direct and Indirect Approaches to Hypnotic Deafness

Q. In discussing the inducement of physiological deafness and blindness, you said that you prefer an indirect technique because of the fact that a direct technique might result in faking on the part of the patient. But is it not true that this type of physiological deafness may also be a direct result of the patient's awareness of what you want him to do? In other words, might he not be responding in exactly the same way as if you had used a direct technique?

A. I have an experimental subject, and I want to induce hypnotic deafness. I do my level best not to let the subject know what my intentions are. I usually do some fake experiment with him. That is, I carry out a very careful experiment which is beside the point, and then I go through that long procedure of building up those behaviors and associations that I believe are important but generally unrecognized sensory cues in audition. Soon the subject begins to get worried about his hearing. But *he* is the one who gets worried about it and distressed about it; and *he* is the one who tells me that he is getting deaf—I haven't even raised the topic yet, and I have no intention of raising the topic.

Q. In other words, you believe that he does not know or assume that you want him to become deaf?

A. I assume it! I've had some very, very alarmed student subjects who discovered that they were deaf; and I really had a problem on my hands that I had to handle psychiatrically, because they were pretty frantic about suddenly losing their hearing. And they were seriously distressed.

Q. But did that prove that they actually lost their hearing, or were they worried about the suggestion that it had developed?

A. They were definitely worried.

Q. Yes, they were worried, but that's not what I'm saying here. I'm asking whether there was any evidence that they lost their hearing, or were they just worried about the *possibility* of losing it?

A. You go through a couple of hours with one of those students trying to get in contact with him and you'll be convinced. Now I think one of the best proofs [of genuine hearing loss in hypnotic deafness] is the indirect proof where I developed the following procedure, which is well described in one of my published papers:[11] I placed tin pans on my desk ahead of time. Then I produced a hypnotic deafness in my subject, and every so often I would carelessly knock the tin pans onto the cement floor. And you know how you feel when you hear a couple of dish pans fall on a cement floor; and you also know how you would leap out of your chair if those pans fell onto the cement floor and *you didn't hear them!* Well, I had a net fixed up that my subject didn't know about!

Another approach: I don't think I've published this one, but there is no more horrible way of determining [the genuineness of deafness hypnotically induced] than to use one of those professional noisemakers. And you have your pretty girl subject sit in this chair, and then you have her try that chair, and that one, and that one; and then you slip the noisemaker under the cushion in one of the chairs, and she sits down very comfortably, and she doesn't even blush. It's a dirty trick! [Laughter]

Q. That still doesn't answer the fundamental question of whether or not there is an actual loss of hearing. You still don't know whether she was able to control her reaction.

A. But she never knew it!

31

Q. Perhaps she didn't act as though she knew it.

A. But you can run controls on it.

Q. That's the point I'm getting at. Most of the other experiments that have been done on hypnotic deafness indicated that there *isn't* really a loss of hearing—but rather just a [loss of a] fraction of it.

A. It's a suppression and loss on the deafness on 500 items. And you sort those out, and the subject knows all the answers to the things, and knows the answers this way.

Q. Let me ask you one other question, if I may. If the subject is re-hypnotized, will she not be able to tell you what went on?

A. No, *no*. I've tried that repeatedly with deafness. I've done an experiment, induced deafness, pulled some such measure as [hiding that noisemaker?], and then re-hypnotized the subject and given him absolute and convincing instructions to tell my collaborator the full details [of what transpired in the session]. And it is surprising: there is no memory.

Establishing Rapport

Evoking Awareness and Feeling: Utilizing Fallacious
Psychological Syllogisms

Take that patient with no breast development who had a tendency to hide in corners, to hide behind the piano, to hide behind the couch. Her father brought her into my office to see me. Now how are you going to get into contact with a person like that? You just sit there, and you talk to her, and you wait; then you say a few more words, and you wait, and you say a few more words, until she begins to develop some feeling of liking for you. And then you raise the question, "Would you like to have the experience of hand levitation?" And then you go into a long and detailed explanation of hand levitation—boring as can be, but what is your purpose? Your purpose is to help the patient, and most patients will gladly shift to topics other than themselves, you know.

And now you can raise the questions: "Perhaps you would like some kind of help? How do you feel? Are you willing to know what your feelings are? Don't tell me, but are you willing *really willing* to know what your own feelings are? But don't tell me." What are you doing with these questions? You are eliciting her feelings, and you are protecting her at the same time. You are not asking her to share her feelings, but you are asking her to become *aware* of her feelings. And as surely as she becomes aware of her feelings, she can't help but want to share them in some way.

Next you gently raise the point: "I've had other girls like you, I've had other patients. Your father likes me; you like your father." You stop right there with, "Your father likes me; you like your father." What is the logical progression in the mind of the girl?: *I like father; father likes you (Dr. Erickson); therefore I like you (Dr. Erickson)*. It's a fallacious argument, but nevertheless it is highly effective.

And you continue: "Now, I've got an agate on my desk. Do you like rock collections? Do you like that pretty agate? The agate is mine—do you really like it there?" Well, that agate is right *there* in relationship to me right *here;* and if she likes it there in relationship to me, then she likes me. Fallacious? I agree. But I'm willing to commit any kind of sophistry to get a patient to think straight!

Hypnotherapy of a Schizoid Personality

Initiating a Therapeutic Redevelopment via Rapport, Change in Body Image, and Breast Development

Q. Dr. Erickson, that brings up another question in regard to this same girl. Her father described her as a schizoid personality and apparently you concurred, based on your observations of her. Yet, as we listen to this case story, it seems that by the mere induction of hypnosis she not only developed breasts but was cured of her schizoid personality as well. Now I wonder if there might have been another element in addition to hypnotic suggestion that entered into the therapeutic process.

A. The girl's father was a doctor who worked from seven in the morning until eleven at night; the girl's mother was someone whom she hated, and quite rightly. She found in me a person who could be genuine in her life and yet represent her father and be deserving of her father's respect. So she had the freedom to develop her personality.

Q. I think there were other elements in it than just the process...

A. ...just the process, but the process of breast development was tremendously important. Incidentally, you undoubtedly will know that girl because she is rapidly becoming famous.

Symptom Resolution

Substituting ("Trading") Menstrual Pain for an
Agate Antipathy

Q. Getting back to the girl who had the menstrual pain. Did you ever find out what psychological gains she was getting from all that pain?

A. Thanks very much for that question. Whenever a patient comes to me with a complaint of some sort, my tendency is to root out the cause of the pain or difficulty, if I can find it; if I can't find it, I select something to give the patient in return for the symptom. Take the girl who wants to be cured of menstrual pain, and that's all she wants, and she will not tolerate anything more. It is perfectly easy for me to take a card, tear it up in shreds, throw it on the floor, and thereby give her a permanent dislike for that sort of behavior. It's an easy trade; it's a cheap trade. I've just traded: I've given her a new dislike [so that she will still have something to dislike once her menstrual pain is gone]. And I usually try to select a dislike

34

that won't really enter into the girl's life again.

For example, one patient told me emphatically that she would not have an agate on her desk. [Laughter] And she definitely meant it. It was all right for other people to keep agates around, but she wouldn't! Well, that's okay with me. [Laughter] But it was a *trade:* that patient gave me her symptoms in exchange for a definite dislike of agates on her desk. That's okay; she'll get along through life without having an agate on her desk! [Laughter]

Dental Hypnosis

Selecting Desired Sensations and Redirecting Attention

Q. You know, the subject of dental hypnosis should be taken up.

A. Dental hypnosis—I haven't done too much of that. Some of you here today are probably better qualified to discuss it than I am. I've done quite a bit—not quite a bit—I've done *some* wherein I used the same technique as the one I used with Rhea. That is, what did the patient want: Did he want complete anesthesia or analgesia?; How did he want to feel about it before?; How did he want to feel about it afterwards?; How did he want to feel about that dentist grinding away *during* the drilling?; And what particular things about the dentist would interest him while that dentist was grinding away? I had one patient who tried to count the whiskers in the dentist's beard—and he was a smooth-shaven dentist, so it really was a difficult job. The patient didn't get even one cheek counted, because the dentist kept shifting around.

Hypnotic Anesthesia in Dentistry

Choosing Therapeutic Techniques in Accord with the Practitioner's Individual Personality

Q. Is there any particular technique for producing an anesthesia?

35

A. I don't think there is any one technique that can be applied by all practitioners. I've seen my medical students achieve good results using techniques that I wouldn't even walk near! But I could admire their results even though I personally couldn't handle using those particular techniques—I've got the wrong type of personality. But they couldn't use mine. In inducing anesthesia in dentistry, I think it's up to the individual to find a technique that fits him and that includes a recognition of the individual personality.

Direct Versus Indirect Techniques

Doubting the Results of Direct Techniques; Protecting the Personality

Q. Dr. Erickson, do you believe indirect techniques are preferred over the rapid direct technique, or vice versa?

A. I use the indirect technique particularly in research, because I'm much more certain of the lasting results. But now and then I'll use a rapid technique for demonstrations, but I don't like it.

Q. Why not?

A. Why not? In the long run, your subjects don't like it either—they just don't like it. They can't be sure of their amnesias; they can't be sure of their reactions; and there's no reason why you should ever risk offending another person. That brings up another item that I hope I'll mention again: *in all hypnotic work, every effort should be made to protect the personality of the subject. It is tremendously important to protect the personality of the subject in every possible way, because you can get into so much trouble.*

Motivation Versus Analysis

Q. Getting back to that girl without breasts. To what extent did you go into the question of what having no breasts meant to her and what having breasts meant to her? And why was it that she hadn't developed breasts?

A. I didn't go into that at all. I already knew what it meant to her without being told, and so I felt my major task was to give her a *willingness* to feel a growth. And I felt she could carry on from there—and I don't mean to pun either! [Laughter]

Anesthesia and Reactivation of Trance

Q. With regard to this question of anesthesia: I'm not entirely clear if either of the patients you talked about had been in a trance at the time of the surgical procedure, or whether it was a post-hypnotic matter. If it was posthypnotic, isn't it possible for you to throw a patient into a deep trance and while he's in that trance....?

A. I've had them both. As soon as you bring out the anesthesia, whether or not you recognize it, you put the patient into a deep trance. You teach him anesthesia or analgesia; you give him an understanding; you build up the situation in which it is to be used. Now that girl, Rhea, for example, called me up at one o'clock in the morning to tell me that she was going to the hospital to have her baby. She couldn't reach me, and besides, I like my sleep! So when she got to the hospital she walked in, went up the elevator, went to the delivery room, and gave a full account of everything. But later she was able to tell me in a trance state, "You know, when I stepped into that elevator *I went into a trance, but I didn't know it.*" And in the matter of anesthesia, if you really test your subjects you'll find that they have reactivated the previous trance [in which they learned the anesthesia].

Time-Limited Dental Anesthesia

Utilizing the Patient's Wish to Turn Dental Anesthesia
On and Off

Q. I am particularly interested in the possibility of anesthesia as opposed to analgesia. Can you give the patient a time-limited anesthesia?

A. I know one of my subjects said, "I'm going to the dentist, but I'm not going to let you hypnotize me and remove the pain. I've got to have several teeth drilled, and I'm really going to find out what it feels like. I want to really find out what that pain feels like"—he was a psychologist!—"but when I am halfway home, I want to lose that ache in my jaw."

I said, "Well, you've had dental work done before, haven't you?"

"Yes," he said, "and I've had local anesthetics, and afterwards they weren't pleasant either."

I said, "Whereabouts do you want to have the anesthesia begin?" And the patient specified the particular part of Highway 112, and the anesthesia set in there.

I've had a patient with a toothache say, "I want to go to a dentist; my appointment is not for another hour; I want to be relieved of that pain, but I don't want to walk into my dentist's office and try to tell him I've got a toothache when I haven't. So let me have the toothache when I sit down in the chair, and then after he checks me and is satisfied in his own mind, let the toothache disappear." There's another psychologist for you! [Laughter] But that sort of thing is fascinating.

Trance Reactivation Versus Autohypnosis

Posthypnotic Suggestion Reactivating the Original Trance:
Falling Asleep in Autohypnosis

Q. Getting back to this man with the fractured feet. In a case similar to that, have you ever tried inducing a deep state of trance and then dissociating, as you did with Rhea, and asking the dissociated personality to tell you about his stocking anesthesia?

A. I like to use that kind of technique a great deal, but I didn't think it was a good idea with this particular chap. I may have been wrong—but the results were good!

Q. When you spoke of reactivating a trance state, is that the same as self-hypnosis? Would you differentiate?

A. A hypnotized subject can be given the posthypnotic suggestion that at the closing of the door he will close a notebook. And if you want to test him at that exact moment, you will find that he behaves as he did in the trance in which he was first given that posthypnotic suggestion. But self-hypnosis is an entirely different matter. I've induced a deep trance in a subject in the presence of such-and-such people and given him a particular posthypnotic suggestion to perform a week later. A week later as he performed it—I merely took hold of his elbow and induced catalepsy—I asked him to look around the room and tell me who was present. And he named the same people who had been present the previous week, because he was still in that original trance.

In autohypnosis, on the other hand, the person induces his own trance. Unless he has mapped out ahead of time exactly what he wants to do and when he's going to awaken, he's not likely to succeed—but he *is* likely to fall into a physiological sleep!

Audience Hypnosis Versus Autohypnosis

Q. Do you find that same situation when members of an audience go into hypnosis while watching you demonstrate with a subject on stage?

A. That's right.

Q. That's certainly a form of autohypnosis—or is it self-hypnosis?

A. I always had the feeling that when any of my students went to sleep in my presence, it was because I was in front of the group lecturing and they weren't interested. When I find I'm demonstrating hypnosis and the [people] scattered through the audience go into a trance, [I find] they have gone into a trance in relationship to me. I can suggest to the subject sitting here [on stage] that he move his right hand, and the person in the back of the room moves his right hand. That isn't autohypnosis.

Defining Autohypnosis

The Condition for Therapist Rapport in Autohypnosis:
Autohypnosis as a Private Experience

Q. What is autohypnosis?

A. Autohypnosis is when the subject sits down quietly in the room and says, "I am going to stare at that object until I fall into a hypnotic trance, and after I get into the trance I'm going to dictate so many case histories." He then stares, and all of a sudden he starts dictating case histories into the dictaphone. When he finishes the given number [of case histories], he wakes up staring at [the object]. Now it's dinner time! He is alone.

I've had subjects who wanted to learn autohypnosis. I promptly found out that if they went into a trance thinking, "Well, let's see, Dr. Erickson taught me how to go into a trance," then I could walk into the office [where they were going into "autohypnosis"] and be in rapport with them. But when they really went into autohypnosis, I didn't have rapport with them and nobody else had rapport with them. Not even the telephone. Nothing had rapport. They [the subjects themselves] had it! ... Autohypnosis does not use a teacher. When subjects start using me, or any recollection that I taught them such-and-such, then I am in rapport with them. ...

I remember a resident in psychiatry at a seminar in hypnosis who went into a deep trance spontaneously. There was no effort on my part to demonstrate. I was just giving the history and phenomena of hypnosis, and I noticed she was in a deep trance. So at the close of the seminar I created a disturbance trying to figure things at the blackboard. She awakened from that trance without knowing she'd been in one. Subsequently she told me she was interested in autohypnosis. I asked her if she wanted to learn to be hypnotized

40

first, or did she want to experiment herself. She told me she thought she would prefer to experiment first [on her own]. Well, I kept a close watch on her office. One Saturday afternoon she experimented [on her own]. She set up a number of objects to look at. . . . I wasn't in rapport with her. But she went into a very good trance. Then later I asked her if she would like the experience of being hypnotized. She agreed. So I put her in a trance. Her reaction when I questioned her about the autohypnotic trance was: "That's mine! But I'll tell you about it if you really want to know." But that was hers! That's right, it was!

In other words I did not have access to that experience except through her permission. . . . She asked me later to teach her self-hypnosis (which is the same as autohypnosis). I very carefully avoided the set up of paperclips she had on her desk [which she apparently had stared at to go into self-hypnosis]. I had her look at a calendar to go into self-hypnosis. Then later when I walked into her office while she was using the calendar for self-hypnosis, I was in rapport with her. But when she used the paper clips, I was out of rapport with her.

I later asked her to use the paper clips and then I was in rapport with her! [Therefore, the hypnotherapist is not in rapport with subjects who use their own methods of going into self-hypnosis. If, however, subjects are following the hypnotherapist's directives, or are using any strong associative bridges to the therapist, then they will be in rapport with each other during the self-hypnosis.]

Arm Movement in the Breast Development Case

Q. [Question concerns Erickson's utilization of the difference between arm movements in men and women to help a young woman develop breasts.]

A. I'll demonstrate this to you right now, and I'll exaggerate. If you ask me to put my right hand on my left shoulder, I would do it this way. And where's my elbow? But how does a girl do it?— because she has to miss that bump there, and she has learned that movement from the age when her breasts first started to develop.

She's got a different way of lifting her arm. She can't just lift it [like a man does]—it will hurt! And now what did I want? I wanted her to have that somatic feeling that there was something there—a somatic but not necessarily conscious feeling that there was something there.

Q. How old was the girl again?

A. Eighteen.

Personality, Neuroticism, and Autohypnosis

Q. What sort of a personality indulges in this autohypnosis—a sort of neurotic means of fantasy? [Laughter]

A. Well, the best autohypnotists I know are experimentally minded psychologists! [Laughter] They can be psychiatrists, which is a horrible way to go. The really neurotic person who indulges in autohypnosis wears out his interest in an awful hurry, because he'd much rather do something neurotic than something that is educational or really interesting.

Q. Do you mean that autohypnosis is educational? [Might it not be more a way of] withdrawing from reality perhaps?

A. There are better ways of withdrawing from reality—better, neurotic ways.

Indian Yogi Feats as Self-Hypnosis

Q. Dr. Erickson, is the type of demonstration that is done by these Indian fakirs when they lie on a bed of nails or stare at the sun a kind of self-hypnosis?

A. What was that yogi's name—the one who was at Yale University? He had quite a discussion about just that question. I never met him, but I got some of his explanations second-hand. I really don't know too much about it, but I do know that if you have enough nails in a board, the distribution of your weight on each nail doesn't make it uncomfortable at all. And you and I could do it, though we'd have a certain [negative] expectant attitude. But if you distribute the weight over enough nail points, it won't be uncomfortable. . . .

Two of my Hindu friends have told me that autohypnosis and autoanesthesia have been employed—I mean autoanalgesia, not autoanesthesia—for that particular purpose. But that is second-hand information, yet I trust my friends—they're both doctors, they're both psychiatrists.

Risks in Using Hypnosis with Lobotomized Patients

Q. Dr. Erickson, have you had any hypnotic experience with patients who have been subject to frontal-lobe surgery—that is, lobotomized? Did you ever attempt to hypnotize a lobotomized patient?

A. I've attempted to hypnotize several, but then I got cold feet. They were making good adjustments, and I didn't feel that I had the right to intrude. You see, I don't know enough about the effects of lobotomy to know whether or not I might give them some [negative] reactions. But I can hypnotize the normal or the neurotic person and speculate fairly well. With the lobotomized person, however, you run a certain risk if they are well adjusted.

Q. A couple of things are described as occurring in or as characteristic of the hypnotic trance state—that is, the freer access to material and the lesser control over motility—and these same characteristics are also described in relation to lobotomized patients. There are very great similarities, and I wondered how these people would respond if . . .

A. I've got a patient right now whom I would really like to hypnotize. She is a former nurse who is now a legal secretary.

43

Q. She's had a lobotomy?

A. Yes, and she is a legal secretary. And her reason for coming to me was, "I've had a lobotomy, and my family thinks I ought to go back and live with them, but I want to earn my own living, and I can handle myself satisfactorily." Well, it happens that I know her employer very well, and he thinks she is a prize secretary. And she said, "Now, I want a psychiatric examination so that I can report to my parents that I've seen a psychiatrist and that he says it's all right for me to earn my own living."

Q. It's been my experience that they are not even interested in seeing a psychiatrist after a lobotomy.

A. No, she's doing a beautiful job, and there are two other lawyers who are trying to hire her!

Hypnosis and Brain Damage

Q. I recently received a referral from a very fine brain surgeon. A patient with an angioma [a nonmalignant tumor] had had practically the entire left hemisphere of his brain excised. He was sent to me for re-educative therapy. I had quite a time with that chap. Once I got him into a fairly light state of trance (that is all I was ever able to do), he immediately began to weep. We had to work several sessions to clear up all the weeping that was tied in with a family situation. That illustrates what you are pointing out that you never know what you're going to bump into with [the surgically modified brain].

The Direct Technique in Dentistry

Indirect Approaches in Psychotherapy; Dangers of Hypnosis

Q. Dr. Erickson, you made a statement indicating a preference for the indirect technique. Speaking from a dental viewpoint, what would you do with the patient who comes into the office with a toothache, but doesn't want Novocain, doesn't want gas, and is afraid of the needle? Would you tend to use a direct technique in such a case?

A. It helps you tremendously. I'm highly in favor of dentists using the direct technique, but I'm opposed to the psychotherapist using a direct technique indiscriminately.

Q. What are the dangers in using hypnosis?

A. The primary danger is the precipitation of a problem that already exists in the patient or subject by virtue of his reaction to you; and then there are the dangers that exist because of that.

Q. Can you be more specific?

A. The patient comes to you with a paralysis of the left arm, and you go right in and straighten it out without being too careful to know about its source. So the man confesses his infidelities to you. So you know his wife's shame. You've got no business knowing it; he came to you without her consent, and she attacks you. When a patient has some sort of personality difficulty, you can make an enemy out of him if you attack the problem too readily, too quickly.

Q. The dangers, then, are proceeding so rapidly with the material that the patient himself cannot handle it, and you cannot handle it with him?

A. You cannot handle it with him. He's already got the problem, but if you take charge of it you should, in your responsibility to him, keep in control of it—or be ready to give him some distraction from it—so that he doesn't lose control of himself.

. . . . How often have patients come to you with a nice, circumscribed problem that you can think through immediately. But you have to waste a lot of your time and their time to build them up to receiving that insight. You knew the answer within ten minutes of their arrival in the office.

Autohypnosis in Personality Problems

Homosexuality; Insomnia; Hypnosis in Physical Verus
Psychogenic Pathology: Cancer

Q. Dr. Erickson, I would like to know if autohypnosis can be used to resolve one's own personality problems.

A. Oh, I've had subjects use autohypnosis for dental anesthesia or analgesia; I've had subjects use it as an experimental procedure, and they accomplished a good deal. But when it comes to the solving of personality problems, you've got to have the unusual type of person who is willing to think things through. One of my psychiatric residents used autohypnosis on a personality problem. He said, "Well, I'm going to spend an hour each day in trance, but I'm only going to do 5 minutes' work in that hour, and I'm going to do it very slowly." That psychiatric resident was very intelligent; he recognized that there was a serious problem, and he worked on it slowly.

Q. Do you think autohypnosis would help a homosexual problem?

A. Do you mean could he help himself by learning autohypnosis? No, I don't think so. Remember, that's a pretty terrifying problem he's got, and it has many unconscious roots. Autohypnosis could scare the daylights out of him, and thereby intensify his problem. That's something he really ought not to handle by himself.

> Eds: We acknowledge the offensive and dated nature of Erickson's comments regarding homosexuality. In 1954, homosexuality was officially regarded as a clinical problem in both medical and psychological communities. Today, however, it is recognized as a non-pathologic choice in lifestyle.

Q. Dr. Erickson, how do you treat insomnia?

A. Insomnia is a very tricky problem. Dr. Pattie mentioned this morning how you induce a trance without mentioning the word *sleep*. If you've got a patient suffering from insomnia of psychogenic origin, you certainly do not induce hypnotic *sleep*. You can induce hand levitation, you can induce catalepsy, you can induce an inattentiveness to surroundings, you can induce a series of lovely reminiscences—but don't use the word *dream!*

Q. Where do you draw the line between the use of hypnosis to control psychological and physiological behavior?

A. I'll draw the line at psychological control of behavior. I do know that a patient can be sitting perfectly quietly in a chair in my office and be in need of sympathy, and so develop a nosebleed without lifting a hand to his face. How did he do it? I don't know. But I simply give him a Kleenex and proceed to work on that problem: I get the patient unwilling to do that kind of thing again, and then I try to find out why he was willing to do it in the first place. But as for treating actual, physically pathological failings like cancer, hypnotically, I don't think it can be done. I can't see any reason for thinking that it could [be effective in those situations].

> Eds: Recent developments in the field of psychoneuroimmunology indicate that there may now be a scientific rationale for exploring the possibility that hypnosis can mobilize effective psychophysiological processes to influence what were formerly thought to be purely medical problems.[12]

DETERMINING THE GENUINENESS OF HYPNOTIC PHENOMENA

[Following is Erickson's discussion of Dr. Pattie's lecture on determining the genuineness of hypnotic phenomena.]

Hypnotic Rapport as a Multi-Inclusive Phenomenon

Dr. Pattie gave an extremely interesting talk, and yet I want to take exception to some of his remarks.

First, he gave a definition of rapport as being the relationship between subject and hypnotist. But what is rapport? I think it is far more than [just what exists between subject and hypnotist, or between patient and hypnotherapist]. At the present time, all of you are sitting in this room in relationship to this desk, in relationship to a certain chair, in relationship to the people around you, in relationship to the ceiling, and so on. Rapport in hypnotic situations is *not* shown just in relationship to the operator; it also may be shown in relationship to the circumstances in which the hypnosis is done. And often, that is the case.

Idiosyncratic Manifestations of Catalepsy

Catalepsy was another phenomenon discussed. Now how do people show catalepsy? Perhaps I can cite an example to illustrate the answer. A while back, I called my psychiatric residents into the staff room and I brought in a patient for them to deal with. I sat the patient down in a chair, and I let the residents sit there for two, long hours while she looked out the window, combed her hair, scratched her head, scratched her shoulder, and so forth. I had told the residents before she arrived that they should each make a final diagnosis within the first 30 seconds of observing her. So we sat there for two, long hours. What was the diagnosis?—catatonic schizophrenia. And what was characteristic of her?—her catalepsy. For those two hours she kept her feet in an extremely awkward position, but that was the only part of her body that showed catalepsy.

How often does a hypnotic subject show catalepsy *not* when you lift his arm as you may expect, but rather in some other, unexpected part of his body? I've seen catalepsy manifested by a rigidity of the eyeball movements, where subjects move their heads but they do not move their eyeballs. That is, if they want to look over in that direction, they turn their heads rather than moving their eyes. Or, subjects may move their eyes but hold their necks stiff. But they are all showing catalepsy.

Partial Amnesia

Next is this matter of amnesia. What is amnesia? Does it necessarily mean that *everything* is forgotten? Hasn't the subject the right to select which material shall be amnesic and which material shall not be amnesic? And how do you know what is important to the subject? Something may be tremendously important to you as the hypnotist, but to the subject something else may be tremendously important. The result may be that the subject shows no *apparent* amnesia, yet if you really go over your protocol and your records, you will find an amnesia.

Perceiving Reduced Spontaneity

Now, this question of a lack of spontaneity: What is meant by that? How do you measure spontaneity? A subject can reach over the table, pick up a pack of cigarettes, light a cigarette, get an ashtray, offer you a cigarette, and yet be tremendously lacking in spontaneity at the same time. *It is the fineness with which you examine, and look at, and understand, what your subject's behavior really means.*

Minimal Cues

Observing Minimal Behavioral Indicators of Posthypnotic Behavior

He [Dr. Pattie?] mentioned the posthypnotic trance. My wife and I wrote a paper on that subject, and I still believe in that paper.[13] Sometimes subjects do not *show* a posthypnotic trance. Actually you have *not noticed* the fact that they showed the posthypnotic trance because they do not have to show it in relationship to the entire posthypnotic act. For example, the posthypnotic act may be to pick up the pitcher of water, pour a glassful, and drink it. . . . Amnesia consists only of the initial start—the initial picking up of the pitcher. Then the subject makes the rest of the posthypnotic act a conscious one. You never can tell exactly what your subject really understands. You simply have to observe—really observe!

Genuine Age Regression

*An Experiment Illustrating a "Child's" Shock
at Menstruating*

Next there is this matter of regression to an earlier age. Kubie and I wrote a paper on this issue in which we discussed the matter of role taking and the matter of real regression.[14] I'm going to tell you about an experiment I did—and I hope you don't throw bricks at me for it—but being a medical man often allows one to do things that a psychologist cannot do!

The experiment went as follows. My secretary tipped me off that a certain female psychology student, who was interested in learning clinical psychology, was menstruating. I had my secretary leave the office while I put the woman into a deep trance, regressing her back to the age of 10. I took a chance in picking that particular age—I didn't know her history; I really didn't know anything about her, except that she came from a good college and wanted to learn clinical psychology. So we sat there and chatted as little girl talking to big man; and while we were chatting we drank [hallucinated] lemonade, and we kept on drinking lemonade, and we kept on drinking lemonade. And you know what happens then—you have to go to the lavatory! So my subject went to the lavatory, where my secretary was waiting, hidden in a side room. Soon my secretary came running back to me and said, "Dr. Erickson, you are in a helluva mess." And I was! Here was this little girl sobbing her heart out, believing that she must have hurt herself terribly because she was bleeding, and she was really very

50

scared. So I had to get the head nurse and a couple of other secretaries to chaperone me, and we all went into that lavatory. It took me quite a long time to get back in contact with that "little girl," reassure her that everything was perfectly all right, and bring her back to her actual chronological age.

Now I think that was real regression. It was certainly an awakening of something long past. Maybe it was a therapeutic thing to do—it was certainly a risky thing to do experimentally; but it did demonstrate the genuineness of the subject's feelings, and it did contravert White's theory that hypnotic subjects simply do what you suggest to them, or what they think they are expected to do.[*]

Now so far as Martin Orne's Rorschach experiments are concerned: I happen to know Orne, and I have criticized him personally many times; therefore I feel free to repeat my criticism, knowing that he would not object if he were present. My criticism is that Orne has a tendency to spend a total of two whole minutes regressing somebody from the age of 54 back to the age of six. I think it takes a much longer period of time for one to rearrange the patterns and neurological processes involved in getting back to that age of six.

Difficulties in Measuring Hypnosis

. . . . Then there was Dr. Pattie's last remark about interpersonal relationships: that you can't measure friendship, and you can't measure hypnosis. I will agree that I was in error, but I still don't think that you can measure friendship by giving Rorschach tests and then selecting your friends in that way. Nor can you give the TAT [Thematic Apperception Test] and determine who your friends shall be. My feeling is that if we are to employ hypnosis scientifically, then we had better work at these various types of measurements until we find some general patterns, some linkings, that will enable us to understand what hypnosis is. I don't want to dismiss hypnosis as merely an interpersonal relationship that is not

---

[*]*Editors' Note:* The ethics of such an "experiment" would be questioned today. It certainly illustrates another of the possible dangers of hypnosis.

measureable, but I do object to saying that you can really measure hypnosis by certain tests. It just won't work—at least it hasn't so far, but I'm willing to be corrected any time somebody comes along with a test that does work.

Eds: The recent work of Kenneth Bowers and Ernest Hilgard indicate that even today, thirty years after Erickson made these remarks, there is still no generally accepted and scientifically objective measure of hypnosis.[15]

THE ROLE OF HYPNOSIS IN LEARNING AND MEMORY

[Following is Erickson's discussion of Dr. Dorcus's lecture about the influence of hypnosis on learning and habit modification.]

Hypnosis and Memory

Using Hypnosis to Revivify Extraneous Associations in the Recall of Nonsense Syllables

I'd like to make a few points about Dr. Dorcus's discussion this morning. First of all, there is this matter of recall and memory. I'm going to cite an example to make my point. A hypnotic subject of mine (who was also a psychology student) learned some nonsense syllables in relationship to an experimenter who did not know me. Two years later, the subject was tested for recall of those nonsense syllables. I think he succeeded in recalling only two out of some 30 syllables—I'm not certain, but I think it was only two. In the meantime, I got acquainted with the experimenter; I told him that, hypnotically speaking, the subject really ought to be able to recall more than two of those nonsense syllables. He replied, "All right, go ahead and see if you can get him to recall more."

Now how did I proceed? First of all, I drew from the experimenter a very adequate and very complete account of the room in which the original experiment had taken place—I had him really describe it to me. Then I wanted to know about the noises outside the experimental room, and I wanted to know about whatever street noises there were—and I went into those aspects in great detail. [When I finished getting information from the experimenter,] I put the subject into a deep trance, using the description of that original room, the description of the experimental apparatus, ... of the outside noises, of the street noises, and so on—using all those factors that were absolutely extraneous to the learning process. And that's all I did with the subject in the trance state: [revivify those seemingly irrelevant memories from the original situation]. Then I turned him over in the ordinary waking state to the experimenter, and he showed a surprising increase in the number of recallable nonsense syllables. All I did was to awaken extraneous associations which permitted pertinent memories to come forth. Certainly we see the same thing in psychotherapy: *it is the associated memories that are so often the key to evoking the [critical or traumatic] memories.*

> Eds: This is an example of how Erickson was using dissociation to facilitate state-dependent memory, learning, and behavior. See Part III of this volume for a theoretical exposition of this approach.

Q. What do you think would happen if you made those associations in the waking state?

A. I've done that in other instances. You know, it's an awfully boring thing; and it would be boring for any of you if a year from now I asked you to think back clearly and recall that the door just opened and a couple of people just entered. Now you'd think, why not get to the point? But in the hypnotic state, what *is* the point? The point is what you are talking about at that particular moment. In the waking state, however, you really want to get to the nucleus of the matter—and you're not going to be too tolerant of somebody who says, "Let's see, did the door open?; Did two people come in?; Was there somebody sitting in the front chair?", and so on. That is talking beside the point. The point is, what do you remember about a particular, specific instance? And I have found repeatedly that the building up of all these side issues permits a much better recollection.

Now I'll give you that example from my own personal life. Mrs. Erickson and I travelled through the Rockies in 1937, and at that time I had a gear shift on the floor of the car. Many years later I was telling a friend all about that trip [as we drove to the hospital], and as I turned into the hospital I exclaimed, "Now where *is* that gear shift?" I couldn't find the gear shift because I had forgotten that it was on the steering wheel now! The mere relation of the Rocky Mountain trip had brought about these other associations [in so vivid a manner that they momentarily became reality to me]. And you find that kind of phenomenon all the time.

Problems in Controlled Experimental Work

Now, the psychologists—and remember that I'm one, so I can speak with impunity—talk about controlled experiments. What are controlled experiments in, let us say, a nonsense syllable learning situation? It isn't a controlled experiment if you have altered anything from one situation to the next. I find that it's much more controlled when you have the same nonsense syllables, and when the experimenter was just as clean-shaven for the experiment as he is for the follow-up experiment two years later. Even the growing of a mustache is a very serious interference with recollection.

Posthypnotic Suggestion

The Role of Memory, Emotion, and Associative Networks in Experimental and Hypnotherapeutic Work

I have verified that finding on a number of occasions. But, again, memory simply is not an isolated experience. For you to remember me talking to you here today, you will have to bear in

54

mind that so-and-so sat there, that there is a blackboard here, that there are certain types of lights in this particular room, and so on, in order to have a complete memory and an available memory. And what difference does it make by what measure you approach that memory? What matters is that you are trying to find out what the memory is. So to put yourself in a totally different situation from the one associated with the memory—even though you may not recognize that it is a totally different situation—interferes seriously [with your ability to recall it. Recall is] a matter of memory *plus* the assocations that go with it.

Let's touch again briefly on the emotional aspects of hypnosis. Do I need to tell you directly or in any way whatsoever that this is a piece of chalk, and that there is a blackboard there? No, that is a spontaneous process of understanding that you yourselves reach. And in the treatment of the girl with no breast development . . . I covered a great deal of material that I didn't report—that I didn't even mention to the girl—because it wasn't necessary. All I had to do was raise certain topics and let the momentum of those topics carry her on in her own understandings and in her own wishes. When she asked me to examine her breasts, did she mean as a father, a lover, or as an M.D.? I really never did inquire into it. It was her privilege to make that request of me, and she could do it freely, easily, and comfortably in accord with her own needs. All I needed to do was to give her an opportunity to experience within herself all of the associated ideas, memories, feelings, and understandings—not to name them.

My feeling is that experimental psychologists name factors *A* and *B* and *C* and *D,* and that is the experiment. But you see, there are an awful lot of letters in the alphabet—26 to be exact. When you just name four of them, what are you really doing? Whether you know it or not, you are *implying* that there are 22 other letters!

Now this matter of isolating therapeutic and hypnotic techniques. How is it possible, really, to isolate them? In the first place you have a person who has many memories; you have a hypnotist who has many memories and ideas and feelings and attitudes. The tremendously important thing to recognize is that no matter how unimportant and how academic a suggestion may be, it may have a very special significance to an individual by virtue of his experience—yet it may have nothing to do with the experiment.

Dream Interpretation

Recasting the Same Dream via a Spiral Approach to Uncover True Meaning

Q. Dr. Erickson, would you say that [a person can interpret his own dream images?]

A. In LeCron's book on experimental hypnosis[16] which is coming out shortly, I've discussed that topic a bit. I don't believe that patients can, by themselves, interpret their dreams correctly. But you can get them to interpret the dreams correctly by using a rather simple phenomenon.

A patient comes to me with a dream. He tells me all about the dream, what he thinks it means, and so on. I tell the patient, "Well, suppose you dream that same dream tonight, *but with a different cast of characters*. It will have the same meaning, the same emotions; it will be the same dream, *but with a different cast of characters*." What does the patient do? The patient *does* dream that dream again, but with a different cast of characters. The "recasted" dream comes closer to the real meaning.

One of my residents in psychiatry came to me with one of his patient's dreams: "I was wandering in the woods. There was a shack there, and it was horrible, loathesome. I had a wretched feeling." So the resident told his patient in the trance state to recast the dream: "Dream the same dream, *but with a different cast of characters*." It took about eight recastings before the patient very clearly and very distinctly recognized his mother, his brother, his father, and the hateful feelings he had toward all of them.

You may seem to be playing around with this type of technique, yet you're giving patients the opportunity to walk around and around in a spiral that brings them right to where they want to be. But at the same time, you're not asking too much of them.

Therapeutic Implants

*Utilizing Repetition and Association in the Implantation of a
Lasting Feeling Tone[17]*

Q. [Erickson is speaking.] I have another question here, which I think is a rather important question to answer: How do I implant a lasting feeling-tone of hatred in a patient for something like the agate on my desk, or the tree less than 18 inches from the sidewalk?

A. The technique is rather slow and rather elaborate, but it is simply this. I'll give you a parallel example to illustrate. I smoke *Lucky's,* and Tareyton's, and *Lucky's,* and Raleigh's, and Camel's, and *Lucky's,* and Phillip Morris, and *Lucky's.* Now, what are you going to remember? You're going to remember the *Lucky's!* When I want to implant a lasting feeling-tone, I have the patient tell me some of his hatreds, his fears, his anxieties; then I manage to drag that tree or that agate (or whatever it is that he hates) into the narration, so that it becomes colored and a part of it. And don't we do that all the time in everyday life? Isn't that a normal process that we experience all the time? We can't help ourselves.

Therapeutic Depersonalization

*Transforming Pathological Dissociation into a Dissociation "To
Be Proud Of"*

Q. I want to question the statement which Dr. Baker made about the difficulty of inducing depersonalization in the state of hypnosis. I've found that it is very easy to do, and as a matter of fact, very common.

A. [Dr. Baker responds.] What I was pointing out was that when the phenomenon of depersonalization is seen in a patient, it is ordinarily something that one must carefully note; it may be a very severe symptom, as far as personality disintegration is concerned.

Erickson's utilization of a similar phenomenon in the therapeutic setting is what intrigues me.

[Erickson responds.] Perhaps I can add to that in another way. I had a patient whom I had looked over. My secretary had also looked her over, and she said, "Dr. Erickson, don't you dare take that woman as a patient, because if you hypnotize her, everybody will say that you caused her psychosis."

The patient was just about one step from being committed to an institution. As a catatonic, she wasn't always sure who she was. Some of the time she thought she was X, her intimate friend who had been committed. So some of the time this poor girl was herself, and some of the time she was X. Well, that's depersonalization: a loss of personal identity. My feeling was that it could be handled hypnotically.

The patient proved to be a good hypnotic subject, both as herself and as X. What was my approach? I used a group of medical students as an audience. I deliberately depersonalized the patient and had her see herself, and then I had her see that *that* person was really X. I discussed at tremendous length the nature and meaning and scientific significance of dissociation as a phenomenon. What happened? The girl became so proud of her accomplishment that she protected it, and so that was the end of being X. She was willing to see herself away from herself, and who was she? "All I know is that I'm an intelligence looking at Jane, but me . . . *me* . . . what does that mean? I suppose I should call that person *me* [instead of X]."

She was so terribly proud of having contributed to the education of medical students. She was so terribly proud of the fact that her dissociation was of social and educational value that she protected it. And that was the end of her pathological dissociation. It became transformed into a good, controlled dissociation, *at my request*.[18] Do I make myself clear?

Psychogenic Stuttering as Aggression?

Q. Did I understand you to say earlier that stuttering is *always* a form of aggression? Or would you like to modify that a wee bit? [laughter]

A. I certainly will modify it. I know that you can get stuttering from neurological causes, but I was speaking of psychogenic causes.

Q. Would you say, then, that psychogenic stuttering is *always* a form of aggression?

A. Now we're quibbling about terms. What is aggression to me might not be aggression to you. We define it in terms of the patient, and of his reactions.

The Dangers of Hypnosis

A Matter of Social Attitudes, Ignorance, and Prejudice

Q. Dr. Erickson, we hear so much about [the dangers of hypnosis]. Have you had any experiences that were disagreeable?

A. I have had a lot of disagreeable experiences. People think that I can do practically anything because I'm a hypnotist— especially anything that's wrong! [laughter] T'aint so! It's the social implications. People avoid my eyes because, well, I don't use them in the right way. It seems I overemphasize the way I look at some part of the anatomy, or something of that sort. There are a lot of social implications in that. But as far as causing actual harm to the patient, I don't think so. The harm comes when people convince a patient that he's an awful idiot for even allowing himself to consult a hypnotherapist. Plenty of people are harmed by others convincing them that they shouldn't have that cancer removed. But I don't think it's inherent in medicine; I think it's a matter of social attitudes. That's where the harm lies.

Temporal Considerations in the Recasting of Dreams

Q. [Question was inaudible.]

A. You tell a patient to recast his dream characters, and it may be a week or two before he does so. What happens? The patient may be building up his courage, or thinking things through; he may be waiting for a certain stimulus that he is confident will come along and open his eyes to a certain thing, or open his understanding. One really doesn't know. Sometimes the patient will go to sleep that same day and recast the dream. More than once, I've told a patient in a deep trance, "Well, you really ought to let your conscious mind know about it. When do you think you'll do it?" I've had patients postpone it for three months. Why? Well, in one instance I discovered why it took three months quite by accident. It happened to be exactly three months until Christmas. At Christmas, Father and Mother were coming to visit; and when they came to visit, the patient really developed the understanding. I hadn't paid attention to the calendar, because I knew I'd find out sooner or later. But there is always a purpose served by time.

Hypnotherapy with Children

Nonresistance and Double Binding Suggestions
Juxtaposing the Positive and the Negative to
Depotentiate Behavior Problems

Q. [Question concerns the use of hypnotherapy with children].

A. I haven't had much practice in working with children. Most of the children with whom I've worked have had bedwetting problems, or some other such behavior problem. Then the question comes of *not* using hypnosis, because the child can learn much more about misbehavior that might alarm his parents. The behavior-problem child is really something more than that; it is a parental-misbehavior problem, also. Your primary emphasis has to be on the parent.

For example, an eight-year-old boy was brought to me as a patient. He devoted the first two hours in my office to an effort to exasperate me beyond all control. And he really did a beautiful job if it! [laughter] However, he found out that I could lean back in my chair, and sit, and watch him; and he couldn't quite understand that. By the third hour, he sat down in a chair and started acting like a gentleman. Then I was able to call in his mother.

The mother said, "You know, I think the whole trouble is this. Just because I'm a war bride, everybody thinks I'm a prostitute!"

She was really taking that out on her child. It was no wonder he had behavior problems! We discussed the matter, and she found out, to her amazement, that I didn't really believe she was a prostitute. It was the first time she had ever verbalized her fear to a stranger. And she had that terribly tense feeling.

She was also very much amazed that Sonny hadn't taken my office apart. But my nonresistance, my just sitting there, left him in an awful quandry, which I further secured by saying the following: "I don't think you ought to open my cigarette box, but it's there, isn't it? And you *can* open it, can you *not?* It's just that I think you *shouldn't,* but I'm *sure* you can. And it's right there." With those statements, I had given *and* denied permission; he had to make a choice. Naturally his choice was, "I don't need to punish that guy." He was quite correct.

I very seldom use hypnosis on children for the reason that it's too much of an argument with the parents.[19]

Hypnotherapy and Habit Problems

*Problems in the Use of Hypnotherapy as a Treatment
Approach to Alcoholism and Smoking*

Q. [Question concerns the use of hypnotherapy in the breaking of bad habits, such as smoking and drinking.]

A. One can build up a variety of techniques, and some hypnotherapists succeed in doing so. I don't like to use hypnosis with alcoholics, because they very promptly try to place a dependency of the wrong sort upon me. As for cigarette smoking, I'd rather go into the matter of, do you or do you not want to quit? I let patients make their own decisions rather than trying to force them.

I've got a dentist friend, for example, who has been making

appointments with me for three years now: he wants me to use hypnosis to cure him of smoking. I give him the appointments regularly, but I fill them with somebody else's name. [laughter] I know the man doesn't want to give up smoking.

As for alcohol, some therapists are actually successful in handling it hypnotically. I've never really had any success, and I don't really want to try. I am experimentally minded, yet it seems psychologically wrong to me (to use hypnosis in treating alcoholism)—because once you get a drink under your belt, you're psychologically a different sort of creature. And then what happens to those hypnotic suggestions?

> Eds: In the 1970s Erickson told the senior editor many anecdotal, therapeutic examples of his successful treatment of alcoholism and smoking. His approaches usually involved the use of strong behavioral controls and changes in the environment, with hypnosis used in a supporting role.

ANTISOCIAL APPLICATIONS OF HYPNOSIS

Legal Considerations in Hypnosis

Q. [Question concerns the antisocial use of hypnosis.]

A. You know what Gladstone says about the law: precedents determine outcome, not facts. I conducted rather extensive experiments in which I actually created situations where there would be definite antisocial acts.[20] But I didn't get any true antisocial acts. Sure, I got certain types of antisocial acts. Do you know the old trick about taking Papa's cigarette? You hold your hand like this, and you tell your friend to watch you blow smoke out of your eyes. Now you've really got the cigarette like this, and you carefully burn your friend's hands. [Laughter] I induced a subject to believe that that would be a beautiful trick to play on a friend of hers. Well, she rehearsed it on me, and decided that the burn I got was much too painful. But I got what was coming to me!

Criminal Applications of Hypnosis?

Q. Is it possible to commit a crime such as murder in the state of hypnosis, if it is against the moral code of the person?

A. I'll tell you a story I think you'll like to answer that question. Tony was a very good friend of mine. He was an excellent hypnotic subject, and an adept pickpocket. I knew all about his "special" talent. Tony's favorite trick was to circulate among the guests at a gathering, pick their pockets, and exchange the wallets he had lifted. Then, after he had completed his rounds, he would haul out the wallet in his pocket on some pretext—to check his driver's license, or whatever—and promptly look very surprised. Somebody else from the group would glance at the wallet Tony was holding, and exclaim, "Why, that's my wallet!"—whereupon *he* would reach into *his* pocket and discover a strange wallet. And so forth. It would create a nice bit of confusion!

Knowing all this, I decided it would be very nice to put Tony in a trance and instruct him to pick the pockets of the doctors and psychologists at my gathering, all of whom he knew. Well, Tony told me in the trance state, "That's *my* trick." He wasn't going to be instrumentalized by me, and that was that! I awakened him, gave him a full recollection of his attitude, whereupon he apologized saying, "After all I owe you, I really ought to be willing to do a thing like that. Besides, it would be a lot of fun." So I put him back in the trance and gave him instructions. Again he said, "That's *my* trick!" [Laughter] There was nothing I could do about it. I even gave him a few cocktails to weaken him a bit. It didn't work. That was Tony's trick, and it didn't belong to me. If I wanted to do it myself, okay, but that was his own trick.

Hypnosis as a Scapegoat

You hear a lot of people claiming that they did things under the influence of hypnosis. Well, yes, but I wonder why they have to resort to that defense. I've had patients come to me and tell me various stories about how a doctor gave them a drug which caused them to have an automobile accident. What was the drug? Well, the doctor had written a prescription, that's correct; and he'd written it on a certain drugstore. But the prescription was still in their pockets—it hadn't even been filled! I don't think the drug caused them to meet with that automobile accident. Yet they claim it was the drug the doctor gave them, even though it was a drug they couldn't get in the doctor's office, and even though there was no record of it. And when you confront such people with the absolute truth, they break down. You hear of that sort of situation. People are always making a scapegoat of something, and hypnosis is awfully handy.

Unrealistic Expectations About Hypnosis

Q. [Question again concerns the use of hypnosis to influence people in antisocial directions.]

A. The one answer I can give to that question is this. You have perfectly honest, sincere people come into your office *wanting* to by hypnotized. They work hard at therapy. But no matter how good a hypnotist you are, it is a long, slow, hard, and difficult process to get them well; to get them the way they want to be . To get patients to do something that is *contrary* to their natures—I certainly wouldn't want that job. Getting them to do things they *want* to do is hard enough!

> Eds: Erickson's remarks about how hypnotherapy can be a slow and difficult process need to be emphasized to counteract the unrealistic expectation for rapid and miraculous cures that has been associated with his work. In the last decade of his life, Erickson recounted many such slow and tedious therapeutic processes to the senior editor. During this entire period (eight years), for example, the Erickson family received a daily visit from one of Erickson's former patients who had been a hospitalized schizophrenic. Erickson was able to bring the patient to a marginal adjustment where he could care for himself and his own apartment, but the "vis-

its" to the Erickson household were still a necessary support eight years later. The necessity of the visits was only partially disguised by the pretext that the patient had to board his dog at the Ericksons' home because he was not allowed to keep a dog in his apartment.

MILTON H. ERICKSON:
A PHOTOGRAPHIC PORTFOLIO

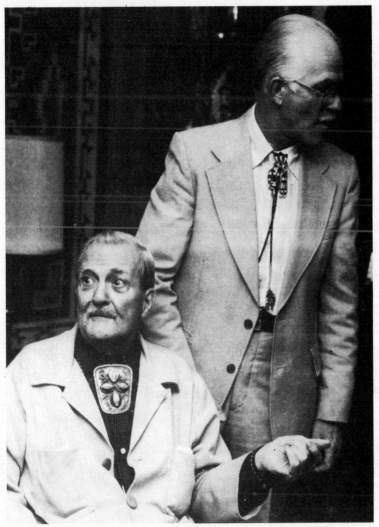

A surprised Erickson with Dr. Marion Moore, his personal physician. February, 1980.

Erickson inducing a moment of cataleptic fascination with his student, Lee Boeke Burke. February, 1980.

Lee's astonished delight at seeing her hand remain cataleptic even while apparently out of trance. February, 1980.

Ernest Rossi, reflecting upon the Erickson manuscripts.
June, 1978.

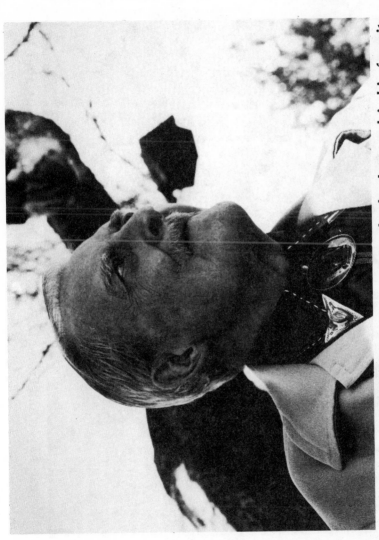

Erickson in a contemplative moment. In the background is his favorite paloverde tree. February, 1980.

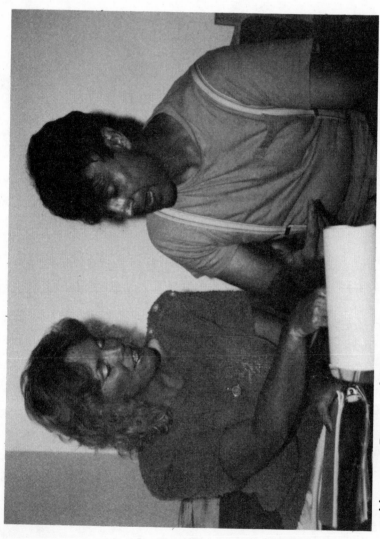

Margaret Ryan and Ernest Rossi at work on this series. August, 1986.

PART II

SYMPTOM-BASED APPROACHES IN
MIND-BODY PROBLEMS*

Therapeutic Hypnosis as the Communication of
Ideas

The Reinterpretation of Terminal Cancer Pain as an Itch;
Producing Numbness Instead of an Itch

The first topic I want to present concerns what you legitimately can expect of your patient. I am going to cite an example. I have a 23-year-old daughter, Betty Alice, who is a school teacher; she is also a good hypnotic subject. She teaches English. She doesn't know very much about anatomy or physiology except what she has gained from her own life experiences. I took her and her mother to visit a cancer patient last night. The cancer patient is troubled with nausea and vomiting. She has been rather difficult to handle in this regard because she does not have much belief in herself. So I asked

*Seminar presented in San Diego, California, in July of 1961. *Note:* Occasionally, well-known cases are repeated in Erickson's lectures. Sometimes greater detail or a different contextual emphasis is provided by Erickson's re-telling. For these reasons, and in the interest of continuity, we have left repeated stories intact.

my daughter to go into a trance and then I explained to her: "This lady has cancer; she suffers from nausea and vomiting. I would like to have your advice about what suggestions I should give her."

Here is a 23-year-old girl in a very profound trance, a school teacher, teaching English, asked to be a medical consultant. My daughter replied, "Let me think." She thought for a while and then she said, "I can answer." I asked her how she knew she could answer and she said, "I made myself sick. First I became nauseous; then I felt all of the stomach muscles of my stomach as I started to heave; and then I cut it off. I produced a cut-off right through here [apparently her stomach]. I lost all that feeling of nausea, and I cut off the contractions of the muscles."

I asked my daughter where she felt the nausea and she said, "I felt it first right there, down here [pointing to her abdomen], and then I felt it back here." Immediately her mother spoke up to explain, "Those are the semicircular canals that are so often involved in nausea and vomiting." Then I asked Betty Alice, "What did you do about this feeling back here? You cut it off— what do you mean by that?

"You produce an anesthesia for it; you direct your attention elsewhere; you change the way you are thinking," was her wise response.

Now, I cite this experience as an example because it is so awfully important for you to realize that when you ask patients to do things, you have to depend upon them to do it in their own way. I didn't know what my daughter was going to do. I knew that my patient could lie there in the bed and watch my daughter, listen to my daughter, become tremendously impressed, and perhaps gain the feeling that she could go ahead and work out her own way of handling her problem.

I want to cite this same point in another regard. I first saw her on February 27th. At that time, she was lying in her bed curled up on her right side. She had been fed so much morphine and Demerol that the drugs had become inactive. She had had X-ray therapy for metastases from breast carcinoma, metastases to the hips, throughout her abdomen, and her lungs. She was in absolute pain throughout most of her body. She had been referred to me in the hope that hypnosis might help her to resolve the pain.

I went out to see her and as I walked into her room she exclaimed, "Don't hurt me, don't hurt me, don't hurt me, don't hurt me, don't hurt me." She uttered this continuous, monotonous recitation; and now and then she would intersperse, "Don't scare me, don't scare me, don't scare me, don't hurt me."

It was very difficult to get her attention. I did it in this particular way. I told her, "I am going to hurt you, I really am going to hurt you. I am going to hurt you quite a bit—I bet more than you are hurting right now—and I am going to scare you, too. Not too much, but I am definitely going to scare you."

She paused in her monotonous verbalizations to say, "Please don't hurt me, please don't scare me."

I said, "But I must hurt you; I must scare you. What we've got to find out is, how much do I have to hurt you? How much do I have to scare you? In what way am I going to scare you? Why am I going to scare you?"

I am reminded of Dr. Brody's "W's"; Why, what, where and so on. I finally had her attention. I pointed out that the hurt would be this: I knew that she had been lying on her right side for some time. I wanted her to think about turning over in bed. The X-rays had revealed metastases on the neck of the femur, and her doctor thought one femur had been fractured. So I got her to think all that over, and she said she didn't even want to remember how she turned over. I told her to go to sleep, sound asleep; but in doing so she was to keep her mind wide awake; that her body was to go to sleep—just her body—but her mind was to remain wide awake.

I emphasize this point because it is a most important technique in trance induction—especially for your patients who cannot understand the division between the unconscious and the conscious mind. You need a willingness to tell them to keep the mind wide awake, let the body go sound asleep; fixate your attention on what I am saying; stay wide awake as your body goes more and more asleep.

The patient finally agreed that her body was sound asleep. Then I told her:*

*Eds: In this presentation, we will highlight some of Erickson's hypnotic suggestions by offsetting them in **bold face** type.

"There are certain things I want you to do. You don't have to think of turning over in bed—that would really hurt. But I want you to develop a horrible, a very horrible and terrible itch on the sole of your right foot. And really develop it there and make it horrible, terrible."

The patient replied, "Why? I have enough pain."

I said, "Yes, you know what pain is. I want to use your knowledge of pain to develop a horrible itch."

Here is a patient conditioned to suffering, expecting to die within a few months' time, and I am asking her to develop a serious itch on the sole of her foot! I told her she would not understand why, but that she ought to do it. She finally agreed. She tried hard, but the best she could do was to develop a numb feeling on the back of the foot. I let her apologize for it and I let her point out that she couldn't help it. She had tried very hard to get an itch, but instead that numb feeling developed and she just couldn't help it. I was very glad to have her tell me she couldn't help it, because then I could agree with her that she couldn't help it. She couldn't help that numb feeling from spreading and spreading and spreading all over her body. The woman had pain throughout her entire body, terminal cancer pain, and so I taught her to have a numb feeling throughout her body. Within three hours the patient was pain-free, and she has remained pain-free since last February.

The X-rays taken recently showed a virtual disappearance of the masses in her body, and the bone seemed to be in good condition. But she still has nausea and vomiting. I want to correct that nausea and vomiting, but I want to emphasize this sort of peculiar approach. It was mentioned this morning. You need to say something to patients that helps them make their own responses. You can have your ideas. *You offer ideas to patients in such a way that they have an opportunity to interpret what you have said in their own way; and whatever patients produce, you accept and abide by.*

Now, getting that itch on her foot: I'd better talk about something horrible, terrible, distressing, because that patient was already oriented around something horrible and distressing. Why should I talk about pleasant things against a background of her experience, her expectations? I would be acting wrongfully to talk about pleasant things. Therefore, I could talk about a horrible itch.

She wouldn't want to add a horrible itch; she would want to add a numb feeling. I would have the totality of *her* desires to bring about a numb feeling rather than a horrible itch. That is what I wanted, but I didn't have to tell the patient. *I merely presented ideas in such a way that the patient could abide by them, and accept them, and develop them.*

Hypnosis as the Communication of Ideas

Stuttering as One Variety of Communication; Segregating the English Language from Stuttering Language

Hypnosis is a matter of communicating ideas to people. It is the presentation of understandings. Patients come to you because they do not understand certain things.

I can think of the stutterer who came to me and explained with great difficulty that he had been stuttering all of his life. He couldn't talk; he stuttered. And would I cure him of his stuttering? Well, of course, that is what the stutterer wants—to be cured of the stutter.

My patient became rather disgusted as I began discussing another subject entirely. I mentioned that stuttering was a form of speech. He knew that, and so did I. I mentioned that there are male stutterers and female stutterers; that stuttering was a kind of communication, just as a foreign language is a kind of communication. Some people can be taught German, some can be taught French, some can be taught Spanish. Even though they know English, they can still learn Polish, or Italian, or Spanish. While that stutterer was listening to me and wondering why I was talking about foreign languages, I made my point: *even though you know English, you can learn another language.*

As soon as I could see him thinking clearly along these lines, I said:

"Of course you do stutter, and you say you want me to cure you of stuttering. Would you like, rather, to have me teach you how to talk?"

71

He immediately translated that question into the possibility of keeping his stutter *and* learning to talk as another variety of communication. In other words, he would be able to stutter and also be able to talk.

> **"You know, little babies learn to talk; they learn to talk by making senseless noises, repetitiously, frequently, over and over again. They try out every kind of a sound. They finally say, "ma," and then they say "mama." By repeating *da, da, da,* they get lots of praise from others and from themselves. Suppose you are willing to learn to make some kind of noises, intentionally."**

When stutterers start learning to make noises *intentionally,* then they have laid the foundation for learning to talk. You see, the stutterer has the idea that he cannot possibly learn to talk. He has stuttered all of his life, and he cannot *talk without stuttering.* Stuttering is his way of communication. *You need to segregate his stuttering from this matter of learning to talk.*

Misconceptions About Psychotherapy

The Myth of Symptom Substitution; Crafting Healthy Habits from Old Problems: Interjecting Exercise into Obsessive Debating

Let us discuss this matter of the correction of symptoms and the development of symptom substitution. I would like to emphasize my belief that this is a most unfortunate, unhappy, medical superstition that is old enough to be retired! The practice of medicine and dentistry is, in large part, symptomatic treatment.

The patient comes in and says, "I have a headache. Can you give me some aspirin?" You relieve the headache, but does the patient then go out and develop a backache because you took the headache away? The patient comes in and says, "I have a broken tooth. Will you repair it?" So you repair the broken tooth. Does the patient then go out and break his leg? No.

In medicine and in dentistry, a large part of your practice is symptom removal. Wouldn't it really be reasonable to expect your patient to replace a symptom with something *less* serious? I think it is awfully important for you to recognize that possibility, instead of listening to the alarmist who shouts that if you remove a symptom, it will be replaced by something much worse. I can think of the unfounded declaration by certain critics that curing cigarette smoking with hypnosis will lead to obesity in the patient. If you cure a patient of alcoholism with hypnosis, he will become a drug addict. If you cure the patient with drug addiction, then a psychotic depression develops. I wonder if these critics have ever discovered the fact that when you fail to cure the cigarette habit, patients go right back to smoking cigarettes; and obese patients go back to shoveling food into their faces. They do not develop alcoholism, or drug addiction, or psychotic depression. They go back to their old familiar patterns. I do think it is desirable when treating a patient for symptoms to suggest that they develop some other constructive way of utilizing the energy that went into the bad habit.

I had a patient who could not decide anything: Shall I go to bed now, or shall I go to bed half an hour from now? Do I take off my right shoe first, or do I take off my left shoe first? No, the right; no, the left; no, the right; the left. My statement to the patient was the following: "Why not utilize that energy in some constructive way, because you use a lot of energy debating right shoe, left shoe, right shoe, left shoe. You can also use that energy in some other way." Now, of course, the patient has enough energy to debate that question, and perhaps to read two or three chapters in the geology book. But do you have to tell the patient that he will still have the energy left over to debate the question? The satisfactions that derive from reading the extra chapters in the geology book serve to allow the patient to skip that horrible debate.

I can think of a third-year medical student who has had to drop out of school. Shall he divorce his wife? Shall he remain married to her? Shall he divorce his wife, or shall he remain married to her? That question plagued him night after night, disturbing him so much that he often had to wait until 2:00 or 3:00 a.m. to fall asleep. My statement to him was the following: "Yes, you can actually debate that question, but not in this sort of a fashion, every night as

73

you try to fall asleep. You are a little bit overweight; you need the exercise; you are a third-year medical student.

"Why don't you walk around the block, round and around and around—while you debate that question. You can debate that question this way, sitting in your room leaning on your desk; or you can debate that same question, right foot, left foot, walking around the block: *Right foot,* shall I divorce my wife, *left foot,* shall I remain married to her? And enjoy the walk, enjoy the exercise, enjoy developing fatigue, enjoy getting ready for bed.

"Before you start out, first map out a reasonable walk, a long enough walk, so that you will feel tired at the end of it; so that you can come back to your apartment and go to bed. You have thoroughly debated the question."

It was a tremendously important thing for him to continue debating about his marriage because he wasn't debating that he had substituted exercise and walking for debating! He feels better about it, and he thinks that he'd better have psychotherapy for his condition rather than devoting himself to this question: Shall I divorce her? Shall I remain married to her?

Misconceptions About Psychotherapy

Reinstating the Need for Unconscious Knowledge; Questions Investigating and Depotentiating a Fainting Symptom to Evoke Unconscious Resolution

Another misconception is that you should make conscious the unconscious mind. I think it is imperative for all of you to realize that therapy of any sort, the instruction of any patient, does not depend upon making the unconscious conscious. All you need to do is examine the history of the human race. You will note that the unconscious mind and the conscious mind have co-existed throughout the entire history of the human being, and that the conscious mind and the unconscious mind are still co-existent.

74

They don't always agree, but they are co-existent! It is necessary for us to have a great deal of our knowledge at the unconscious level.

Did you ever consciously try to tie your shoestring? Let's see, you put it over this way, that way; and how do you really tie a double bow knot in your shoestring? It is very difficult for you to describe which finger, which thumb, and so on, and how you do it? You need to do it automatically, at the unconscious level. When you first learned to drive a car, you held the wheel tightly in your hands and you figured, there is a corner coming ahead, and when do I turn the wheel? When you go through a lot of conscious thinking, you are an *in*expert driver. As soon as you become an expert, you casually note the corner ahead, or the stoplight ahead. You roll gently up to the stop light and stop with the right amount of pressure on the brake without failing to put the clutch in, and so on. And you do it all automatically. In fact, you drive across town in traffic conversing with a friend, never realizing that you have gone through town because you have done it automatically. So it is in everyday, ordinary living.

When you are dealing with a patient, you can ask that patient to realize that there is an explanation for your gagging; there is an explanation for your fainting; there is an explanation for your symptomatology. Maybe you need to know it consciously, and maybe you don't. The important questions are: Do you need to keep that particular symptom? Do you need to keep it in part? Do you need to change it for something better? Neither you nor I know consciously what you ought to do about it. But, if you let your unconscious mind think it through, it can arrive at some way of handling that particular symptom.

I think of the concert pianist who had the unfortunate experience of fainting the first time he was supposed to give a concert. Thereafter, for the next fifteen years, he just simply fainted if he tried to go on the platform to give a concert. He could play for no more than a total of three friends in his own home, but he could not play publicly. He couldn't even play in an empty public hall, because as surely as he got up on the platform he would faint.

I asked him rather simple questions: Do you really need to keep that symptom? Would you like to play concerts publicly? Do you suppose your unconscious mind has some kind of a solution for this problem? Has it ever occurred to you to be curious about your symptom? Are you willing to have that symptom?

This matter of human behavior is a very important thing. You should respect human behavior, and you should allow all human beings to *behave,* no matter what kind of behavior it is. You try to guide them intelligently, but you need to meet their weaknesses as well as their strengths. With this particular man, I suggested the following approach:

> **"Now, the piano is over there, and there is the beginning of the platform. Suppose we take this red towel, and this blue towel, and this green towel, and this yellow towel, and we will drop them [along the platform]. The question is, as you walk across the platform, will you faint at the red towel, or the blue one, or the yellow one, or the purple one, or the white one? Let's see at which one will you faint, and there is one on the piano. One other color. Now, let's see which towel will you faint at. And with the second trip, will you faint at the same towel, or will you faint at a different one?"**

Why not find that out? Why should that man ever be afraid of fainting? Fainting is simply: syncope, and drop down to the floor. You don't fall very far. Any drunk can fall down without hurting himself, and he ought to be able to do the same. Now, the man became very interested in these issues. He didn't faint at the first towel, and that astonished him. He didn't faint at the second; surely it will be the third. No, wrong again! Fourth? No. Do you suppose he'll get clear to the piano before he faints? He did, and then I broke the bad news to him. "Well, maybe, you can faint *after* you start playing. Maybe you can."

Why should I be scared or terrified or threatened of his fainting? Or why should he? That was the question. The man is now playing concerts in public. Do I need to know what was in his unconscious mind that caused him to faint? Did I need to make it conscious? The essential point is this: There was something in his unconscious mind that caused him to faint. It had been there some fifteen years ago. Would any one of you really like to tell me what kind of thinking you did in frightening circumstances fifteen years ago? I don't think you could give a very accurate account of it. It would be awfully, awfully difficult. Most patients are afraid of their symptoms. They ought not to be afraid of their symptoms. They've got their symptoms. Therefore, you had better deal with those symptoms.

Age Regression in Dentistry and General Medicine

Let's discuss this matter of age regression in dentistry, and, I would add, age regression in medicine. Some say that dentists are unqualified to do age regression, or that general practitioners are unqualified to do age regression. But I think that any dentist or any practitioner is able to ask me: "When you were eight years old, where did you live?" And, I am able to think back in my memory and say, "On a farm near Lowell, Wisconsin."

"What kind of things interested you when you were eight years old in the summertime?"

"Well, I know what interested me: wading in puddles, barefooted, interested me tremendously."

Isn't that a matter of regression so far as my memories are concerned? I think the dentist is entitled to ask a patient in the trance state: "Now here is a specific problem of yours—gagging. What are you understanding about that gagging?" I do not think the dentist is at all interested in the totality of the patient's experiences way back in that patient's childhood. The dentist is interested only in the specific experiences that resulted in gagging. If the patient says, "I had a tonsillectomy," the dentist can say, "You know, a tonsillectomy is a medical problem, and your gagging is a dental problem. Therefore, you don't need the gagging in that connection." The dentist is not exploring a medical problem; he is defining the dental aspect of it.

"I don't think you need the gagging as part of your tonsillectomy, because the gagging that you have is a dental problem."

I think the general practitioner is also entitled to regress a patient for any specific goal. I think the psychiatrist is properly trained to regress the patient, not only in regard to specific experiences, but in relationship to related and even remote experiences.

Age Regression, Amnesia, and Resistance

Utilizing Direct, Authoritative Suggestions to Depotentiate Resistance; Revivifying Past Trance States; Specific Amnesias as Statements of Resistance

Now, at what level of trance can you secure any regression? A patient was recently referred to me who is being sued for an enormous sum of money. He is awfully afraid that he will lose the suit because he has an amnesia for something that would prevent the loss of the suit: the location of some papers he had hidden which contained some specific information. He is being sued by a swindler. The man came to me and said that this doctor had trained him to be a good hypnotic subject but didn't feel that he could handle the problem. Therefore, he sent the patient to me, writing that the patient was very highly resistant and could only develop a medium trance.

The patient came and told me that his doctor said I should put him in a trance, a deep trance, and that I should regress him. The patient said he was very, very cooperative. I have never seen a more resistant patient in my life than this particular man! He resisted going into a trance in every possible way. What could I do with the man? I explained to him very simply:

"You are highly resistant; you aren't letting me put you in a trance; you aren't letting me teach you anything about hypnosis; you have the idea that *I* put you in a trance,

which is false. You have to learn to go into a trance. You can go into the trance that your doctor taught you.''

The patient said he was sorry he was so resistant. So then we agreed that in no way would I try to influence him; in no way would I try to direct him; that I would merely sit here, and he could sit there; and he could go into a trance all by himself, on his own terms.

He went into an excellent light trance. He regressed to the year of 1932. He lost all contact with me except that he realized someone was standing over there somewhere, sitting over there somewhere, some stranger whom he didn't know; whom his mother didn't know. In that state of regression he was talking to his mother, and he was telling her that he wasn't going to let anything happen. It was a nice regression state. Shortly, he aroused from it with the realization that he had been in a trance, that he had regressed.

He said, ''That rather looks like I can regress but I am not going to regress for your benefit.''

I asked him why and he said, ''What are you talking about?''

I said, ''Why aren't you going to regress?''

He said, ''What are you talking about?''

He had developed an amnesia for his trance state and for his regression.

So we talked a while on casual topics and then he said, ''That is interesting. I went into a trance and I regressed to the year 1932. I was talking to my mother and I was explaining that I wouldn't do something.''

''What was it you wouldn't do?'' I asked.

''What are you talking about?'' he responded.

He had developed another spontaneous amnesia. In other words, he was demonstrating that he would not cooperate with me. Yet he was in a light trance and he did regress on his own terms. If I didn't interrupt him, he could give me details about the year 1932. The events he wanted to recover were in the year 1950, or thereabouts. The patient demonstrated his absolute resistance. After the trial I will hear from the patient's doctor about what he finally did. I gave him posthypnotic suggestions that he might recall the amnesiac material just before the trial, during the trial, just after the trial, a week before; and I listed various other possibilities of behavior.

Utilizing Psychological Processes in Pain Control

Pain Reduction via Sensory Displacement, Fragmentation, Fractional Diminution, Reinterpretation, and Transformation

Now this same principle applies to recovery from any kind of illness or distress. You want your patient to utilize various psychological processes. Let us take this matter of cancer pain. How does one lose pain from cancer? You can do it by anesthesia. However, some patients cannot develop anesthesia. But *your* patient needs to be free of pain. Maybe your patient has some other painful condition and can't develop anesthesia. I think you need to bear in mind that the human body is capable of a wealth of manifestations. You teach your patient in the trance state—light, medium, or deep— the possibilities of a variety of functions. That is, you can develop anesthesia, and that is one thing, you can develop analgesia, and that is another thing. Maybe you are unable to develop a total anesthesia, but maybe you *can* develop an analgesia for the pain.

You point out to the patient: "You know, a businessman can have worries that hurt and trouble him up here in the mind, and he can have ulcers in the stomach as a result. He can have that displacement, that conversion.

"Now, you've got cancer pain. Why not have another kind of pain also? Why not have pain out here in your hand? You have cancer pain in your body. It is very, very troublesome; it is very, very threatening; it is going to kill you. You know that. You wouldn't mind any amount of pain out here in your hand, because that wouldn't kill you. It is the pain in your torso that is going to kill you, and if you only had pain out here you could stand any amount."

You can teach your patient to displace the pain from the torso out into the hand where it is gladly experienced, because it has lost its threatening quality.

Stop to consider how people treat this matter of pain. How do people describe pain? It is a *dragging* pain; it is a *gnawing* pain; it is a *cutting* pain; it is a *burning* pain; it is a *cold* pain; it is a *hard* pain; it is a *dull* pain. Consider all of the adjectives that are applied to pain. You tell your patients in the trance state to think over their pain. Maybe they can't cut out the *nagging* quality of the pain, but maybe they can cut out the *burning* quality; maybe they can cut out the *heavy* quality. Or maybe they can keep the heavy, dull aspect of the pain, and lose the burning, the cutting, the lancinating, shooting qualities of the pain. And what have you done? You have asked your patients to take the total experience of pain and to fragment it into a variety of sensations; and as surely as your patients fragment their pain into a variety of sensations, they have reduced it.

I think I can give you a nice illustration of this idea. What happens when you fragment things? A pretty girl is a very kissable person. She is awfully nice to look at; she is pretty; she has pretty eyes; a pretty mouth; pretty lips. And you would really like to kiss her. But, you know, her eyes are a little too wide apart, her upper lip is a little bit short, her lower lip sticks out just a little bit too far, her face is too narrow. What happens to all of her kissable qualities? They slowly vanish as you get hypercritical in that fashion. You would be a lot happier to say she is kissable!

The same thing happens when you start picking a pain apart. The same thing happens when you start picking apart any kind of a symptom. That cancer patient I described last night: The next time I see her, if she still has nausea and vomiting, I am going to ask her to describe the location of the nausea. Is it more on the right than on the left? Is it mid-abdomen, or slightly below the mid-abdomen? Is there a warm quality to part of that nausea? Is there a cool quality to part of that nausea? Is there a little twitch to some of that nausea? And I am going to ask her to examine that nausea in every possible detail until she literally fragments it.

Now, another matter that was mentioned this morning which I want to discuss is this matter of symptom diminution. "How much of that cancer pain do you have now? Let us rate it on the basis of

100 percent. If you lost one percent of it, you wouldn't notice the loss—you would still feel it as if it were 100 percent." Your purpose, of course, is to get the patient to recognize the possibility of *unnoticeable losses*.

> **"Perhaps you can lose even two percent, and you won't notice the loss of two percent of that pain. The remaining 98 percent will seem just as painful as 100 percent. In fact, you could lose 10 percent of the pain, and the remaining 90 percent would still seem as bad as 100 percent."**

You see, you have changed your wording, your verbalization.

> **"Suppose you lost 15 percent and you had only 85 percent left? That would be a big improvement, even if you didn't realize how big an improvement it was."**

The trouble with patients is to get them to accept the initial premise, the initial idea; so you offer it to them in a way that can be accepted. Then you diminish the pain unnoticeably until, finally, they can accept the idea that pain can be diminished. *Then you suggest the alteration of pain by a reinterpretation.* You know, a very severe pain can be a heavy pain, a dragging pain, a distressing pain. Why not point out to your patient that a heavy pain ought to be accompanied by a feeling of weakness? I can think of the dying man, a doctor, to whom I described this matter of heavy pain. I described it more and more in terms of weakness of his muscles, and weakness of his legs, so that eventually the heavy, dull pain became a nice feeling of comfortable relaxation of his legs. I utilized only the weakness of his body. This transformation of pain—whatever your patient's symptoms are, you ought to be able to transform them into something of another character. Remember that in ordinary everday life, there are tremendous transformations that occur. A woman with a wandering husband describes him to her doctor in terms of, "There is something wrong with my neck. It hurts." Her husband is a pain in the neck! It may be a headache. That is right; a man may talk about his headache, and as you take his history you discover it is really his wife who is the headache, or his teenage son who is the headache, or something of that sort. These transformations occur all the time in everyday life. Your own awareness of this ought to make you willing to transform your patient's complaints into something much less troublesome, much more agreeable, much less handicapping.

Pain as Habit

Reversing the Fourteen Years of Distress in a Case of Tic Douloureux

There is another problem that I would like to bring to your attention, and that concerns this matter of *habit*. You can have habits of speech, habits of eating, habits of sleeping, habits of elimination, muscle habits, all kinds of habits. But does it occur to you that a traumatic experience, a painful experience, might give you the habit of interpreting normal sensations as pain? In *tic douloureux*, the patient may have a severe attack and recover, but still continue to interpret every sensation of the face as a painful sort of thing. I can think of the retired soldier who came to me having suffered from *tic douloureux* for 14 years. He had had two operations, and I don't know how many alcohol injections, for his *tic douloureux*, but he still had the pain. As he talked to me, I watched his pupils dilating and contracting; I watched the changes in his breathing, indicating that he was in pain; I watched the twitching of the muscles in his face, indicating that he was in pain; I noted the change in the tone of his voice, indicating that he was in pain; and I believed the man when he said he had pain. So, in the medium trance state, I asked him to try to understand what I meant by a *pain habit*. It took four interviews to relieve him of his 14 years of distress, which he had suffered since the age of 56. He remained free of that pain for seven years. He died at the age of 77. Your willingness to understand the possible ways the body can function, and this matter of *habit*, are very, very significant factors in dealing with pain.

Symptom-Based Approaches

Utilizing Experiential Learnings in the Control of Blood Pressure; Prescribing the Symptom; Increasing Hand-Tic Behavior

This morning Dr. Brody mentioned this matter of high blood pressure. Now, you know, it is so easy to say that one cannot influence blood pressure by a silly measure such as hypnosis. But when you stop to consider human behavior, and this matter of psychological stimuli that can raise your blood pressure so easily, so thoroughly, and so very, very high—then you wonder. I can think of some naughty words you could say down South that would elevate the Governor's blood pressure so quickly and so easily. That is right—we do have the capacity of responding by increasing the blood pressure. But how do we bring it about? When you get suddenly very, very cold, your blood vessels contract, you alter the circulation of the blood, you throw a burden on the heart, and you alter the blood pressure. When you get very, very angry, you alter the blood vessels, you alter the blood pressure, you alter your heart rate. Your body has a wealth of experience in elevating your blood pressure, but it also has a wealth of experience in lowering the blood pressure. I think *you ought to be willing to call upon the human body to utilize its experience* in lowering blood pressure. You can call upon it to use its experience in elevating blood pressure, and you know various ways of doing that.

Now, another approach for patients is this matter of spreading symptoms. There is the patient who tells you about various symptoms. He has a terrific itch on a certain part of his body—on the elbows, for example—and as you listen to him, you realize that he has some emotional problem centering around his elbow. What do you want to do with that? The patient may be very, very resistant to therapy. But you can ask him to keep that itch right there, and temporarily to develop an itch right here; and temporarily to develop an itch right here; and temporarily to develop an itch here, and here, and here. You can get your patient thoroughly interested in the spreading of his symptoms. The reason is rather simple. Once the patient lets you maneuver or manipulate a symptom, he is turning over the control to you. Therefore, the best way of doing it is to exaggerate it, to increase it, because you never want to let your patient get frightened.

I can think of a paper I published a long time ago about a patient who had a tic, a motor habit. He moved his hand back and forth at the rate of 135 times a minute, and there was nothing that could be done with that particular patient. I had the intern count the number of times per minute for a week, so as to impress upon the patient that I really knew that it was 135 times a minute. Then in the trance state I suggested that his hand would move back and forth 145 times a minute, and sure enough it did! I was going in the direction of the patient's symptomatology, and that is an awfully important matter. Then I got it up to 145, and then I put it back where it belonged, at the patient's level of 135. I put it back up to 145, reduced it to 140, up to 145, down to 135, up to 140, down to 135, up to 140, down to 130. You see the sort of graph that I introduced into that arm movement? One hundred-and-thirty, up to 135, down to 125, up to 130, down to 120, up to 125, down to 115—a progressive, downhill movement. *With patients, you often want to exaggerate their symptoms. Once they turn over control to you, then you are in charge for them. But you had better take control by going in the direction that patients demonstrate: that is, you exaggerate or increase their symptoms.* The patient with her cancer: "I am going to hurt you, and I am going to scare you." I had better say it that way. She wouldn't believe me if I had said to her, "I am going to reduce your pain." I wanted her to agree with me. That is what you want your patients to do.

Variations in Body Image

Adjustments to Organic Diseases; Correcting an Inferior Self-Image; the Relativity of Childhood Perceptions of Size

In this matter of organic disease, I just lectured at the meeting in Indianapolis on Physical Medicine and Rehabilitation. I think physical medicine and rehabilitation of patients is a most important issue. You come across some of the most horrible things because your patients have such fixed and rigid ideas. I thought of this point this morning when mention was made of the multiple sclerosis patients. They get the idea that they have to have a certain limp; that there is nothing they can do about it; that it is going to get progressively worse. You have the patient who says; "Well, I do have a transverse myelitis; my back was broken. I am paralyzed from the waist down. There is nothing left for me in life. I am just absolutely helpless, and I can't do anything." Yet there is a great deal that can be done in the way of physical medicine and rehabilitation.

In the April issue of the *The American Journal of Clinical Hypnosis,* Dr. Chappell has described her experimental work with cases of transverse myelitis. And in the July issue, Dr. Blair is publishing a brief clinical note about teaching patients with transverse myelitis or multiple sclerosis certain things they need to know in order to adjust to life. You see, patients can learn a tremendous amount, even though they may have transverse myelitis.

People have a general view of themselves, of their body images. I can think of the man who came into my office with the statement: "I am a poor, miserable s.o.b. of a shrimp. A poor miserable shrimp. I am a tenth-rate salesman on a tenth-rate, second-hand car lot." In others words, he worked on a car lot of the inferior type to the 10th power, and he was a poor salesman to the 10th power—and it was a 2nd-power car that he was selling! He really was a poor, miserable s.o.b., and he was a shrimp.

> I asked him: "How tall should a man be, to be a man?"
> His statement was, "Six feet."
> "How much should a man weigh, to be a man?"
> "Between 190 and 200 pounds."
> "All right," I said. "How tall are you?"
> "I am only 5 feet 11 and 3/4 inches."
> "How much do you weigh?"
> "Only 170 pounds."

He was a 10th-rate salesman on a 10th-rate, second-hand used car lot; and he was a poor s.o.b. of a shrimp! He said he was very tired of looking up in order to look other men in the eye; that he would give anything in the world to look right straight into a man's eyes. His body image was so exceedingly defective that he saw himself as no taller than that.

Now let me give you a reverse example, which undoubtedly you have had in your own experience.

I left the farm and went to college. I was away from home for some years, and when I got back and stood by the old wood range in the kitchen and started reaching up for the warming oven, something was very wrong. The warming oven was down here, not up there. But I had had a childhood of standing on tiptoes and reaching way up there. That kitchen stove looked to me as if it had shrunk; the sewing machine, the table, and everything. I had spent my childhood there, and I grew quite a bit after I went to college. We all have had that sort of experience.

I can think of a friend of mine who told his sons about that great big island, with that great big tree, with a great big boulder on it—right out there in the middle of that great big river. He talked so much about his childhood play on that great big island that he took his 10-year-old and 8-year-old sons up there purposely to see his great big island with the great big tree and the great big boulder. Then he was so embarrassed at that little bit of a miserable stream, with the tiny little bit of dirt out in the middle, with a tiny little bit of rock on it, and a little sapling. His two boys looked at it and said, "It is just the way you said it was, Daddy!" But they saw it with childhood eyes.

Now my patient who is a poor, miserable shrimp saw himself as he had seen himself in his childhood when he was only that tall. He still asked his father, "What magazine can I read?" He still asked his mother, "What can I have for breakfast?", and he lived at home. I moved him out of his parental home, and now he is the manager of the new car department—first degree, first class.

Consider this matter of body image with your multiple sclerosis patient, with your polio patient, with your man who has lost a leg by amputation, with your patient with the phantom limb. You need to investigate each type of body image. Usually, you use hypnosis or hypnotic techniques in order to get the patient's attention so that you can deal with the patient, so that you can get the patient to cooperate with you, so that you can get the patient to be willing to understand what you have to say.

Hypnotic Deconditioning in Acute Asthma

Retracing the Steps of the Trauma to Create a Positive Outcome

I had a patient who lived in San Diego for a long, long time. She and her husband were saving money to build a new house. They were living in a converted garage that had not yet been wired for electricity. Somehow or other, the savings account did not build fast enough and the wife got rather curious about it. She discovered that her husband was slipping some funds out of the savings account and she wondered why. Then she accidentally discovered a note in his shirt pocket when putting the laundry into the wash; and then she discovered that her husband had a mistress. She looked at the address on the piece of paper and she went and looked up the mistress. She tried to talk to the mistress, but the mistress would have nothing to do with her and jeered at her. She took the matter up with the husband but she just couldn't "catch her breath" over the entire situation; she went into an acute asthmatic state and wound up in the hospital in an oxygen tent, where she stayed for three days until she was released. As soon as she got outside of the hospital, she developed an asthmatic attack and was rehospitalized. Her doctors finally sent her up to Los Angeles, but the smog caused such a severe attack that she was sent out in the country somewhere. For the next couple of years, that woman was treated by first one physician and then another. Every time she entered the environs of San Diego, she landed in the hospital for several days. She came to Phoenix, where she was treated by several allergists and internists, and given a great deal of medication despite the fact she was obviously an asthmatic. Finally, in desperation, she came to me and asked me if I could teach her how to live in San Diego. Her husband was now behaving himself and would behave himself, but the husband could not stand to live in a town such as Phoenix. Now, what is wrong with him, I don't know. But he just couldn't stand to live in Phoenix [laughter]. He just

88

craved to get back to this place [San Diego] and the wife wanted to know if there was any possible way I could condition her so that she could return to San Diego.

She proved to be an excellent hypnotic subject. We went over the entire story in every detail, and I told her that it was enough to make any woman catch her breath! I used all the cliches that people in ordinary life develop about their breathing and their reactions to shocks, and so on. I suggested after, I think it was four hours, that she might return to San Diego all by herself. She might drive back cautiously, a block within the city limits. Drive another block; drive three, four blocks; see how she took the city. Then gradually approach the place where she had lived with her husband and ask the people there if she could look at the place; then go and look at the place where the mistress had lived in better quarters and see if she could find the mistress and talk to the mistress.

The woman drove in San Diego very cautiously. She spent about a day just driving, stopping, looking around. She started circling San Diego because she said it was a beautiful city to see. She finally got to the garage apartment. She asked the people if she could look through it. Then she went and looked at the house where the mistress had lived. The mistress wasn't living there, but the people allowed her to go through the place. Then she looked up the mistress and went to visit her. The meeting between the two women was not the epitome of happiness; it was rather a frosty sort of thing. Then, having talked to the woman, she went all around San Diego; she visited Balboa Park and smelled the flowers, and looked at the trees and bushes and plants there. She spent the night in a motel, then wired her husband to come back to San Diego.

I called her up last night and she said, "I am never going to live away from this beautiful city ever again. It is a year ago, last August, that I came back to San Diego. I am sorry to have left Phoenix, but I am really enjoying living here. My husband is well placed in his work, and we are getting along happily. I don't need to see a doctor about my asthma, or anything of that sort."

I think she had had a total of six or seven hospitalizations with oxygen tents. Now, that gives you some idea of the intensity with which a patient can react. I also suggest to you the importance of following up on patients. I follow up on patient sometimes 25 years later, and even longer.

Questions to Alter Symptoms

Focusing, Accessing, and Indirectly Suggesting Via Questions:
Moving a Migraine from the Right Side to the Left

Now, there are some additional remarks that I want to make concerning pain. My remarks about pain concern every other medical and dental condition that you treat. Too often, you take the patient's complaint and you accept that complaint as if it were sufficient in itself. The patient tells you about the pain, about the asthma, about an aching back or headache. You need to know a great many things about it. Is the headache acute and what were the immediate precipitating events? Is the headache chronic? Is it transient? Is it persistent? Is the pain acute, chronic, transient, persistent? What type of distress is the patient feeling? You need to inquire into all these issues because the patient needs to know, first of all, that you are getting as well informed on the problem as the patient is.

Now, when the patient tells you that the headache is acute, severe, drastic, unbearable, the patient is thinking that you are listening. You are, but there is the point at which you begin offering your suggestions. The patient says, "I suffer from migraine. I have suffered from it for the past five years. It is migraine on the right side of my head, and it is always on the right side of my head."

Now that is something that you need to know. You need to know it thoroughly, and you are listening to that description. You also ought to know that that is the time when you offer another suggestion. You say:

> **"It is always on the right side of your head. Now how often does it slip silently beyond the midline in the back? How often does it slip beyond the midline at the vertex?"**

That is your honest, earnest inquiry. *Actually, it is your honest, earnest suggestion that the patient start altering ideas about the migraine headache. Your reason is that you want to discover how open that patient is to suggestions.* If you can start getting that headache a little past the midline at the axis point, a little past the midline at the vertex—and your own general medical judgments say that the migraine headache is a reaction pattern—then you have begun your therapy. *If you can move the headache a little bit, the patient has accepted that suggestion in a state of unawareness.* Then you have offered that suggestion. The patient has no opportunity to offer you unnecessary resistances. *Therefore, you have offered a suggestion and the patient has accepted it, and you have actually begun your therapy on the patient.*

I can think of the patient in whom I raised that question of slipping just a little past the midline of the head, a little past the midline of the vertex. And I wondered if the headache always reached down to the eye, or if it limited itself to the mid-forehead line? *I got the patient interested not in telling me, but in looking within the self to see what the feelings were with the self. Then it was a relatively easy procedure to suggest to that patient that it was time for there to be a shifting from the right side to the left side.* This patient has a fairly frequent history of migraine. So far as I could understand, a shifting from the right side after five years to the left side would be a welcome experience, in as much as five years of migraine headaches on the right side would lead to the development of physiological habits that would intensify the headache. Therefore, to slip it over to the left side of the head would allow the patient to have the migraine headache, allow the patient to analyze it more adequately, and allow the patient to build up better physiological responses under medical direction.

Indirect Versus Direct Suggestion

Allowing the Unconscious to Direct Symptom Resolution

Now, that sounded like perfectly good thinking and reasoning to the patient, and I pointed out that I did not know when it would happen. It might happen with the next migraine headache; the headache might slip over only half an inch, an inch, two inches, two and one-half inches. *I didn't know, but sooner or later we would let the patient's own unconscious mind direct the process.*

You see, too often the effort is made to tell the patient directly: "Don't have a headache; do feel comfortable; do not suffer pain"—instead of bringing about an alteration.

When a patient comes to you because of pain and distress, both you and the patient know that the patient wants to get rid of that pain and distress. Therefore, you do not have to explain to the patient: "You have come here to get rid of the pain and distress." The patient does not have to tell you more than once; you want to get rid of the pain and distress. You accept the situation as it is, know the patient understands, and know the patient knows that you understand. You do not have to keep defining and specifying your goals and your purposes. Instead you assume very definitely, very emphatically, that *this* is the goal we are working for, and that is all there is to it. *This* is the goal. Now the question is: What are the means, what are the steps, what are the little procedures? Let's bear in mind that one walks a mile just one step at a time, and you impress this upon the patient.

Now, with an acute or chronic situation, you treat it in essentially the same sort of way. An acute symptom—well, that took some time to develop. *Acute symptomatology is a manifestation of the ability of the body to respond in one direction.* "You have been suffering this acute pain for some time. Now let's give your body a reasonable length of time to correct this acute pain, this acute distress." Never try to tell the patient something that seems literally absurd, ridiculous, and wrong.

[Next, Erickson tells the story of "Robert's Red Blood," which is published previously in *Healing in Hypnosis,* pp. 177-179.]

Focusing Attention

Utilizing a Threat as a Distraction for Airplane Nausea

I shouldn't really tell this group what I did to a young lady sitting next to me on the plane. I was sitting here, a young man was sitting here, and this young lady was sitting between the two of us. As the plane started down the runway, the young lady said, "I am scared, I am scared. I'm afraid I'm going to get sick to my stomach when this plane starts going up."

Well, who wants to sit next to a girl when she is vomiting? I don't. There is nothing charming about it. It doesn't even sound good, and so I turned to her and I said: "Well, you know, I can put a stop to that, if you want me to, rather easily."

She said, "Okay."

I said, *"It is very easy. When the plane starts going up, I'll pinch you in exactly the right spot. You won't like it."*

The young man laughed and the young lady looked at me rather horrified. I said, "Oh! I'll enjoy it."

The plane went up and she was still looking at me when all of a sudden she said, "Say, it *is* up!"

"That is right," I said. "It is up, and you are enjoying the ride."

Why should I waste time with a lot of hypnotic techniques? I had her attention, and her attention was not on her stomach.

Questions Structuring Therapeutic Frames of Reference

Establishing a Yes Set with the "Pleasant Aspects" of the Symptom that Leads into a Double Bind Facilitating Cure

Now the next thing about any condition—that pain, that headache, that backache, that asthma, that bronchostenosis, that coughing—is whether or not it is a troublesome condition. *Now you are asking earnest, serious questions.* You say *troublesome*, and the dictionary says: "A darned nuisance, an annoyance." *Troublesome—nuisance—annoyance. What are you doing except diminishing it by your choice of words?* Now is it *threatening?* That is rather a serious word. A very threatening word. If you think you can take it, all right. But you are altering the nature and the character of the patient's understanding of that particular difficulty, and so you raise that question of threat. Is it intractable, or can you control it at times? Can you direct it? Are there times of freedom? That is one of the important things that you need to note. Does the patient have a sense of freedom from the condition? Even in cancer patients in whom the pain is continuous, it is not at all difficult to get them to tell you, "There are times when I don't seem to notice it." Well, that is what you want the patient to tell you, because then the patient has told you, "I can ignore it, I can overlook it."

Now, the next thing you do about the patient's complaint, no matter what it is, is to raise the issue:

> **"There are certain things about your problem. And if you view your problem honestly and comprehensively and earnestly—and I am going to say this to you in words that at first do not seem right—if you will view your problem, however distressing it is to you, there are certain pleasant aspects to it. There are also—and these are the things that brought you to me—unpleasant aspects to it. Now, what are these pleasant aspects?"**

Well, you know, any doctor who looks at the X-ray film likes to see a good clean break in a bone. Now, a broken bone is an unpleasant thing, but a *good clean break* is a good thing. A doctor likes to look at a boil and see a good, clear line of diminutation and the patient begins to take a new view of the difficulty. A nice, walled-off abcess means that it is really separated from the rest of the body. The rest of the body is protected from it and, therefore, that is a very pleasant bit of knowledge, a very pleasant aspect of the condition. So you point out to the patient that there are pleasant as well as unpleasant aspects. Your patient seems to agree with you that there are pleasant aspects. As surely as the patient agrees with you, you have opened the door wide for the presentation of another type of suggestion: a therapeutic, corrective suggestion. The patient is willing to listen to you because you have presented something that contradicts all previous understandings.

"Now, that is a horrible, emphysematous cough that you have. You know it, I know it, everybody is alarmed by it. You can wonder what the pleasant aspect of it is, and it is rather a deep cough, isn't it? It is not a shallow, ineffectual cough, is it? It is a rather deep, good, strong cough." And your patient begins to look at the emphysematous cough with a totally different attitude. You've gotten the patient willing to change his mind about this disease for which he is consulting you. Then the next thing you do is build up the contrast.

"Now, of course, with disease you do expect a continuation of certain unpleasant aspects. You really ought to expect a continuation of certain unpleasant aspects *until the disease is cured*, and I want you to continue to expect those unpleasant aspects for some time yet. I don't know for how long."

There is my double bind: You are to expect those unpleasant aspects for a while until it is cured. Patients have to accept the expectation [of the unpleasant aspects], and so they have to accept the curing of the condition as well, because I have tied the two things together.

Pain as Learning

Autohypnotic Age Regression for the Dissociation and Reinterpretation of Pain in an Emergency Burn; Childhood Perceptions of Sensations; Trance Not Contingent Upon Therapy

There are certain things I would like to impress upon you in regard to reactions to disease and pain. There is the Canadian study about rearing animals under pain-free, stimulation-free situations. When those puppies were three-quarters grown, they were allowed to get out of their stimulus-free cages. The investigators put lighted cigarettes up to the noses of the puppies and the puppies would let their noses rest against the lighted cigarettes. You could step on a puppy's foot and the puppy would look down at its foot. It had not yet learned pain and it needed to learn pain.

How many of you have had the unfortunate experience of holding a baby, and the baby is laughing and very happy, and it bumps its head against your forehead; you see stars, but the baby just giggles and giggles. The baby hasn't learned the painfulness of knocking its noggin against yours. It is a painful experience to you, but to the baby it is funny. How many babies rock back and forth in their cribs, pounding their heads against the headboards because they like the noise? If you tried it, it would hurt you. Babies haven't yet learned pain, just as babies haven't yet learned colors as various sorts. They haven't learned cold—all the various sensations. *Pain is a learning.* When a patient gets sick, and especially a child, it is your obligation to that child to help it to interpret its various sensations so that the various distresses of the illness are felt in a less painful way.

Recently, my 23-year-old daughter burnt her wrist rather severely. It was very painful, and she could smell the odor of burning flesh. She didn't like that, and her stomach started feeling queasy, so she said to herself: *I wonder what I would think about this if I were a little baby?* She promptly went into an autohypnotic trance and looked at that burn on her wrist, and she noticed all the feelings of it. It was a very, very curious experience on her part. It didn't hurt, but there were different sensations there, and she examined them all. Having done so, she decided that some of the feelings were very, very nice. She was so pleased when she awakened with a nice feeling in her wrist, and she looked at the wrist and had an immediate recollection of her regression, and of her examination and retention of certain feelings.

Now, I have done that same sort of thing with adult subjects in other regards, with the result that they discovered that they experience sensations quite differently in regressing to childhood. Take somebody with a severe migraine headache. You tell him: "I don't believe that hypnosis is going to help you, but what I would like to do is a rather simple thing of finding out if you can learn hypnosis. If you can learn hypnosis—after you have learned it—then we can investigate the possibility of using hypnosis for your migraine headache. I am not the least bit certain that we can, but let us find out if you can learn to go into a trance." *So you have the induction of a trance not contingent upon therapy; you have therapy contingent upon their ability to learn hypnosis first.* That makes using hypnosis with the patient much easier, because when he tries to go into a trance for therapeutic purposes he has a double goal and all of the anxiety and fears with the trance induction. [But when he tries to go into a trance just for the sake of the trance, then he is risking nothing.] Then, in the trance state, you raise the question about regression.

Age Regression and Therapeutic Contrasts

Questions Facilitating Direct and Indirect Approaches; Shifting Past to Present Tense; Diluting the Unpleasant Present with the Pleasant Past; Presenting Acceptable Ideas to Patients

Now regression directly or regression indirectly? What is the best way of regressing a person? Right now as I sit here and ask you that question, "What is the best way of regression?", I immediately notice that old childhood feeling in the soles of my feet of walking barefooted on the frosty grass, and that tingling, disagreeable sensation. One can regress totally to the ideational content of the moment, of the minutes, of the hour, or one can revive intensely a memory that belongs to the past. Very often as a regression technique, I raise questions with the patient: "Whereabouts in a small village did you grow up? Do you remember if the house had a front porch? Did it face west? Did you ever sit on that porch and watch the sun set? Can you remember any particular sunset?"

You haven't asked your patient to go into a trance; you haven't asked him to regress. You have asked him to single out a single memory of a single sunset belonging to the past, and if the patient responds he is likely to say something to the effect of: "Yes, I used to sit on the front porch and look at the sunset. I was awfully pleased with the tree that highlighted the sunset. I always saw the sunset through that tree."

"And did anybody else sit on the porch with you?"

"My father and my mother."

"And on which side is your father, and on which side is your mother?"

The patient doesn't notice the change in his tense and he is looking at that sunset. You have used a single memory, and he is looking at the sunset right there, and he is feeling mother over here and father over here. You've gotten a regression.

Are patients in a trance state? I don't know if they are in a trance state, but I do know that they are doing a great deal of thinking in terms of a sunset, let us say, 30 years ago, or 40 years ago, or longer.

"And as you continue to look at that sunset, and you did tell me about your headache, and you are still looking at the sunset. And how does that headache really feel now?"

You have introduced a wealth of memory; you have altered the mental furniture of the patient so that he is dealing not only with the headache, but he is dealing with past memories, happy memories. You have diluted the entire situation, and you have effected a most significant contrast. There is a contrast between a regressive memory of pleasure, and you are speaking about his headache of today. You are doing so, comfortably and easily, and it seems just like a casual conversation. The patient doesn't have to say: "Now, will this therapy work? Is it working?" He doesn't need to have any anxiety about it. *Your task as the therapist is to present understandings and ideas so that patients can accept and act upon and incorporate those understandings into their total understandings of the entire situation.* Now, I am not the least bit hesitant about effecting those contrasts.

As I mentioned before, pain is a learned experience; distresses of various sorts are learned experiences. Certain primitive women are utterly astonished at the civilized woman's attitude toward childbirth. Just where do they get the idea that it is a painful thing? And one wonders. I can remember the startled reaction I got in Rhode Island when I first went there after finishing my internship. An attendant in the hospital came to me on morning and said, "Doctor, I am brooding." Well, what does that mean? (I see some rather blank looks on the faces in the audience.) He was brooding, so I asked him, "How does it show itself?" He said, "I have morning sickness." That is what he had. His wife was pregnant and he had morning sickness. I soon found out that whenever the wife was pregnant, the man had morning sickness in that entire French Canadian Colony in Providence, Rhode Island. It was standard procedure. No wife in her right mind would have morning sickness; she had enough, she had the pregnancy. But how many people can understand that? And yet culture causes people to learn that sort of thing.

Now, when a patient comes to you [with aches and pains from flu or infections], you can begin by asking him when his body feels comfortable: "We will come to the question of the aches and the pain later, but first tell me where your body feels comfortable." With certain virus infections, patients are apt to complain about aching muscles, aching feelings here and there, a feeling a weakness. You ask: "Where do you feel relaxed? Where do you feel heavy? Where do you feel rather comfortable, as if you were too lazy to move from sheer comfort?" *You get patients to establish the contrasts within their own minds; and they are those contrasts that enable you to build up your hypnotherapeutic point of view for patients.*

A Comprehensive View for Learning

I mentioned the Canadian studies on pain as learning. Hunt [inaudible] has conducted a long, long study of what pain means to people, and how they react to it, and how they intensify it.

The little child comes to you and says, "See, I wrote the sentence, 'see the cat.'" And the child insists that you look at every word in "see the cat." And you really ought to look at *s e e;* you ought to look at *t h e;* you ought to look at *c a t;* you ought to look at the period. You also ought to look at the chalk in the child's hand. You also ought to look at the eraser. You also ought to look at the blackboard, so that the child gets the comprehensive idea: "I picked up a piece of chalk with my right hand and I wrote 'see the cat.' I put the chalk down, and I have an eraser here so I could erase the entire thing." You want the child to have a comprehensive view of what he has done: pick up the chalk, write, put the chalk down, and be prepared to erase it. Whenever you give the child a comprehensive view, the child has learned a great deal.

Impact of Internal and External Stimuli

*Questions Evoking Psychological Stimuli Extraneous to Organic
Pain; Implication of Sensory Deprivation Experiments; Utilizing
Past Positive Sensory Stimuli to Offset Present Painful Stimuli*

The doctor who walks into the office and asks the patient about pain forgets to consider other things. A dentist's wife was complaining to her husband, a friend of mine, about her temporal mandibular pain. The dentist said, "This is interesting," and he asked his wife to continue the description. When she finished, I said the following:

"You know, I think you inquired into your wife's pain very well, but did you really build up the situation for her? Did you get a very careful description of her bite, as well as she could give it? Did you ask her when she had that temporal mandibular pain? Was it when she was eating steak, or roast beef, or whatever? Where does she sit at the table? On what days of the week does the pain seem worse?" And so on.

The patient was listening to me and she said, "Oh, yes, there are all of these other psychological factors, because my temporal mandibular pain is worse when the kids are having a fight at the table."

That is right—that is when you would expect it to be worse. The patient was the one who was specifying that extraneous, psychological, emotional factors were a significant part of her organic, temporal, mandibular pain. Then it was a very easy thing to get her to accept psychological suggestion, because the patient, herself, had specified that her problem did have a psychological emotional component.

Extensive studies on sensory deprivation have been conducted in various places: the University of Hawaii, in Oklahoma, the Canadian Studies at the Wright-Patterson Air Base, the Aerospace Medical Laboratory. In these deprivation studies, the subject is immersed in water wearing a mask; there is complete silence floating in the water. The subject can push a button at any time to be hauled out of the tank. The longest any subject remained immersed at the Aerospace Laboratory was for 24 hours. One of my friends stayed four hours; he said he was rather alarmed at his psychotic auditory hallucinations. There is a tremendous need for people to have sensory stimulation of various sorts. A person can stay in the sensory deprivation chamber much longer when some auditory stimuli is present. You can give subjects alternating currents of a minimal degree to give them a little electrical stimulus, and they can endure that life in absolute silence for a longer period of time.

When patients are sick, what about this question of giving them the opportunity of paying attention to various stimuli? I think it is most important for patients lying in bed to have sensory stimuli of some sort, and hypnotically you can provide it very, very nicely. Now, in the heat chamber experiment the question came up: What should we do with that chap in the heat chamber? We didn't want him to feel that horrible high temperature. Therefore, I produced a general state of body unawareness so that he could endure that heat, so that his heart wouldn't pound, so that his sweating would not become excessive. I gave him a nice, comfortable feeling, along with a forgetfulness:

"Now, while you are losing your body awareness, what about this possibility of having an awareness of another kind? Why not have a wealth of memories of walking in the snow, of shoveling snow?" And the chap shoveled a great deal of snow. I don't know how many tons of snow he shoveled; but his comment was that he could literally feel every shovelful; he could feel his elbows, his back, his shoulders, his knees. The snow was nice and heavy, and the wind was blowing so nicely on his cheeks, and it felt so cold and so wonderful, so comfortable; and it was a completely delightful thing. Sensory experience? No, he had a constant sensory experience of excessive heat, but he had a wealth of other sensory experiences that enabled him to withstand the excessive heat in the chamber in a much better fashion. With sick patients, *you ought to be willing to suggest that they utilize sensory memories of the past as a measure of protecting themselves from the sensory experience of the immediate present.*

Extensive Scope of Medical Purposes

*A Case of Organic Brain Dysfunction Misdiagnosed as
Hysterical: Questions to Evoke Individual Sensory
Manifestations: Perceiving the Quality of Patient Behavior:
Altering, Not Abolishing, Pain and Symptoms*

Now in this matter of dealing with pains, sickness, and distress of all sorts, the usual history is: The patient comes to you and says, "Get rid of my headache for me; get rid of my broken arm for me; get rid of my cancer for me; remove all of these distresses from me; I want freedom from my stomachache." That is the general attitude, medically and dentally. *"Stop* my toothache; *take* my toothache *away* from me; *take* that cavity *away* from me, and so on. Patients learn indirectly over a period of years that medical-dental purposes center primarily around *abolition. Medical and dental purposes should actually be represented to patients not just as abolitions, but possibly as developments, extensions, alterations, and changes of various sorts.* When they stop to think about it, of course, patients know that this is true; but they do come in with the fundamental attitude that you are going to *abolish* certain things. You should abolish this severe headache, or this aching back, or the pain in that broken leg, when actually, what ought you to do? I tell a patient: "Now, you have rather a bad headache there. I think you ought to make some kind of use of it."

I am thinking of the patient who was sent to me from Baja, California. The patient said: "I have been to at least a dozen doctors. They have all told me that my problem is just 'in my head.' I have some miserable feelings throughout my body, and those miserable feelings bring about a paralysis of my arm. Sometimes it lasts half a day, sometimes it lasts 20 minutes; and the next thing I know, I get a paralysis of the leg. That might last one hour, two hours; and then I get absentminded and say things unexpectedly; and sometimes I really don't talk sense. The doctors have all said that it is a hysterical matter, and so now they have sent me to you to hypnotize me and to suggest away my paralysis, and to suggest away my absentmindedness."

My feeling toward the patient was this: A hysterical paralysis of the arm ought to last more than 20 minutes; and when it shifts to the leg it ought to last quite a long time. You don't expect a patient to give you that sort of a reasonable explanation, and you start wondering and wondering about it. I told the woman, "You really ought to tell me some more of the things that happen to you."

The woman said, "My body doesn't feel right; it just doesn't feel right in any way. I have been thoroughly examined; I have had the brain waves; I have had neurological examinations, and everything."

I asked her to tell me every possible detail she could think of so that I could get the information I needed. I noticed that she would begin a sentence and then it would drop off; she would put in part of another sentence; then come up to another level in another sentence. It was the most fragmented train of thought when you drew her out at any length, and so I sent her back to the doctor with a diagnosis of organic brain disease.

I wanted the woman to become aware of every sensory change in her body. Psychiatrically, I knew that her problem just couldn't be a hysterical one, a psychoneurotic one. It had to have some organic basis—possibly a circulatory change of some sort—that her doctors ought to study. Her family physician took her back, hypnotized her, got her over her paralysis, got her over a lot of her feelings. He saw her about two or three weeks ago. She said she was developing the paralysis again, and again he put her in a trance. He didn't like her general appearance, but she got over that special weakness of her leg that she was complaining about. The next day he was called to her home: she had dropped dead very suddenly.

Later he phoned me to tell me that he was sending me a new patient, and that he would mail the autopsy findings on the woman to me; he already had a preliminary report. She had had a very diffuse brain tumor. A neurological friend of his said it was probably a tumor in one of the silent areas of the brain. I mention this because it is so awfully important for you to check on the individual sensory manifestations of patients.

When I listen to patients talk, I ask myself: How consistent is their train of thought? Do they show a fragmentation of it? Do they seem to talk at different levels? You see, there is too much of a tendency to examine patients and to pass judgment only on certain

103

rigid things—how much pain, how much fever, what are the laboratory findings, what are the physical findings—*instead of looking at the quality of the patient's behavior.* I was concerned about that peculiar, interrupted train of thought; that interrupted train of associations and ideas. I knew it was not neurotic, but I certainly didn't know what it was. Was it an encephalitis? A tumor of the brain? A circulatory disturbance? I was simply unqualified to answer the question. When you deal with patients, you want to be aware of the multiplicity of their manifestations. Then, in dealing with them therapeutically, you want to cover the possible ways of appealing to them. It is not just a matter of the abolition of a problem.

I tell the patient: "Yes, you have a hot burning sensation on the side of your head that always goes with your migraine headache. But, you know, if you will examine the periphery of that hot burning spot, there is a warm feeling, there is a gradation. Now how about the use of that warm feeling?"

"You have aching pains in your legs that distress you very greatly; you are suffering from arthritis. But if you will examine those sensations, you will find, perhaps, a feeling of warmth; perhaps a feeling of coolness; perhaps a feeling of coldness; and now how about extending some of those sensations?"

Your task is that of altering, not abolishing. There are a lot of problems you cannot abolish; therefore, *you need to reconstruct them in a way that is endurable to the patient.*

Indirect and Direct Approaches to Symptom Correction

Altering the "Attendant Manifestations" of the Symptom;
Building Rapport by Acknowledging the Patient's Reality;
Utilizing Anticipation in the Acceptance of Therapeutic
Suggestion: Headaches and Toothaches

Now, whenever a patient complains to you about any particular matter, I think you'd better recognize a number of things. The patient who talks to you about that splitting headache: if you watch and listen to him carefully, you will notice that the muscles of the neck and the hands tense up. And you know from your own experience in physiology and physical examination that if you do not get a good knee jerk, you ask the patient to pull like this and exaggerate the knee jerk. Certainly you ought to expect a patient who is complaining about a headache to show an increased knee jerk, just from general tension. How, then, do you handle that headache? Well, I think, a little relaxation in the legs will improve the exaggerated knee jerk; and I think that the relaxation there will extend to the torso, will extend to the chest, will extend to the neck, extend to the face, extend to the headache.

I think you ought to be willing to begin working away from the actual problem. How do you examine an abdomen for acute appendicitis? You do not jab right down over the appendicular area; you start way over on the left side and work your way over by palpating the abdomen. *The same thing should be true in your hypnotic approach to any patient's difficulty. You take the attendant manifestations of that particular difficulty and you begin altering the attendant manifestations; and as surely as you begin altering the attendant manifestations, then you have opened the way for the patient to accept your suggested alterations of the particular difficulty.*

The patient says, "I have a splitting headache; it makes me ready to scream." You add to that, "And the sound of loud noises splits your head still more, doesn't it?" And the patient readily agrees with you. The patient knows that you are intelligent; the patient knows that you understand; the patient is in agreement with you and you are in agreement with the patient. You have built up your accord and rapport with the patient. Then you point out to the patient: "You know, when you get that tense with your headache and you are ready to scream at the sound of a noise, there must be quite a bit of tension in your face, in your hands. You must feel like picking up something and throwing it." And the patient can agree with you. He has told you, he has confirmed for you that there is tension in his hand, tension in his feet. By implication I think you had better mention that because if you want to deal with that headache, you will begin with the hand and the feet. And you have begun with the hand and the feet in a way that the patient can understand.

You have a bad toothache but it is not constant; you notice it more when you are eating. It is rather troublesome then. In fact, it rather interferes with you on the way home when you are thinking about that good steak dinner. Yes, the thought of a good steak dinner—the thought of an aching tooth when you are eating that good steak dinner—interferes. But you have taken the patient out of that painful eating situation, and you have the patient thinking about his feelings on the way home, anticipating the good steak dinner. *You have the patient wide open for suggestions of therapy, and that is what you want, because on his way home he is anticipating certain things. Well, let him use that anticipation in the acceptance of therapeutic suggestion.*

Public Education and Medical Attitudes

Viewing Patients as Intelligent, Questioning Evaluators: "The Successful Doctor is the Doctor Who Really Explains"

You see, in dealing with patients, there is an increasing recognition of *patients as thinking, feeling, emotional creatures—people who want to understand;* who demand to understand; who increasingly are accepting things on the basis of their own intellectual evaluation rather than on a blind evaluation. Therefore, the patient is going to ask you to approach him more and more on a psychological level: *the successful doctor is the doctor who really explains.* I have had more than one pregnant woman come into my office and say, "I am going to change obstetricians. I want to know something about my pregnancy, and my obstetrician is too darned busy! He doesn't tell me a thing, and so I want you to give me an hour of your time, and I want you to tell me all you know about pregnancy and everything you think would interest me about my pregnancy, and just tell it to me so I understand it."

I have had patients come in to get my dental advice about dentures. They ask: "How will I feel wearing dentures? How embarrassed will I get? Will I be self-conscious? Just how will my mouth feel with dentures? What about this gagging that dentures cause? Should I go to Dr. P who advertises in Phoenix and says he can remove my teeth and give me the dentures in exactly the same day and there will be no pain involved?"

So I have my dental practice, my obstetrical practice, and my psychiatric practice; but people are demanding. [Laughter] You look through the *Readers Digest,* and *The Ladies Home Companion,* and the *House Beautiful,* you will see a tremendous number of articles on medical subjects. Do tranquilizers really work? How many tranquilizers should you take each day, and what variety? All these lay articles and these laymen that practice medicine. You had better be aware of the public's increasing reading, and the importance of you, yourselves, looking at your patients as thinking, feeling human beings who are coming to you first for information, and secondarily for treatment of the condition, bearing in mind that the patient's motivation is primarily his pain and distress. But as long as you go to the doctor, you might as well get educated in the process!

Transforming the Body

Altering Physiological Behavior via Suggestions Evoking
Comfort and Responsiveness in Non-Problematic Areas:
Sciatica, Dental, and Arthritis Approaches

I have listed the approaches to disease, pain, and distress. Bear in mind that there is the physiological in which you transform the body. Tension in one place alters the behavior of another part of the body: the knee jerk becomes exaggerated; relaxation of the body results in alteration of the knee jerk. Your first approach to patients is that of altering their physiological behavior. For example, there is the sciatica patient who sits down in his one-hipped style in the chair. You ought to recognize that one-hipped style of sitting in a chair. Now, what are you going to do for that patient?

107

"You know you are resting your arms in your lap. Let's see. You are about 5-feet 11-inches tall, and in that chair I think your arms would rest more comfortably on the arms of the chair." Of course, you know he is 5-feet 11-inches, and you see that one-hipped sitting procedure. Therefore, you suggest an increased comfort of his arms. You haven't told him: "Because you have sciatica, and your sciatic nerve hurts, let's get comfort in your arms." You have rationalized it on the basis:

"You are 5-feet 11-inches or thereabouts, and with your height, your arms would rest more comfortably on the arms of the chair."

So he puts his hands and arms on the arms of the chair, *but he has made a response to you, and it is a response in relationship to comfort of an extremity—in fact, to the comfort of two extremities. And so, whenever possible, you transform the body in some way to bring about physiological responses.*

There are several things you can do while sitting in the dental chair. You can really tighten up your hands this way, and that drill feels all the worse; or you can actually study the sensations of relaxation in your arms. Oh, yes, the dentist is drilling. That is right, but your interest is focused on that feeling of relaxation. You keep your patient's attention; therefore, you keep your own attention on the matter of relaxation while the dentist is drilling, and you keep forgetting that he is drilling. Then you transform the body in some way, and then you utilize physiological changes.

If I had an arthritis patient—say, with ankle arthritis or knee arthritis—who wanted relief of pain (no arm, hand, or wrist arthritis), I would immediately suggest the placing of the arm there.

"Now, I would like to investigate your understanding of various things. Do you really know what a warm feeling would be like in your arm? Can you really sense a warm feeling in your wrist joint there, or do you notice it more between the elbow and the wrist?"

It isn't a question of, "Do you really feel it?" It is a question of, "Do you feel it in the wrist, or more in between the wrist and the elbow?" *What I want to do is, of course, bring about physiological change and alteration of circulation of the blood through increasing attention.*

Transforming the Symptom

Questions Accessing and Reframing Symptomatic Experience:
Reducing a Splitting Headache

The next matter is this issue of transformation—transformation of symptomatology. You have a splitting headache. I don't know exactly what you mean by a *splitting* headache, but you know what you mean by it. I would like to suggest to you that you try to make me understand. Now, a *splitting* headache: Does that mean a shooting pain, where one pain after the other shoots through your head? Or does it mean that pain shoots through your head this way? Now I want an anterior-posterior view there; I want a lateral view there. The patient doesn't know that I am asking him to shift from an anterior-posterior view to a lateral view, but why shouldn't I shift? "And is it a shooting pain? And now does that shooting pain seem to have a cutting feeling? Did you ever dip your hands into the dishwater and run your fingertips against the edge of a sharp knife and get that horrible cutting sensation?" Where is the patient in relation to that question? In my office, or in the patient's kitchen?

I've gotten regressive behavior in listening right there. "And before you got that cutting sensation in your finger, your finger really felt so nice, didn't it? But it was such a shock when you got the cutting feeling." What have I done? I have asked the patient to realize that even right now he can recall nice feelings. Well, what do I want my patient to do but develop nice feelings? It is my task to point out to patients that they can do so, not by belaboring the point, but by the simple process of presenting ideas to them. I can shift that shooting pain from the splitting headache to a shooting pain in the anterior, posterior, or lateral locations.

Then there is the matter of cutting pain, and then there is this matter of a pleasant feeling in the fingertips. "You know, when shooting pains go through here, the front of your head can actually feel comfortable. And it really can, you know, because it is here that you are beginning to feel the sensations."

What have I done? I have pointed out to the patient that he can actually have nice feelings here, and so I am bringing about, systematically, the physiological change. I am bringing about an alteration of the [symptomatic] manifestations, and I am talking about it casually. Yet I know the words that I am saying; I know the steps. How do you reduce a splitting headache in your office in the course of a few minutes? You ought to dictate your ideas into your tape recorder, or you ought to write them down on paper and examine them, outline them. Then improve that outline, and then outline them from the improved outline, and so on, until you know the variety of things that you can say to your patients.

Directing Attention Inward

Utilizing the Hangover Experience; Utilizing Doubt to Enhance Receptivity

Now, patients are always afraid that you really don't understand their complaint, because their complaint is peculiar to themselves. How can you really be sure the other person understands when you know, out of your own experience, that other people don't understand you? Therefore, you offer patients some little example wherein they can take an amused attitude toward this situation.

"Did you ever have a hangover? Did you ever wake up one morning with a terrific hangover—the granddaddy of all hangovers—and watch that fly stomp his feet on the carpet? You really have a hangover when you hear that fly stomping his feet on the carpet!"

And the patient thinks about that as you roll your eyes at that miserable fly. And the patient starts thinking: "Oh, yes, and I have all these other feelings." *The patient's attention is directed within the self. It is no longer a question of, "Do you understand?" It is a question of, "Do I understand all of my feelings?"* I want the patient to be in a state of doubt, because as surely as that patient is in a state of doubt, then he is going to be receptive to ideas. So I use that little illustration of the hangover—of the fly stomping its feet, or the kitten stomping its feet on the Persian rug—so that the patient starts looking within the self.

Reframing Symptomatic Compensations

Now whenever you have a disease, an injury, an illness of any kind, you know very well that the body is going to compensate. The patient is going to look upon those body compensations as indicators of something being wrong. The patient says, "I have a backache and I am stiff all over." I tell the patient, "I am awfully glad that your body is making so adequate a response. You really don't know very much about medicine. You really don't know very much about anatomy. You didn't go to medical school, but you've got a backache and your body is automatically going to splint the back. It is going to tense the muscles in order to protect the back movements and cut down the pain. You splint the muscles in your hand, you notice your forearm tightens up too, and so, of course, you feel stiff all over. I think you ought to be pleased for that indication of the adequacy of your back muscles splinting the backache.

Then the patient begins to have a respectable understanding of body compensations, and so instead of reacting to body compensations, he begins to think you know what you are talking about. He is willing to listen to you, and he is willing to let his body start healing itself, and that is an awfully important thing.

Body Confusion in Symptomatology

I don't know what David Cheek did with that girl who had the menstruation and the retinal hemorrhages. I know what I would have done. The first thing I would have done is give the girl a very nice feeling about menstruation. I would make her feel that it was a

111

wonderful experience, that it was the badge of femininity, and that it was something that she could actually enjoy in a physiological way. Now, how extensively should her body participate in menstruation, and in what fashion? I think that the body should participate by pelvic congestion. I think there should be an increased flow of blood to the inner surfaces of the thighs; I think there should be increased flow of blood to the breasts, to the thyroid. I don't think there should be an increase of the blood flow to the eyes, but I do think there should be an increase to the breasts, to the pelvis, to the thighs. With that increased flow of blood in the pelvis, there is going to be an alteration in the appetite. But I really think the alteration in the appetite should not call for an increase circulation of blood in the retina of the eye. And I would enable her to differentiate between the eyes and the urogenital system, and so I would get the patient thinking about her body in a totally different way.

I know that this is the sort of approach I used with a patient who had menstruated vicariously through the nose and through the mouth every time she had normal menstruation. I thought it was unnecessary to have a nosebleed. Her preliminary manifestation at the onset of the menses was: a spotting and a sting from the nose, and then a gush of serum and blood from the nose. I didn't think that was necessary, so I pointed out where I thought there *should* be an increased flow of blood. I pointed out that there could be a body confusion that was justified, because in the genital system you have rectal tissue and in the nose you also have rectal tissue. Because of the rectal tissue in the nose and genital system, the body çould get confused about menstruation and have increased blood supply in both areas. But, really, it isn't necessary. So I would analyze the situation comprehensively for the patient.

DEMONSTRATION

Using the Double Bind

Subject Selection via a Double-Bind Question; Teaching Subjects a Mutual Trance Induction; Hand Levitation

112

The double bind means presenting an idea to patients so that they have no way out of the situation. I will demonstrate a double bind right now. I don't know if it is going to work, but at least it will be very illuminating.

Erickson (E): Will the pretty blond bring the pretty brunette up? And will the pretty brunette bring the pretty blond up?

I use this opening as an illustration of the double bind. I didn't ask either one of them to come up. They did not volunteer. The blond brought the brunette up, and that brought the blond up! But, you see, it is the double bind.

E: All right. [To first subject] How do you think you would induce a trance?
Subject (S): I have already experienced it before.
E: [To second subject] And have you? How would you hypnotize her?
S: I don't know if I could. I don't know if I would want to.
E: And how would you hypnotize her?
S: I really don't know.
E: Put your hand on your knees, and unwrap, and just sit comfortably there. Now, put your hands here and I would like to have the two of you ... this should be very, very informative for the entire group. I would like to have you [first subject] tell her to look at your right hand, and I would like you [second subject] to tell her to look at your left hand. Go ahead and tell each other that. Right hand and left hand. Then each of you tell the other to watch that hand continuously. Don't be polite about this. You speak the same time as she speaks.
S: Watch my hand.
E: Now, each of you tell the other: "Watch that hand lifting higher and higher."
S: Watch that hand lifting higher and higher.
E: Keep repeating.
S: Watch that hand lifting higher and higher.
E: Keep on repeating, and mean what you say, and hope her

113

hand lifts higher and higher.

S: Watch that hand go higher and higher. Watch that hand go higher and higher. Watch that hand go higher and higher. Watch that hand lift higher and higher—higher and higher.

E: And tell her that her eyes are going to close.

S: And your eyes are going to close. Higher. Your eyes are open. Watch that hand go higher and higher and higher.

E: Tell her that her eyes are closing and mean it.

S: Your eyes are closing. Watch that hand go higher and higher. Higher and higher. Watch that hand go higher and higher. Your eyes are closing. Watch that hand go higher and higher, higher and higher.

E: Close your eyes. Close your eyes.

Giving and Experiencing Hypnotic Suggestion

Inducing Self-Trance via the Giving of Suggestion to Another; The "My-Friend-John" Technique; Autohypnosis

Now, this is something I want to illustrate because it is so exceedingly important if you are going to understand hypnotic techniques. I am going to interrupt it.

E: **Now each of you tell the other to lower the hand slowly, and to open the eyes slowly, and to awaken slowly. Now start telling the other.**

S: **Lower your hand slowly. Let your hand lower slowly. Let your eyes open slowly. I am awake.**

E: **You can do it. Missing out on things.**

This is a technique that I have employed more than once with resistant patients. It is a very, very nice group technique. It is a nice technique to enable you to discover something about hypnotic phenomenon for yourself. Now this is what you did:

E: **You each told the other what to do. I told you to mean what you said.** *As surely as you mean what you say—your hand* *is lifting, lifting, lifting—and when you really mean it, you have a tendency to execute your own suggestion. Ideomotor activity.* Your eyes are closing, and there is a tendency for you to close your own eyes; thus, you are offering suggestions, and you are meaning them. You are also learning something about the timing of suggestions. You suddenly discover that you are really interested in your own feeling, and when did you forget about her?

S: Almost right away.

E: Almost right away. Yes, you became interested in yourself, interested in your own sensations, in your own responses, and in hypnosis. What do you want? You are not really concerned about the external world. You are concerned about yourself, and what you can learn, and what you can achieve. Now, actually, of course, you can imagine my friend John—the one who is sitting right there. And you can visualize someone sitting in a chair, and you can offer him suggestions; you can suggest ideomotor activity and you can carry it out; and you can suggest the closing of his eyes and you can carry it out. You can induce a trance in that imaginary person but, of course, you are actually developing a trance yourself. You are learning autohypnosis in that particular way. [Several sentences inaudible]

E: Do you mind staying up here? Do you mind staying awake?

S: No.

E: That is right.

Good Hypnotic Technique

Attracting Attention; Dealing with Resistance via Direct Suggestion to "Stay Wide Awake"; Amnesia as Trance Indicator

Now, what do you mean by "staying awake?" What is a good hypnotic technique? What do you mean by "hypnotic technique?" You mean, the attraction of a subject's attention; the holding of that attention. I allowed her to rouse up several times so that you could see; and she smiled. She didn't quite know what the situation was, but I attracted her attention again and so she went back into the trance state. You have the highly resistant patient come into your office who says: "So-and-so tried to hypnotize me, and so-and-so, and so-and-so; and they say that maybe you can but I don't think you can. But I have come here to see if you can." And you look the patient over, and you know that the patient really ought to go into a trance.

E: What happened? You just woke up. Did you rest up a bit? That is fine. Do you mind sitting up here? You have good company here.

So you say to that highly resistant patient: "All right, you find yourself resistant. You have your doubts that I can put you in a trance. Well, I too, have my doubts about it. I really don't think I can, but I would like to have you be attentive to what I say. I notice you have emphysema; I notice that you are having difficulty in breathing. I would diagnose you as having asthma, emphysema, probably bronchiectasis, I don't know what all. I notice that you are a chain smoker, and I don't think you are ordering your life very well. *Therefore, I would like to discuss a number of things with you, so will you just keep looking at this spot right here? And stay wide awake, stay very wide awake; stay very, very wide awake. And just look at that spot, and listen to me, and hear everything I say on whatever topic I discuss. Listen carefully and stay wide awake, and just pay attention to that; and just keep looking at that and listening to everything I say about your problem."*
Now, how many of you recognize that the subject is in the trance state even though her eyes are open?

E: Did you forget the audience?
S: Yes.
E: That is right, you forgot the audience. What did you see?
S: I didn't see. I was listening.
E: I didn't really see. I was listening.

Now, you never tell your highly resistant patients what they are doing, because why should you tell them that? They don't come to find out how much you really know in the practice of medicine. They come to get help from you. I don't think a surgeon ought to explain to a surgical patient, "I know all of these stitches and all of these knots." I don't think you, in using hypnosis, ought to tell your patients: "I know this technique, and I know that technique, and I know that you are in a trance right now." Instead, I think you ought to talk to your patients and present the ideas they need to have presented.

Reducing Cigarette Smoking

Fractional Diminution of Cigarettes: "Forty Taste Better than Eighty"; Assessing Trance via Time Distortion; An "Unnoticed" Trance Awakening

Regarding that particular patient with emphysema, bronchiectasis, asthma, and four packages of cigarettes a day. What did I need to talk about? I had her look at the clock on my desk; I had her keep her eyes wide open; I told her to stay wide awake; I told her to listen to me and try to understand what I was talking about. I told her that I really didn't know whether or not she needed 80 cigarettes a day. To me, I really believed 79 were enough, even though she thought 80 were sufficient. I really didn't think she needed to have four cartons of cigarettes in her car—two cartons in the glove compartment and two cartons in the back seat. I really didn't think so. It seemed to me that one carton the back seat and one carton in the glove compartment would be enough. In fact, according to my way of thinking, one carton in the car would be enough, and the same for her home. Why should she really have a carton in the livingroom and a carton in the library, so that she wouldn't run out? Why did she think 80 cigarettes a day were necessary when 79 or 78, or for that matter 73, might be enough?

I kept on talking in that sort of fashion because in taking the history I had found out that she had a carton in the kitchen, a carton in the bathroom, a couple of cartons in the bedroom, a carton in the library, a carton in the livingroom, two cartons in the glove compartment, two cartons in the back seat, and two cartons in her handbag. She was not going to run out of cigarettes. And so she looked at the clock, and she listened to me with her eyes wide open, and I reduced the 80 cigarettes down to 70, and down to 60, down to 50; and I wondered if 40 couldn't taste just as good as 80. In fact, I honestly believe that 40 would taste better than 80 cigarettes, and anything that makes cigarettes taste better would certainly be worthwhile. Therefore I justified cutting down to 40 cigarettes on the basis of tasting better. Now, if half taste better than the whole, then a quarter ought to taste still better!

E: By the way, are you in a trance state?
S: I don't know.
E: You don't know.

But why should I tell that resistant patient that she was in a trance state? The two hours passed and I said, "Now, you have been looking at the clock. (She wanted a two-hour appointment.) Time has passed and I really think it is time for you to leave the office now. I think you ought to leave it as you came in." How did she come into the office? Wide awake. I thought she ought to leave the office as she came in. Why should I tell her to wake up? So she did leave but she said, "Is that clock wrong? I haven't been here over five minutes—ten minutes at the most." She checked on her watch. She said, "Did I get here late? I thought I got here at two o'clock. Your clock and my watch say four o'clock." I said, "Well, you know, time does have a habit of slipping away un-noticed." Why shouldn't I say it that way? And I wanted to emphasize that word *unnoticed*, because I trusted to her intellect that she could listen to me.

Trance Without Awareness Of It

Focusing Attention in Non-Traditional Ways; Inducing Emergency Surgical Anesthesia; Dental Anesthesia; Childbirth with Hypnotic Anesthesia: Choosing to Feel a Stage of Labor

You see, I want to stress this approach because with many
118

patients you can avoid the ritual and routine of a traditional induction: "Now put both hands on your knees and your feet flat on the floor, and lean back in your chair and relax. Take a deep breath and fixate a spot on the wall." Actually, *why not fixate patients' attention by the manner in which you are talking to them? By the manner in which you are presenting ideas to them? By fixating their attention on a particular problem for which they have come to you?* In fixating their attention thusly, you are going to get the same results as fixating their attention on that spot right there. You are talking about their problem; you are talking about relaxation in the feet, in the calves, in the thighs, in the arms and so on. It is only preliminary to talking about their problem.

I can think of a colleague of mine, Dan S. from Seattle, Washington, who was called in on an emergency car accident. The patient's face was all gashed up, all ground up, with gravel and so on. He needed a lot of stitches, and Dan told the patient, "You know, I would really like to use hypnosis on you."

The patient said, "I don't believe in that stuff."

Dan said, "You know, your face needs a lot of mopping up; it needs a lot of stitching. I would probably have to start right about there, and I would put so many stitches here. There are a lot of stones I am going to have to get out. I have to mop up this, and you know, if you were in a hypnotic trance, you wouldn't feel anything. I could do the the work and there wouldn't be the the effect of the anesthetic. I would put in a stitch here, and I would put another one in here.

Finally the patient said, "When are you going to start work instead of talking about it?"

Dan said, "I am just about through."

Well, why shouldn't you do it in that particular way? Dan was mopping up the face, he was putting in the stitches. The nurse stood there with her mouth wide open, but Dan was using an excellent attention-absorbing technique of trance induction and hypnotic anesthesia.

In a trance state you would have no pain, no distress. Of course, the patient would listen to that; would hear that; and would unconsciously carry it out. So many, many times instead of telling the patient, "I want you to develop an anesthesia of the hand, or of the face, or of the jaw," you mention anesthesia as something of

119

interest. The patient comes into your office fully aware of the fact that you are going to do dental work. Do you really have to tell the patient, "I want you to have an oral anesthesia?" If your patient has had a grade-school education, he knows you are going to work in the mouth. You don't have to tell him to have the anesthesia, but you can tell him how wonderful the anesthesia is, and how very, very comfortable. And you also can tell him that the reduction of salivation is a very, very desirable thing.

You tell the woman who is pregnant that it is delightful to have a delivery under hypnosis; that she can learn it in various ways; that every human being has learned anesthesia as a part of life's experiences. For example, there are the shoes on your feet. You haven't been feeling them while I have been talking, have you? But now you can feel them. So how did you get that anesthesia for the shoes on your feet? Not because there is a drug put into the nerve; not because you were told to have the anesthesia; but because in your lifelong learning you have acquired the automatic ability to turn off sensations and to turn them on again.

Since you are a pregnant woman, you are expecting a baby, and you would like to have that baby in the way that is most comfortable to you. I want you to be sure to have it in the way that is most pleasing and most comfortable to you. If that means that you have to get a cramp in your arm from holding on to that grip, be sure to get that cramp because, you see, I don't know what kind of pain or distress you might want to have during the labor. All I know is that you want to have a very happy, very agreeable labor. You want to look upon the arrival of this child as a completely pleasing thing. Therefore, you might want a cramp in the right arm, a cramp in the left arm; you might want an itch on your leg; you might want to feel a labor contraction here and there. If you do want to feel a labor contraction I would like to suggest the following. You know that labor comes in three stages. The first stage gives you much more time to feel a labor contraction than the second or third stage. So if you really want to feel a labor contraction, do it in the first part of the first stage; because that gives you more time to study and to experience and to feel it. But, of course, you can also have a contraction that you feel in the second or the third stage, if you want to. In case you do wish to feel a labor contraction, I just want you to feel it in the most adequate way possible.

Being a medical man, I suggest the first stage, and the first part of the first stage; because that is the best time for the patient to feel a labor contraction. But I also give her permission to feel it in the second stage, or in the third stage; "But in the third stage, you are going to be busy with a lot of other things." There is that impending question: What sex is the baby going to be? Let's really get her interested in the very vital question. Let's take her mind off the discomfort. You see, in all techniques of hypnotic induction, you offer ideas in a wealth of ways so that patients can sort through their own personal understandings.

Protecting Patients

Dispelling "Aloneness" of Patient via Casual Remarks about Yesterday's Patients: "This Is a Chair of Very, Very Pleasant Memories"

Now, in having these two ladies up here—I chose two for a reason other than to illustrate the double bind.

E: Aren't you a bit more comfortable, knowing that she is up here?

S: Yes.

E: And she is more comfortable, knowing that you are up here.

That sense of comfort and satisfaction in knowing that she is not the only one on the platform. You try to protect your patients that way. How do you do that in the office, where the patient is the only one present? You mention to the patient: "You know, I am delighted to see you sitting in that chair. Yesterday there was another pretty girl sitting in that chair." I have thereby introduced the fact that this chair—the one that she is sitting in—is one that accommodated another pretty girl. Or, I can say, "Yesterday there was another mother sitting in that chair." That makes the patient feel much more comfortable. It is not just a chair that I have here all alone; *this* is a chair of very, very pleasant memories—memories of other people, even if the patient doesn't know them. And, obviously I liked the patient of yesterday. Therefore, the patient of today feels much less alone, and doesn't feel the self to be in such a forbidding situation as a psychiatrist's office. I think that in the obstetrician's office, in the dermatologist's office, there should be a willingness to help the patient experience the self as not just alone.

Fundamentals of Hypnotic Induction Techniques

Centering Attention Upon the Self: Evoking Ideomotor and Ideosensory Activity; Visualization and Relaxation; Kinesthetic Memories

Now I mentioned the identity of techniques—the ideomotor technique, such as I was using here, and this matter of visualization. It was a visualization technique the subjects were using as they were looking at each other and visualizing how the other's hand should move and responding in that way. You can visualize the technique in any other way—visualize a picture, visualize someone sitting in a chair—but in all techniques you have certain fundamental considerations. You have relaxation. What is relaxation? Relaxation is a muscular phenomenon; it is an ideomotor phenomenon of a negative character. It is the relaxation instead of the contraction. It is ideomotor. It is also ideosensory because you get a feeling of relaxation, a feeling of comfort. You get a feeling of kinesthesia of some sort, a feeling of relaxation. So you are relying on ideomotor activity, and you are relying on ideosensory activity, and then you are asking the patient to remember. What are you asking the patient to remember?—the memories of relaxation, the memories of kinesthesia, the memories of joint activity, of muscle activity. You are asking patients to look within their own minds; so *you are centering their attention away from that spot on the wall and upon themselves as remembering creatures.* You haven't told them directly to remember kinesthesia; you haven't told them directly to remember the feeling of warmth and comfort and relaxation; but you are literally telling them to remember previous states of relaxation.

Most hypnotic techniques are built around this simple matter of ideomotor activity, ideosensory activity, and the focusing of the attention—not externally but internally. As soon as the hand starts levitating, what happens? The movie this morning demonstrated a hand levitation that involved the cog-wheel movement which is very characteristic of hypnotic muscular activity. What does it mean? It means that you have the unconcscious taking a look at muscle feeling, muscle memories, and then moving the arm; taking another look, moving it; taking another look and moving it. And you are very, very certain where the patient's attention is directed. It is within the self. *Every good hypnotic technique is directed toward centering the patient's attention upon the self.*

Now, when you ask the patient to look at that clock, to see the clock, to hear the clock, and the patient looks at it and listens to it—are you really asking him to do something external to himself? You are asking him to *hear the clock, which is an internal experience;* you are asking him to *see the clock, which is an internal experience.* And then you can tell him, "After your eyes get tired." But when you say, "After your eyes get tired," you are directing the patient's attention to his eyes, *to inner feelings and to memories of tiredness;* and so you are directing his attention away from the clock. "After your eyes begin to get tired they can close, but you will still have a mental picture of that clock." You have thereby suggested extensive ideomotor activity; you have suggested the visualization of a clock without expressly telling the patient to visualize the clock. More than one patient will tell you, "But I couldn't possibly visualize anything." Yet those same patients can tell you about dreams in which they have all manner of experiences visualized. Now, I think it is incumbent upon all of you: every time you put a patient in a trance, with each suggestion that you give them, that you, yourself, analyze your suggestion for ideomotor activity, for ideosensory activity, for an internal direction of attention that utilizes memories.

Playing with Resistance

Depotentiating Resistance via the Expression of It; Talking in a Straightforward Manner; Presenting Ideas in An Acceptable Manner

E: How is [inaudible]

S: I don't think I am very resistant.

E: You don't think you are very resistant. How do you like sitting up here in front of the group?

S: [Inaudible]

E: Do you mind being very resistant?

S: I don't think I would like to be resistant.

E: Would you try?

S: I could try.

E: All right. I am going to take hold of your wrist and lift it up in the air. Don't let me lift your arm up, but I will pull quite hard. I will get it up. That is right. What is the matter?

S: I kept changing my mind. I didn't know if I wanted to be resistant or not.

E: That is right. You did it very, very nicely, because I wanted the audience to see how one doesn't have to be troubled about resistance.

Just because a patient is resistant, why be offended or disappointed or heartbroken about it? The patient is entitled to be resistant, and if you accept that resistance and play the same game, what happens? The patient doesn't know whether he wants to keep on being resistant or not. It doesn't make me feel angry; it doesn't make me feel distressed. My tendency is to get amused. Even with patients whose psychiatric problems, whose resentment problems [are great]: you can ask them to express their resistances; you can ask them to express their hostilities toward you; and if patients can do that so easily and so comfortably, [then resistance is thereby depotentiated].

I think it is distressing when doctors feel offended just because a patient describes them in unflattering terms. I think it is very complimentary if the patient respects you enough to tell you what an s.o.b. you are, because he is trusting you to take it straight from the shoulder. How do you feel about the alcoholic patient to whom you can talk turkey—straight from the shoulder—and you lay it out to him: "That is the sort of person you are; this is the sort of home situation you are creating; now what do you want to do about it?" AA is helpful to alcoholics because one alcoholic talks straight from the shoulder to another alcoholic, and they can take it. You ought to employ that [same straightforwardness] in the matter of the practice of medicine and dentistry. You tell the patient in a straightforward fashion: "This is what is wrong with you." You try to do it in a way that the patient can actually understand.

If a patient is going to be terrified by your statement that she has a benign tumor, you tell her: "You know, there are various things that can happen to you: 1) you can have a cancer; 2) you can have a benign tumor; 3) you can have a cellular growth, if you know what I mean. Perhaps the best way of explaining it to you is the following. You know what callouses are on the hand; you get a cellular growth as a result of irritation, and I think you have some cellular growth in your breast that needs to be examined." Once the patient has accepted that concept, you can move on to a concept of a benign tumor, and then you move on to this question of a carcinoma. Your first problem is to get the patient to accept one-tenth of one percent, then one percent, then ten percent, then 50 percent, finally 100 per cent of the situation. Your task is the educational one of presenting ideas.

Changes in Body Image

Hypnotic Focus on the Self and Conditions of Sensory Deprivation; Using Hypnosis to Investigate the Problems of Space Medicine

E: Are there any questions you want to ask?
[Question from audience member directed at one of sub-

125

jects] Do you have [sensory] changes at this time? The feeling of sickness you had yesterday? Do you have that today? Do you know why you had it yesterday?

E: [To subject] This feeling you had yesterday?

S: I felt enormous.

E: Enormous. Big and heavy. And how did it begin? Where did it begin?

S: It began in my right arm.

E: It began in your right arm and moving up over your right arm.

Now, you see, if she were a patient in my office, I would never let her catch on; but I paused here long enough and it was slow enough so that she could catch on. So that you could catch on. And I was rather exaggerated in the way I did it. In the office, I do it much more gently and much more unnoticeably.

Now, that enormous feeling is one that should interest you very greatly because it is a topic of interest at the present time on a national scale. I was lecturing at the Aerospace Medical Laboratory in Dayton, Ohio—at the Wright-Patterson Field—for three days and participating in experiments intended to study the physiology of the astronauts in this matter of body field-body size in non-gravity situations, heat situations, and so on. This matter of the effect on the body of stimulation deprivation in emersion chambers—what happens to the body physiology and alterations in body image—was a fascinating problem. It is a tremendously important area for those astronauts. The person interested in hypnosis very often discovers that the body image changes very greatly because of the increased attention on the self and the withdrawal of attention from the surroundings. [To subject] When your arm started to get big again, you forgot the audience just that quickly. [Back to audience] In space, the astronauts are going to be free of gravity; they are going to be free of sound; they are going to be free of an awful lot of body stimuli that are imperative to our daily functioning—though we don't know in what way they are imperative. I think hypnosis is a nice way of studying this area, and so does the Aerospace Laboratory. Various branches are setting up study projects using hypnosis to investigate the problems of space medicine.

126

Vocal Dynamics in Demonstration Hypnosis

In the teaching situation you usually have subjects without high motivation and, therefore, you try to control the situation. With highly resistant patients you have a situation without the right kind of motivation, so you try to control the situation. Here I did everything I could to illustrate to you the use of words, of intonation, of inflection, as a means of controlling the situation and holding it. In the office I would have talked much more slowly, much more gently, used a lot more time, spaced my words, because I would have had only myself and my patient to deal with. Here I had my subject and the audience, the entire room, the teaching situation, the microphone, and so on, to deal with. The simplicity of the office makes it possible to do the same thing much more easily.

Autohypnotic and Heterohypnotic Limits

Utilizing a Conscious "Set" or Frame of Reference for Trance and Awakening; "Checking Up" in Obstetrical, Surgical, and Dental Situations

These various phenomena are phenomena that all of you can do, and I hope that all of you will become interested in acting as subjects—if not for others, at least for yourself. In acting as subjects for yourselves, you can use the my-friend-John technique (or whatever it was called yesterday) and go into a trance. All you have to do is set a limit for yourself: that is, if I were to go into an autohypnotic trance I'd say to myself, "I have an hour and a half here." When my wife wants to use autohypnosis for any particular reason, she takes a look at the clock and then considers the possibilities: the doorbell will ring, the phone will ring, maybe one of the kids will come dashing into the house, or there may be some interruption; so she sets herself to meet the interruptions. Just as in the case of the mother with a very sick baby who falls into bed exhausted; she drops into a profound physiological sleep so

127

that the house could fall down and she wouldn't wake up. But let the baby let out one yap and she is wide awake. *She has set herself in a certain frame of reference.* In this matter of hypnosis you can do the same thing for yourself and for your patient. I like to reassure my patients in that regard by stressing the fact that they can rouse up at any necessary time, and that any time they want to check up on me, in the waking state, they can rouse up and check up on me—because I have psychiatric patients, and they will want to check up.

The obstetrical patient sometimes may want to check up to see if everything is going well, because there is often a distinct separation between unconscious understandings and conscious understandings. So you always give your patients that *set,* that *frame of reference,* to the effect that they can rouse up at any time. You give your surgical patients that same understanding, but you give it to them so that they know they can rouse up and then can go right back into the trance. You ought to give them the understanding that if they inadvertantly, unintentionally rouse up from the trance—well that is all right. Anybody can be absentminded and fail to pay attention to the things at hand. That can happen when you are in the trance state, and it can happen when are in the ordinary waking state. But when it does happen you can again redirect your attention to the thing in hand, and if the thing in hand is a trance state, you redirect your attention to the trance state and go right back into a trance. You do not have to be alarmed and apologetic for having come out of the trance. I have had patients come to me who had been to the dentist and come out of the trance in the middle of the procedure. Then they couldn't go back into the trance because they were scared that they had done something wrong, that they had been unfair to the dentist, and so on. I had to explain to them that that was all right. *There is your willingness to approve of patients' behavior—and to ask them to utilize that behavior to their profit is a most important thing.* ... Accentuate the positive and eliminate the negative. Sometimes the positive happens to be the negative, because to the patient's understanding, according to the patient's orientation, the negative is the important thing.

Redirecting the Patient's Attention

Depotentiating Resistance Via the Repetitious Building of an
"Unchangeable Frame of Reference"; Hallucination Training;
Fragmenting Attention Via Confusion and Distraction

[Question from the audience] How do you redirect the patient's attention?

> **"Now, you have undoubtedly noticed that while you looked at the clock, your eyes showed a tendency to wander. Actually, of course, in all the psychological studies made of human attention, it has a very limited span. Therefore, I think you ought to be interested in noticing that your eyes drifted away, and sooner or later they will drift back; then they will drift away again, and then they will drift back. And I have stated a simple, psychological fact."**

I haven't corrected the subjects' experience. I have *explained* something to them, because you do not want to *correct* patients. Correcting them gives them a feeling of inferiority and uncertainty; a feeling of failure. You want to stress to them how normal they are, because you do want normal behavior from them; and you want to give them the feeling that they are normal, and that they do stray away.

Now, there is another technique that I ought to illustrate, and that is this. I can think of the man and the woman with whom I worked. They had some thirty hours [of therapy] apiece by various other doctors, and they were exceedingly resistant. I began with the man in this fashion:

> **"As you sit there in this chair, and you sit there in that chair, you will notice there is a picture on the wall there. There is a curtain there, and there is a doctor sitting**

> "there, and a doctor sitting there. There is a carpet on the floor, there is a tape recorder there and, of course, you are going to have difficulty cooperating with me in hypnosis because you are a resistant patient. You know it, and you are not quite certain about it. But there is a picture on the wall there, you couldn't help noticing, and there is a curtain on the wall there, and there is a doctor there, and a doctor there, and a doctor there, and a picture there on the wall. And while you are sitting there in that chair with your feet on the floor just as easily as you see a picture on the wall, the doctor there, the doctor there, the curtain there, the picture there, the doctor there. And you can feel the shoes on your feet, and keep right on feeling the shoes on your feet until you direct your attention to the picture on the wall; and the doctor there and the doctor there, the picture there, the carpet on the floor and the tape recorder."

Now, what is that patient going to do, round and around and around again? I am going to get his feet in it, I am going to get his knees in it, I am going to get his thighs in it; and you know he is going to forget about that wall entirely, because that is the picture on the wall. He will see just that picture. He will see just that doctor, and that doctor, and that doctor, and that curtain, and that carpet, and that tape recorder, and he's got himself all fixed up just on those things, and you can pick up that tape recorder and move it over there. He won't notice it, because he is already set on seeing the tape recorder right there. And somebody else can walk in and the doctor sitting there can move elsewhere, but he will still continue to see the doctor over there. All you have done is *built up a frame of reference by repetition that is unchangeable*.

You have mentioned his feet, his left foot and his right foot; and his knee and his thigh; and he has been trying to follow you and to make sense out of this endless verbalization.

> "And after a while you can literally see the doctor sitting there, and the doctor sitting there, and the doctor there, and the curtain on the wall, the picture there, the picture

there, and the tape recorder there, even with your eyes closed. And you know you can keep right on remembering the picture on the wall, the doctor sitting there, the doctor sitting over here; and you keep right on remembering the picture on the wall, the doctor there, the carpet on the floor, and tape recorder over there. While you are thinking to understand other things, you really don't need to think about those things at all. *The important thing is yourself and your problem and what you want to do about it, and the various thoughts that are flitting through your unconscious mind.*

I have given this technique to you very rapidly, but it will give you an idea of how you direct patients' thinking so that they very promptly forget about everything and just close their eyes and start thinking about the problem. A very nice trance.

Then the woman was brought in. She was very resistant too, and I used essentially the same technique, altering it to make it a little bit briefer and emphasizing her feet and her hands, her gloves, her elbows, and so on.

"You can remember your right foot but you can forget your left foot, but, of course, your right hand is on your knee and your left hand is on the arm of the chair. But it really wouldn't make a bit of difference if your left hand were on your knee and your right hand was on the arm of the chair."

Well, that is right. So the patient is listening to you, but where is her attention? Right hand, left hand, right foot, left foot, your right leg—no, your left leg, and so on. You are directing the attention.

"But, of course, it isn't a question of your right hand or your left hand, your right elbow, your left elbow, or your right foot or your left foot. The question is about that breathing trouble of yours and the complaint you have of coughing. But your right hand is on your knee—you feel it there, and you would like to feel the same comfort in your

throat and in your chest as you feel in your hand and in your knee."

You could call it a fragmentation technique, if you wish, wherein you fragment the body; or you could call it a confusion technique, or you could call it a distraction technique. But it is all a matter of asking the patient: "Give your attention to this, to this; and let me keep your attention moving in an ever narrowing spiral until your attention is directed to the thing for which you came to see me."

"Keep On Wishing"

Utilizing Wishing to Depotentiate Rigid Ideas and Avoid Argument

When patients have a fixed and rigid idea, why argue with them about it? They know better than you do. They know their condition, and when you try to dispute them you are on the losing end of the argument. When the patient says, "There is no possibility whatsoever that I can do such-and-such," you agree with him and you can tell him: "Yes, you will probably keep right on doing it for the next ten years, and you will probably keep on wishing that it would only be for nine years." You have agreed that he will keep right on doing it for the next ten years, but it may be only for nine years. [When you say, "You will probably keep wishing"], you have altered that direction immediately. Then you've gotten the patient's attention focused not on what he tells you he is going to do, because he can't help himself; you've gotten his attention focused on his *wishes* of what he *hopes* may be so. And you, knowing what he has said, knowing what you have said, have somehow slipped over to this question of the patient's actual therapy. Now, there is your willingness not to try to compel patients to do what *you* wish or to think what *you* wish them to think, but your willingness to present understandings to them. They can believe, "I will do this for the next twenty years," and you'd better agree. "I am going to do it for the next twenty years; I can't help myself; there is nothing I can do about it; I will keep right on." But along with [those emphatic statements], you know that they must have a wish or they wouldn't be in to see you. So you start dealing with their wishes, you start dealing with their emotional attitudes, you start dealing with their fears, but you do it gently. You never engage in a losing argument.

Offering Ideas Via the Double Bind[1]

*Reinforcing the Double Bind Via a Simple Question: "Never?";
Utilizing Agreement to Move Patient into a Therapeutic, Self-
Designed Double Bind*

I want to mention this question of the double bind again because [it is so pertinent to] this matter of presenting ideas so that patients can find them acceptable. You tell your children, "Do you want to go to bed at ten minutes to eight, or at eight o'clock?", and they will tell you eight o'clock. They don't want ten minutes to eight; they want to stay up until eight. They have specified the bedtime. What if they tell you, "Oh, I don't want to go to bed at all." "Never?" you ask. You have asked a question. You have taken them at their word. They are the ones who must back up in their understanding immediately. They have weakened their understanding, but you should know that. Why should you tell them: "Now let's be sensible. You have to go to bed sometime." Let them do the thinking [by your simple asking of the question, "Never?"]. *This is the way you offer ideas to patients: not by forcibly shoving ideas at them but by just giving them the opportunity. When you offer an idea in this manner, you ought to know that you have placed the patient in a double bind.* Don't jeer at him because he came to you for help. You ought to be pleased that you can think in a way that is helpful to him, and you ought to let him know that you are always respectful of his need to save face. Therefore, you ought to be willing to lose face for your patient, because your patient hates to admit that he is wrong.

I had a patient come to me recently and explain: "I have seen plenty of psychiatrists and they are all crackpots. Every one of them says I have a psychological problem, and it is obvious it is physiological!"

I told him rather simply, "All right. You are positive that it is physiological. Well, that is a settled argument. Now let's deal with it as a physiological problem."

I said, "Unquestionably that is true, too."

Now he is asking me to emphasize the physiological, and he thinks the psychological is a very minor consideration. Why should I dispute him? Why should I protest that psychiatrists aren't crackpots? How about some questions on double bind?

Therapeutic Versus Pathological Double Bind

Reversing Schizogenic Binds in the Family: Creating New Identities; Weight Loss; Utilizing the Double Bind in Trance Induction

[Question from the audience] What about the type of person who has been living in the double bind all his life and this is the big problem? You, as a physician, put him back in the double bind for different purposes. How is he going to react to something that he is always reacting to? [How do you deal with the] schizoid type?

E: The schizoid types. I can think of quite a number of illustrations. If they are intelligent enough, I ask them to understand what a double bind is: *"If you don't get your mother a present, she is going to be heartbroken; if you do, she is going to tell you you shouldn't have done it. Either way you lose.* Or if you take the job your father insists you take, he will then tell you that you should have gotten a job all on your own. So you lose either way."* You get the patient to understand and then you tell him:

"You know, I would like to put you in a double bind, but I would like to put you in a double bind to *your* advantage. What kind of a double bind can we work out? You are in a double bind with your father, and you are in a double bind with your mother. Your father is going to insist that you take that job, and he is going to be as disappointed as can be. Your mother is going to insist that you live at home, and she is going to be as disappointed as can be if you do. Well, any way you are going to be wrong. All right, this is what you do: Fortunately your family owns both a country house and a city house. Live at home. While your parents are in the city house, you live in the country house; while they are in the country house, you live in the city house. Work half time on that job, one week in the forenoon; the next week in the afternoon. Your father is going to be wrong each way."

That is exactly what the chap is doing. He has his parents very much wrought up because he isn't doing anything they want him to, and yet he is doing *everything* they want him to! It is a nice double bind, and he is thoroughly enjoying it, and his father has written me: "My son seems to be improving greatly and I can't understand it." There is your willingness to work out a double bind in those cases.

"Your mother wants you to eat at a certain restaurant, she wants you to go to a certain college, she wants you to take certain subjects—and she is going to be disappointed if you do any one of those three things. Tell her, "Mother, you want me to go to college—fine; you want me to eat at a certain restaurant—that is fine; you want me to take certain subjects, so I am going to sign up for these subjects. I am going to take these subjects at Phoenix College, and the other subjects at night school in Tempe at the Arizona State University."

So I split that up for the chap so that he is taking a full course—night school, day school. Mother can't find fault because he is going to Arizona State University; Father can't find fault because he is going to Phoenix College. He can't eat in a certain restaurant *some* of the time, but he *can* eat in it some of the time. It is really a mess, and the boy is enjoying himself thoroughly because his parents can't handle that sort of a combination! It is either that approach, or let the boy be committed as a schizophrenic. He has a tremendous sense of accomplishment by virtue of my assisting him in getting some double binds going for his parents. Parents that I have treated in this way via their children have finally agreed that they were delighted with what happened to the children. They are glad that the children finally matured, which is what they wanted in the first place, and so they save face with the children.

[Question concerns a weight loss double bind situation in which

135

the mother insists that the child lose weight, and so takes the child to a doctor. The child begins to lose weight, which pleases the doctor, but then the mother insists that the child eat more to keep his strength up for school. The mother is sabatoging the plan in some way so that the child is wrong. The bind for the child is: "If I lose weight, I am going to be too weak; and if I eat as much as mother wants, I won't lose weight and she'll yell at me that it was a waste of money."]

E: I know, that is a horrible mess. "You've got to eat to keep up your strength so you'll have enough strength to lose weight." What I usually do is get the mother and the child together. The mother doesn't know what I am doing. I point out to the mother: "Now, listen, let's be reasonable about this child's loss of weight. How tall is your daughter? What do you think is the average weight? How much should she weigh? Well, let's allow for an extra fifteen pounds, and I want you to see to it that she does not lose more than two and a half pounds a week, or not more than one pound a week. That is your responsibility, Mother, and you see to it that she doesn't lose more that that."

I turn to the child. "It is your obligation to cooperate with your mother so that you lose at least a pound a week." Now the tug of war is between *more than* and not *less than,* and they are both working for the pound a week—or whatever is set. And I have satisfied that double bind need on their part.

[Question from the audience] Can you use the double bind to keep subjects in a trance?

E: Oh, yes. Let's see. Whenever you are using the double bind, you try to derive it from the immediate situation with the patient— out of the situation in which you find the patient: "Now, you are in a light trance and you are having difficulty going deeper." Examine that statement.

"You are having difficulty going deeper, and I want you to keep on experiencing that difficulty. There is only one way of keeping on experiencing that difficulty. Go deeper. I don't know when you will enter the deep trance. You don't know and I don't know. It really isn't important, but perhaps you would like to know. But I don't think you will

know when you go into the deep trance, but you will suddenly discover it when your hand plunks into your lap, or maybe you won't even notice that."

Whichever way [the subject responds is acceptable]. You have a double bind in all directions.

"You are in a light trance and you are undoubtedly going to notice that you keep awakening, but, of course, you are cooperative. You go back into a light trance, but you awaken again; but since you are cooperative you will go back into a light trance."

How much practice, how much rehearsal do patients need? And each time they awaken and go back, awaken and go back, awaken and go back, awaken and go back, they become less and less interested in the waking state. "But you will go back. Of course you will awaken, but you will go back." So they go back, back, back into the trance.

Giving a Wealth of Suggestions

Learning to Use and Examine the Meanings of Words; Listening with the Unconscious Mind; Expecting "Adequate Functioning" of the Unconscious Mind

This morning, emphasis was placed on this matter of the use of words. I think that you should be very, very careful to use your words in a manner that expresses meanings that are important to your patients. I think all of you ought to verbalize the technique into a tape recorder. Then listen to it and notice what you said, and think through what you intended to say, and then repeat it again and again and again until you have learned how to offer suggestions. I know that when I work with the patient, I throw out a tremendous number of suggestions and that as I continue with the patient, I will start picking up various of those suggestions.

Do you remember the issue of the Journal in which Haley and

Weekland and I published the article on the techniques with a resistant subject?[2] The subject said she was sorry she couldn't be hypnotized but that she would be glad to act as a subject. Haley and Weekland had a tape recorder, and I sat down beside the patient to go through an induction technique. After the first ten minutes I mentioned that I could count to 20 in various ways—by ones, by twos, by fours, fives, tens. Then I offered a wealth of suggestions about five minutes later, and about ten minutes later I mentioned that I've got eight children. You know, they are cheaper by the dozen—and that is one way of counting to twenty! I used that as a posthypnotic suggestion on her. Count to 20 in various ways—ones, fours, fives, tens. There are various way of counting to 20. Very simple things. You ought to examine your words and their meanings, and how you can communicate those ideas.

[Question from the audience] Why do they go back into trance?

E: They don't know.

Q: They really don't know—part of them is counting?

E: Part of them is counting, and they learned to count that way a long, long time ago. Remember that tremendous pride you had in learning to count by fives. That tremendous pride when you first discovered you had five digits—that pride that little children have? You are talking to your hypnotic subjects, and you give them posthypnotic suggestions, and they go into a trance when you count to 20. So they are in a trance. They don't know why. Consciously they wonder if you have departed from your wits, or what has happened to you! Unconsciously, they are at 5, 10, 15, 20. It is just like that, and your awareness that the unconscious pays attention. I tell my patient:

> **"You know when you walked into this office you brought your unconscious mind with you. Your unconscious mind is at liberty to listen to me or not to listen to me, but it will undoubtedly listen. Now, consciously you listen to me, or you let your attention get distracted and not listen to me. I am close enough to you so that your unconscious mind will hear me."**

What have I told that patient right then and there? *"Don't bother to*

listen to me consciously; your unconscious mind will listen to me."
Quite often that is an adequate technique to induce a trance state,
and it is so utterly simple, so utterly direct.

You ought to expect your patient's unconscious mind to function in an adequate fashion. When you rely upon patients—when you give them the feeling, the expectation, that they will respond— then they can respond.

> **"I just don't know how you are going to quit smoking four packages of cigarettes a day. I think it ought to be interesting for you to find out. I don't know whether you will find out today, tomorrow, next week, or next month."**
> **"I don't know when you will stop wetting the bed, I really don't care. It isn't my bed."**

When I say, "It isn't my bed," I am saying a whole volume. I am telling the patient I would literally rub his nose in his own bed. It is his bed, and he knows it, and I don't care. But he does, and I have told him to care and to care with utter intensity.

Iatrogenic Health Versus Iatrogenic Disease

The Different Outcomes of "Dr. Serious's" and "Dr. Jovial's"
Patients: Understanding the Significance of Everything Said to
the Patient

That reminds me of another point I thought of this morning. Johnny was brought to me because he was a bedwetter. Well, Johnny had been informed that he is a bedwetter, very emphatically. A question that has been written on recently, and also has been written on periodically, for I don't know how long, is the question of iagtrogenic disease—that is, disease caused by the doctor. "I think you have rather a bad heart, and you'd better watch it." So the patient promptly becomes a cardiac invalid. I have such a patient at the present time. The doctor merely said: "You may have something wrong with your heart. You'd better watch it." And the patient was bedridden for three months as a result of the remark—iatrogenic disease. While I have read a number of articles on this subject of iatrogenic disease, and heard many discussions about it, there is one topic on which I haven't seen much written about and that is *iatrogenic health*. Iatrogenic health is a most important consideration—much more important than iatrogenic disease.

I can remember a study that I conducted a long time ago. There were two surgeons. We all agreed that they were of equal skill. Dr. Serious was a long-faced, solemn soul who would walk in and look at the patient, do a careful examination, very tersely express his opinion, and tell exactly how bad the condition was. He always expected to take one, two, three, four hours for the operation. After the operation he would come into the post surgical: "You are not doing too badly"—solemn, serious—and that was the limit of his interpersonal contact with the patients.

Dr. Jovial, on the other hand, was another sort of a chap. He always bounced in to see his patient, he always had a story to tell, he always had some wisecrack, some compliment to give; he always minimized the patient's condition even though he would say: "Of course, it is possible for this [to happen] but from the looks of you, it is going to be a relatively easy thing."

In studying the 300 cases of each of these two surgeons, Dr. Serious's patients had a much longer postoperative stay; he had a higher morbidity rate, a higher mortality rate, and more complications. Dr. Jovial's patients came along perfectly beautifully with fewer complications and much shorter hospital stays. In other words, *there was this matter of iatrogenic illness and iatrogenic health resulting from the attitudes of the two surgeons*. I wanted to publish that finding but I was forbidden by the "authorities" because they said it would be too serious a reflection upon hospital staff. You know, the AMA can take some very stupid attitudes. I think you ought to bear that in mind whenever you deal with patients: *everything that you say to them is of significance*.

Different Levels of Conversation

Talking to the Different Levels of Conscious and Unconscious Processes

Just before lunch a question came up about this conversation I carry on with patients at different levels. Let me illustrate it in another way because, you see, people are used to conversing at different levels. The parents will say, "Why can't you have good manners just for the family as well as when we have company." The children put on another set of manners and another set of conversation. You can be talking to yourself on a subject, discussing it aloud to formulate your opinion. Let somebody else come into the room and you try to repeat what you said to yourself, but you will modify your remarks because of the other person. Let two other people come in and you will modify your remarks still more. From the very beginning of childhood we learn to modify our remarks, to carry on different levels of conversation. When you work with a patient you ought to think continuously: *I have a patient here, and I have his unconscious mind. I have his conscious wishes and I have his unconscious wishes, and I really ought to talk to both of my patients, the conscious one and the unconscious one also.* In that way, you learn to develop more and more skill in this matter of saying things to convey double meanings, triple meanings, and so on.

Real Life Versus Laboratory Learning

There is another matter I want to emphasize to the group and that is the rapidity with which people learn. In the psychology laboratory, anybody, everybody knows that you flash a light, ring a bell, give an electical stimulus, and you get a conditioned response. It may take 20, 30, 40, 50, 100 combined stimuli to get a conditioned response that lasts for a reasonable length of time. But I can assure you that in real life, the learning process is entirely different. It is just the same as it is with laboratory medicine. In the test tube you get one set of results; in people, in the human body, you get another set of results. In this matter of learning: in the laboratory you get one kind of result, in real life you get another. How many times do you need to touch a red-hot stove to remember it forevermore? How many times does the little child need to touch an angry cat to realize that you don't touch an angry cat? Just once, and the next time the child sees the cat, the child is afraid. In real-life experience, one drastic lesson is sufficient. In the laboratory you can give very drastic stimulation, over and over again, because it is a laboratory—a make-believe situation. You do not get learning as rapidly. When you get this learning, how is it manifested? In the laboratory you can give very drastic stimuli—electrical stimuli—and your patient gets a conditioned response, a muscle response, a pupillary response, or something of that sort. And it can be a very serious electrical shock that constitutes the stimulus. But your subject knows that this is a laboratory, knows that this is an experiment, and you get a conditioned response that lasts a certain length of time. In real life, however, you can have a much less serious stimulus that you remember for weeks and months.

To iullustrate this point, I can think of the woman who was visiting with some friends. They went down north Central Avenue in a car, and on the way they stopped and got a frozen custard. They were driving along and eating the frozen custard. My patient had just finished her custard and, being a litter bug, threw the box out on the street. About a block further, a little girl dashed out on the other side of the street between parked cars, and an oncoming car traveling at a legitimate speed struck the little girl and killed her. It was a horrible sight and it distressed my patient very much, but she forgot about it.

A month later at a party, ice cream was served and the women went into a state of shock. Her stomach tightened up and she was in a serious state. She didn't know why. She thought it was a sudden attack of appendicitis or something worse. I saw her after about a month. I don't recall exactly how long. It was a psychiatric problem to get that story: tossing that frozen custard container out in the street, realizing at the same time that it was a litter-bug act, a block further seeing the little girl on the other side of the street hit by another car. Nobody was really at fault—it was simply a shocking experience. A month later at a party, when she had forgotten all about the little girl—she didn't know the little girl or any of the friends of the little girl—she was served a dessert. And a dessert equals a dessert: a frozen custard equals ice cream. So she went into a state of shock and required medical attention. How quickly did she learn a very violent response without there ever being adequate stimulation for that particular kind of response? There was nothing in the accident that warranted her developing a stomach reaction, but she had gone only a block after finishing the frozen custard.

Reframing Symptoms as Healthy Responses

Overcoming a Dog-Biting Trauma Via Negative Praise: Rebecca Twice Bitten; The Body's Knowledge of the Forces That Affect Us

Now, I can think of little Rebecca. Rebecca was a nice, little seven-year-old girl. She was coming home from school when a great, big German police dog bit her (not very badly) and frightened her horribly. The owners of the dog came out and scolded little Rebecca for bothering that great, big German police dog; and they really scolded Rebecca. They resented sending the dog for observation, and they resented paying the bill for that period of observation. Rebecca recovered from the bite and was coming home from school again. The owners of the dog had been ordered to keep him behind a fence, but they said he was entitled to have some exercise. So, Rebecca was coming home from school; she was some blocks from the dog's home when the dog came along and bit her again. The owners told the little girl that they were going to sue her parents. They really scolded her, and it resulted in a very nasty, disagreeable event.

Rebecca went home and the doctor checked her over; he also had the dog sent for observation. Rebecca stayed at home that weekend recovering from the dog bite—Saturday, Sunday. On Monday, Rebecca started out for school, got as far as the side walk, turned around and came home, saying that she was not feeling well. The next day she got as far as the front porch before she got sick; the day after, she wouldn't leave the house. Her symptomatology was: looseness of the bowels, incontinence of the bladder, violent perspiration, a racing heart—tachycardium, vomiting, and syncope. She *had* to stay in the house: the mere thought of going outside the house was incredibly painful to Rebecca. This situation continued for some weeks, and then her doctor (a general practitioner)

143

decided to send her to me. Getting Rebecca to my office was a rather difficult task, but the importance was explained to her by the general practitioner.

Rebecca was brought in wrapped up in a blanket so that she could see me. A seven-year-old girl—with all of those violent reactions. The question was how much should I unwrap her from the blanket, and how willing was she to talk to me. It was a slow, systematic approach, but before the hour was over, Rebecca was laughing and joking. She even wanted to see my dog, which I had explained to her was a Bassett and not a German police dog. I saw Rebecca for a total of seven sessions in which I raised this question of the dog bite. The first thing I did was to justify her fear to her. I justified to her the diarrhea, the bladder incontinence; I justified to her the sweating, the tachycardium. I told her I was surprised that since she was such a strong and healthy girl, that her heart didn't beat faster; I was surprised that since she was so strong and healthy, that she didn't have more diarrhea, that her fainting didn't last longer, and so on. I had to give that little girl some good opinion of her body and her behavior, and so I was just surprised that it wasn't a lot worse—which gave Rebecca a much different opinion of herself. In talking to her I praised her body in that negative sort of way, because it was a negative praising which had positive results. Rebecca just listened to me, forgetting the rest of the office and developing a very nice trance. This is the kind of story that demonstrates the capacity of the human being to learn a tremendous number of things.

The question was raised this morning: How can the suggestion of a high altitude result in vascular changes when the direct suggestion of coldness will not produce vascular changes? I offered the response that we all have had the experience of being at sea level and at mountain level. Our bodies know a great deal about the different forces that affect us in a multitude of ways. How quickly can you detect a change in humidity? Ordinarily you overlook such a matter, but if you up the humidity one percent in the heat chamber, the man can tell you right then and there that humidity has gone up; and he describes it as a terrific blast of hot air. but you have only upped it one percent, yet he knows it immediately.

Now, Rebecca was bitten; what is the response of the body to that type of stimulation? Rebecca was only seven years old. Should she say: "Well, I was bitten on the face here, so I should bleed there and only there; and I was bitten on the knee, so I should only bleed there. I think Rebecca didn't have much chance to do any thinking at all. The fright caused her heart to react; the fright would cause her sweat glands to react; the fright would cause the change in her body's peripheral circulation. Everything about her would change—her smooth muscles would contract, tension would develop in all the muscles, and then the sight of a dog would really precipitate a lot ot things.

Life After Symptom Removal

Rechanneling the Energy of Symptoms into Constructive Developments: Treating Insomnia and Other Bad Habits; The Case of the Skilled Failure

In this matter of symptom removal is an awfully important question. I want to reiterate what I said about symptom removal. It is perfectly proper. There is no law that says symptom removal must be replaced by a worse symptom. There is at least a 50/50 chance that it will be replaced by a *better* symptom, but there is something you ought to do whenever you alter a patient's life. You need to point out to the patient when you alter his life that he has his daily equipment of energy, his daily allotment of energy, and the question arises: How should he use it? What does he want to do about that energy? Previously he had a very serious symptom and you removed it. *What is he going to do with the energy that went into the manifestation of that symptom? He's got to find some way of using that energy.* I tell the patient suffering from insomnia:

"You use an awful lot of energy staying awake. You resort to every conceivable measure of preventing sleep. Now, if you sleep and rest yourself thoroughly, you will have an over-supply of energy. What would you really like to do with that energy? What constructive or instructive or developmental project would you like to undertake to use

145

up that extra daily allotment of energy? You've got to direct it elsewhere than in keeping yourself awake. That nice rest each night is going to replenish your energy. How are you going to use it?''

You need to get the patient interested in a wealth of new things. I can think of the 21-year-old patient who, in getting through high school, went to endless trouble to get grades that kept him at the bottom of a class of 112 students. He wanted to get through high school. He was a very brilliant chap, and he came from an excellent home; but he did want to be low man on the totum pole. It was perfectly remarkable the way his grades put him in position 112 in a class of 112. And I pointed out to him that it took an awful lot of skill and maneuvering to make sure that he passed and yet was bottom man. He thought that over and started to laugh at my analysis. In every course he was bottom man in the class, and yet he scored just high enough to pass. Now that took energy. Then after high school he managed to flunk out of college; he managed to get kicked out of the Academy at Annapolis; he managed to get himself fired from half a dozen different jobs; he managed everything in the wrong way—always putting forth an awful lot of energy. He stole a car, and he stole it with the greatest of care. As I pointed out to him, he made even the stealing of the car into a failure.

"You cased the various parking lots; you discovered a car with the keys left in it; you made note of the attendant's habits; and one day, when the attendant went across the street to get a Coke or ice cream, you slipped into the lot and just casually drove off on the other side. You drove within the speed limit; you drove the car a total of 25 miles; you parked it very prominently on the top of a hill about six blocks from home; you got out and walked the rest of the way home, leaving the car to be discovered by the police. You weren't caught, you didn't violate the speed laws, or anything. You stole the car by driving it like a perfectly good citizen, not like a competent thief. And how are you going to use that energy that you've put into that sort of a failure? How are you going to put it to use? The chap is now studying the problem of getting a job, and performing a job, and using his energy in a highly constructive way.

In a similar manner I took that psychiatric patient and demanded that he use his energy in a constructive way. You ask your insomniac patient to use this energy in a constructive way. You ask the patient who's got a bad habit to use that same energy in another way.

The "Throw Away" Technique

Utilizing Symbolic Acts to Resolve Psychological and Emotional Problems: "Throwing Away" a Father Dependency; The Common Everyday Basics of Symbolic Attitudes

Dr. Brody has a very nice way of asking patients to dispose of things: He has them write down in a notebook something they want to get rid of, and then hand it to Dr. Brody. He had one patient write "five pounds" on a piece of paper and then throw it into the wastebasket. I know I have published on the use of the same sort of mechanism: asking a patient to look through a newspaper, and notice a word, a phrase, a sentence here and there, and then discard the newspaper. What are you really asking the patient to do? *You are asking the patient to open his mind.* He looks at a word here, a phrase there, a sentence there, page after page; and then he throws the newspaper away. He hasn't really read anything; he hasn't learned anything. He is wondering, wondering. Then the next time he comes to see you, he has used all the wonderment as a form of energy to recover and to remember a wealth of forgotten material.

I once asked a patient to write his father's name on a piece of paper and then to dispose of it. I can think of one patient who drew a picture of his father, labelled it "father" and then flushed it down the toilet—which was a very nice way of severing his absolute emotional dependence upon his father. He really got rid of his father without insulting his father, without cussing his father out. He just simply freed himself by writing the word on a piece of paper and flushing it down the toilet. I have had patients do that in many, many regards. What happens when they write "five pounds" on a piece of paper and then throw it in the wastebasket? That's their act. That is their commitment to a certain thing. It is not a commitment to you. I have asked patients to write out the

147

things they couldn't discuss with me, seal it, and then present it to me sealed—knowing that I wouldn't open the envelope. Then they discover that they didn't have to discuss those things with me, but that there are a lot of other things, now uncovered, they could discuss with me.

You see, in the handling of patients you need to meet their psychological needs and their emotional needs. When you ask them to throw away five pounds, two pounds; when you ask them to throw away their dependency upon their father—you are having them go through the symbolic act. But as you consider patients, aren't they pretty much governed by symbolic acts of all kinds? I think your medical/dental approach to patients should be with full cognizance of the fact that we all take a symbolic attitude toward a lot of things: "That is something I would like to sink my fangs into" expresses a whole lot; "If I could only get my teeth into that problem"—what kind of a problem?—social problem, economic problem, mathematical problem—whatever it is, if I only could get my teeth into it. We think about teeth in certain symbolic ways. There is also a philosophical concept: "I really wish I could get my hands on it." Do you want to get your *hands* on a philosophical concept, or do you want to grasp it—to comprehend it in some way?

Utilizing Patients' Language Descriptions in Diagnosis

Globus Hystericus *as a Displacement of Peptic Ulcers;*
"A Pain in the Neck" Positively Correlated with
Cervical Arthritis

Whenever you deal with patients you need to watch their language and then to utilize what they are saying to you.

The patient who told me: "I've got a *globus hystericus*. I have a lump in my throat." I knew the patient was a nurse who couldn't get along with any doctor. She always did the diagnosing and the prescribing and the cussing out of the doctor for being so stupid. She came in and gave me her diagnosis of *globus hystericus*. She recognized it because of the lump in her throat and the peculiar type of pain that she felt. She wanted me to use hypnosis, but I pointed out to that nurse that I had known her for some time and that she had a sister and a niece who called her daily on the telephone. The patient interrupted me to add, "And I can't stomach either one of them."

"That is the point I am raising with you. Everytime anything displeases you, you say you can't *stomach* it. You can't stomach this, and you can't stomach that. Before I treat that lump in your throat, which you say is hysterical in nature, you are going to have an X-ray of your stomach. I want to know what condition your stomach is in. I think from your description of the lump in your throat and the pain you describe that you have a pyloric spasm which you have displaced in your throat. In short, I want to know if you have a peptic ulcer."

The nurse was very disgusted, but I got her X-ray studies. She did have a peptic ulcer, but she was true to form. She flatly refused to let anyone treat her. She was a nurse and could prescribe the right kind of diet and treatment for herself. One month later the X-ray was negative. She had cancelled her sister's and her niece's two-or-three-times-a-day telephone calls and several-times-a-week visits. She just couldn't stomach them.

Last September, in Canada, an orthopedist was relating a number of cases in which patients explained to him that various things were "a pain in the neck." He conducted his own X-ray studies of the necks of these patients to find out how many of them who described things as "a pain in the neck" had cervical arthritis. He reported a positive correlation in his studies and noted the need for acute sensitivity to the body language of patients.

Predicting Patient Behavior

Prediction as a Tool of Learning and Observation: Arthritis of the Feet; Checking Up on Patients as a Learning Tool

I can recall one set of parents to whom I said, "I really feel sorry for your 20-year-old daughter. She has got a rather disagreeable disposition. Everybody has the feeling that she goes around kicking at people right and left. My feeling is that some time in the future—perhaps by the time she is 40—she will have arthritis of the feet." Of course, the parents said that was rather a ridiculous prediction to make. But I've always been interested in this matter of making predictions. I checked up on that patient when she was age 43, and she was on crutches for arthritis of the ankles and the feet. Then after getting acquainted with her, I predicted that by the time she reached her mid-fifties, she probably would be off her crutches and she would have a mellowing of her personality. And she is off her crutches. She uses a cane once in a while.

I think all of you ought to be interested in your patients—in predicting from week to week [how they will behave. This is] not for the purpose of being right in your predictions, but each time you predict something and then you check up on it and find out that you were *wrong*, then you are going to notice all the things that you should have taken into account in order to make a more reliable prediction. After you have done this over a long period of time, you will find out that you can make a few predictions quite accurately. You make the predictions and you check up on them to see what your oversights were.

I checked up on this asthmatic patient last night. I called her up to see how she was getting along. I had a very delightful conversation with her. She was very pleased. Why shouldn't I check up on her? I have checked up on patients after 25 years because that is the sort of thing that enables you to learn.

I like to think over the possibilities of the patient coming in next week. What is the patient going to do? Of course, I am going to overlook a lot of the things today that I will suddenly be aware of next week. Next week, I will do just a little bit better in my handling of the patient because I have become more aware of that patient.

Accepting Resistance as Any Other Symptom

Utilizing Resistance in the One-Hour Therapy of a Neurodermatitis Case: Marrying for Money: Directing Resistance to Where It Is Most Needed

In this matter of handling resistances, I don't think it is too difficult a job. In the first place, the patient comes to you for help of some sort, whether it is dental, medical, or psychiatric. But he has come to you for help. If he brings in an ulcer, you are not going to tell him: "Set that outside the office; I don't want any ulcers in the office." You just don't. You accept the ulcer. If he comes in with a lot of resistance, isn't that just as important a part of him as an ulcer or a skin rash? I think you ought to recognize this point.

I can think of the woman in her sixties who came in with a case of neurodermatitis up to about here, and her statement to me was this: "I've got neurodermatitis. I have been to many dermatologists. They all diagnosed it the same, but not one of them has been able to do a thing about it, so they referred me to a psychiatrist. I have seen several psychiatrists. Every one of them has questioned me and discovered that I married my husband for his money, and I did. He isn't going to live much longer because he has a bad heart, he is an alcoholic, he drinks horribly. I have tried to sober him up. I have been a good wife to him. He's got cardiac disease. He is going to kill himself some night in a drunken bout, but I get fed up with his behavior because every time he takes a couple of drinks he gets awfully obnoxious. But I do want his money. I have been perfectly honest with him, but after I married him I noticed I got the neurodermatitis. I am not going to give up the man but I do want some therapy. Now, will you use hypnosis on me if indicated?" Her attitude then was to fold her arms and lean back.

Well, what better proof of resistance do you want? Then I pointed out to her:

"You know that your present position indicates that you are full of resistance. I don't think unconsciously you want hypnosis. Therefore, my feeling is that first of all, in addition to your neurodermatitis, we recognize your resistance as a part of the problem. You say you married your husband for his money; many a man takes a job for money, and there is nothing wrong with that. Even if he doesn't work for his job he may take it just to have the money. Many a man marries a woman for money. I think he works for it and he earns it if he marries her for her money. If a woman marries a man for his money, I think

151

she is going to earn it, for she is going to have to put up with a lot of things. So, if you have a job that is going to pay you big money, all I can say is, congratulations. Don't ask me to take any moralistic attitude about your marriage because I am awfully, awfully certain that you are earning every cent of it, and that you will keep on earning every cent of it. The question really is this: you are going to have your resistances to a lot of things, because in working at the kind of a job you have elected, you are going to have to resist a lot of emotional distress; you are going to have to resist a lot of unhappiness, a lot of disappointment. Why not use your powers of resistance in that regard and leave your neurodermatitis unprotected for me to handle?"

I kept on that train of thought with her, and then I asked her how she would really like to have her arms feel. Something came up about lying on the beach when she was a young girl sunning herself, and the warmth of the sun on her skin, so I asked her to recall that vividly and to get some of that feeling in her arms. We worked for one hour. Her statement was: "That is enough. I don't see why I should spend any more of my hard-earned money on you."

A year later she came back and said: "You know, that one treatment took care of my neurodermatitis until about a month ago. So I sat down in a chair and relaxed myself, and I recalled everything you did, for I didn't want to spend anymore of my hard-earned money on you. I have tried it for a month and it doesn't work, so here is a check. Give me an hour."

Then I said:

"May I give you a stamped envelope with my address on it? And will you drop me a note in about six months' time to let me know if the therapy I do is still effective?— because I am interested in knowing, and that is much cheaper than coming in to tell me."

I got a letter from her six months later saying that she was still free of the neurodermatitis. But, you see, I differentiated between the neurodermatitis and her life situation. When you do therapy with the patient, you look at the patient as a responsive, living human being with thoughts and ideas and experiences; and you also look at the problem. If it is a physical problem, you had better identify it and you had better consider how far it extends into the patient's personal life. If it is a psychological problem, you had better examine it to see how far it extends into the patient's personal life. In that way, you can differentiate between resistances that the patient needs for himself and resistances that are just generally manifested. Your task is to accept resistances as a part of the total problem and put them aside, but not necessarily to fight those resistances. Yes, you can fight those resistances. If you do need to fight them, do as Joan did yesterday. When I lifted her arm, it wasn't a very difficult matter to tell her, "Go ahead and resist— fight against me." Even the most resistant patient who comes into the office is going to cooperate with you if you openly acknowledge that you understand the resistances, and that you are neither antagonized nor offended.

Utilizing Resistance

Treating Acting-Out Behavior Via the Injunctive to "Throw It on the Floor"

I can think of the mother who came in and said: "Here is a check for fifty dollars. That will pay for the damage done to your office. I want you to see my 12-year-old son."

The mother said: I don't need the check. I will just take it on account for the psychotherapy."

The mother said: "You don't understand. When my son comes in here, he is going to grab this, he is going to grab that, smash it on the floor, and so on."

I said, "Thanks for warning me. I will take care of that when he comes in. What is the rest of his problem?"

When the son came in, he took a very careful look around the room. I handed him a very heavy ashtray and said, "Throw it on the floor." He looked at me and tossed it on floor. Then I handed him an ordinary pencil and said, "Really slam it on the carpet." So he caught on then and really slammed the pencil to the floor. He looked around at the bric-a-brac and then I said, "Grab that piece of Kleenex and now crash it on the floor." He looked at me and grinned. "I can't do that." I said, "All right sissy, now sit down." And that was the end of my difficulties with that boy.

Yes, I had found out previously that he had smashed up several doctor's offices, but when I called him on that with "crash that Kleenex on the floor . . . sit down, sissy"—well, what could he do? The boy came in prepared to show resistances. Why? He wanted a challenge to see if it could be met: could he intimidate me, could he make me fearful, could he make me worried or anxious?

A Double Bind Utilizing Insult

Overcoming Resistance Via the Therapeutic Use of a "Thorough-Going Insult"; Acceptance and Wondering in Response to Resistance

I can think of the 20-year-old boy who said: "I prefer not to talk to you, but my father insists that I talk to you. I am dependent on my father, and my father is a doctor. He is making me do this. My mother is making me, and you'd better say only nice things or I'll clobber you in spite of your age and the fact that you are crippled."

I said, "Well, are you going to begin now, or are you going to wait until I insult you?"

He said, "I will have to wait until you insult me."

I said, "Well, do you want a mild insult, or do you want thorough-going insult?"

What could he say? He couldn't say he wanted something mild. *He had to say he wanted a thorough-going insult.*

"Shall I tell you when I am through, or do you just want to guess?"

So I had an absolutely delightful time talking to him and insulting him. He is my patient now, and he said: "You really made me see myself as I am. All those things you said about me—I sat there wishing I could clobber you, but for some reason I didn't know how to get out of the chair."

Of course, he didn't know how to get out of the chair because I hadn't finished with him yet. He was bound to stay there until I finished my insulting, and the implied agreement was that I was to do a thoroughly good job of insulting. Nothing mild—he wasn't that kind of a chap who would take something mild.

When you get your resistances in a patient with dental work or medical work, you respect those resistances. You are perfectly straightforward and frank and direct in your acknowledgement. You are not offended; your feelings are not hurt when patients say something to the effect, "You aren't such a bright doctor after all. I don't know why I came here. Maybe you can't make a living in a big town." Why should you take offense? The fact that the person is a patient in your office tells you that he thinks you are good enough for him. If he didn't think so, he wouldn't be there. Why take offense? Patients do say offensive things as a measure of expressing resistance. Well, why shouldn't you take that expression as much a part of their condition as their complaint of pain, of headache, backache, or loss of function? There is your willingness to take the patient *as he is:* resistances, antagonisms, complaints. *Whatever it is the patient brings into your office, you accept it and you wonder how to deal with it.*

Posthypnotic Suggestion

Presenting Rather Than Labeling Posthypnotic Suggestions: Letting Patients Create Responses and Define Situations: Indirect Posthypnotic Suggestions That Adjust to Future Events: A New Hairdo, a Postoperative Recovery, a Bedwetter/Class President

In the matter of posthypnotic suggestion, I think it is awfully important to recognize that you ought to use it at every possible opportunity, but I think it is awfully unnecessary to label it as *posthypnotic suggestion.* Just exactly how far do you get when you tell a pretty girl: "Will you please listen to me? I want to say something to you. It is going to be a compliment. I want you to understand the compliment. I want you to be pleased with it." She is going to look at you and think you had better see your psychiatrist in a hurry. You had better just give her the compliment and let her deal with it herself. *You give a posthypnotic suggestion, and you let the patient deal with it. You don't try to label it, you don't try to emphasize the fact that it is posthypnotic suggestion.* You word it so that it is clearly understandable as a posthypnotic suggestion. For example, I looked at the patient and remarked to her: "You know, with that color hair and that kind of a wave in it, you really ought not to wear a tight ponytail." And she really ought not to wear a tight ponytail, with her hair pulled straight back; and that was all the posthypnotic suggestion I gave her. You should have seen the hairdo she walked in wearing the next time I saw her. I didn't want to instruct her: "Now change your hairdo." When she walked in she said, "How do you like my hairdo? My husband has been after me for eight years to change it, and I have flatly refused. But I am glad I changed. I like it this way. I have always worn it tightly drawn back—either in a bun or in a ponytail—but I like it this way." My posthypnotic suggestion was a posthypnotic suggestion, and the implication was that she should change her hairdo. I just left it for her to deal with.

> **"This operation you are going to have, it is going to be a cholecystectomy. The date of the operation has not yet been set. I wonder if the surgeon is going to be pleased with your preoperartive behavior? I know he is going to be pleased with your preoperative behavior. He is going to be pleased and rather surprised—delightfully surprised."**

I am talking about the surgeon, you see. Actually, however, I am talking about the patient. The patient walking postoperatively that same day, going to the bathroom by herself, eating a full meal; and the surgeon was very surprised and very pleased, and so were the nurses. The operation occurred a couple of weeks after I saw the patient. Why shouldn't I give that suggestion? I also said:

> **"Of course you will be very cooperative, and you'll utilize the surgeon's knowledge and abilities to the utmost; and in case of any complications you will rely fully upon him.**

Naturally you can be aware of complications, because they can develop, but you will be aware of them immediately."

I didn't want her doing anything that could injure her in any way, and I wanted her to be sure that she reacted to the full extent of her ability rather than as a bedridden patient, fearful and anxious.

Posthypnotic suggestions should be given primarily in an indirect way. They should be so worded that patients feel obligated to do certain things without knowing exactly what those things are, and so that their adjustment to the future situation will define the situation.

This matter of the bedwetting.

"I don't know when you are going to stop it, but I do have the feeling very strongly that you are going to like celebrating some special way, in some special way of great importance."

Well, what could the boy do? He had to find some special way of great importance to himself. He campaigned for class president and was elected, because, you see, that was a matter of great importance to him. I just had a feeling; I didn't name anything. I didn't even know it would be his class presidency. *I just set it up so that he could define the situation for himself, and by defining the situation for himself he could then compel himself to do things.* You see, we really don't know too much about what meets the personal and emotional needs of the individual patient, but we do know that the patient living his own life has his own wants and his own desires. Therefore, *you use the suggestions to motivate patients to achieve their own wishes, their own desires, in the way that is most constructive for them.*

The things I think are good, many of my patients think aren't too good. Therefore, when I can't define things sufficiently, I tell them:

"Now, this is what I think is good, but you are another person. I am going to look after these interests of mine

because they are valuable to me. I don't know what your interests are, but I'm going to look after my interests because they are valuable to me. But I don't know what your interests are.''

Sooner or later, patients get the idea that what I am really saying, without using the exact words, is: "And you look after your interests, because your interests are important to you.'' All I have said is that *I* am looking after my interests, because they are important to me.

Autohypnosis

Limiting the Use of Autohypnosis in Patients: Using it in a General Way for a Specific Purpose: Allowing the Creative Unconscious Freedom of Choice: Reducing Hypertension; Mrs. Erickson's Peripheral Vision

Now, concerning autohypnosis: Autohypnosis is a very interesting problem and a very interesting topic. Average people cannot use autohypnosis by themselves. They need to use it under instruction from someone who is aware of it. You can teach your patients how to sit down in the chair and relax and go into a trance state or a state of relaxation, but *you always caution them: "Never wear out a good thing. You use a good thing sparingly.* If you had steak for breakfast, lunch, and dinner, seven days a week, you would get fed up with steak. You use steak now and then. You get fed up with anything that you have too frequently. So I am going to teach you autohypnosis, but don't waste it on every little thing that comes along.''

The best way of using autohypnosis is to use it when you have something sufficiently important. I can think of the woman with a blood pressure of 240/140. She said that her internist told her to reduce her blood pressure or consult a mortician on an emergency basis. She came to me, but not because I was a mortician! My statement to her was:

"I think you have a use for autohypnosis, and this is what I am going to suggest to you. I don't think you should drive the twenty miles through traffic. I don't think it is desirable. Therefore, we will spend the next couple of hours letting you learn autohypnosis, and it is rather simple, because all the autohypnosis you need to learn is that which will reduce your blood pressure. You've got no business learning autohypnosis for anything else, because there is nothing else that threatens you; nothing else that really concerns you. Therefore, we will limit the autohypnosis to this question of your blood pressure. Sit back in the chair, hands on your lap, and proceed to learn how to relax."

So I gave her a nice, long, laborious, boring discussion of relaxation, and then I told her: "Now, three times a day, at home, sit down in the chair and relax like that."

It took her a couple of weeks to get her blood pressure down to 140/90, and that was checked by her family physician. But three times a day, for thirty minutes, she leaned back in her chair and relaxed herself. Sometimes she cheated by doing it four times a day, but that was autohypnosis for a definite cause. With patients you need to limit it to a definite goal. Otherwise they will try to use autohypnosis to remember where they put Aunt Nellie's letter; and they will use autohypnosis to try to remember what kind of salad they had two weeks ago; and they will figure out all kinds of ridiculous ways of using autohypnosis in order to achieve a conscious awareness. But for that hypertension, that feeling of relaxation, the feeling of comfort, the feeling of ease, the feeling that the blood pressure is going to go down, the feeling of utter physical comfort, relief of tension, and so on, [the autohypnosis can be used repeatedly]—just remember to limit it for patients to the matter in hand.

When you are experimentally inclined about autohypnosis, you'd better bear in mind that you should rely on your unconscious mind. Mrs. Erickson can use autohypnosis at will. Her technique is that of looking at a piece of jewelry. She simple moves it around, watching the light glinting on it. Her peripheral vision narrows

159

down, narrows down, narrows down, until it is finally just one single glint. As her peripheral vision narrows down, her peripheral awareness also diminishes. But she never goes into the autohypnotic trance without making provision for the telephone ringing, the doorbell ringing, one of the children yelling, or something of that sort. She sometimes says: "When I go into the autohypnotic trance, I would like to reveal to my unconscious mind some particular topic. I would like to review, mentally, a book I read some time ago." That is a very general task. She practically never goes into an autohypnotic trance for a specific accomplishment. It is always for a general accomplishment.

Too many people try to use autohypnosis for a highly specific thing. When you tell a patient to use autohypnosis for high blood pressure reduction, you are asking for a specific thing. [But you use the autohypnosis] for a general feeling of relaxation and comfort. Those are pretty hard terms to define. As a result of that general feeling of relaxation, and that general feeling of comfort, your general memories of how your body felt when your blood pressure was normal [are evoked]. You will have the general feeling that your blood pressure will go down. You are avoiding the specific instruction of, "Reduce your blood pressure." When you try to go into an autohypnotic trance and say to yourself: "I will now go into an autohypnotic trance and memorize this," *you have prescribed a conscious task. By virtue of prescribing a conscious task, you have defeated the purpose of autohypnosis, because you ought to respect your unconscious mind as having just as much intelligence as you have.* What you really ought to do is say:

"I will give you, my unconscious mind, an hour or two hours; and you do something of value to yourself which may, incidentally, be of value to my conscious mind."

In that way your unconscious mind has a freedom of choice. That is why I give general suggestions to patients, because I want them to use their own methods of accomplishing things.

Time Requirements for Somnambulistic and Autohypnotic Training

Betty Alice's Pupillary Variations: "Waiting and Getting the Feeling": Utilizing a General Feeling of Comfort and the Passage of Time to Control or Alter Physiological Behavior

How rapidly can you learn autohypnosis? It took me about three years, with frequent effort, to teach Mrs. Erickson to become a good somnambulistic subject. Then she spent a very considerable period of time, with much effort, learning to be a good autohypnotic subject. Now she can go into an autohypnotic trance, and lecture on her own feelings as she is going in. And you can recognize the development of the trance in the tone of her voice, the alteration of her enunciation, and so on. My daughter, Betty Alice, learned to go into a somnambulistic trance very quickly, very easily, and then she got curious about whether she could induce various hypnotic phenomena in herself. As a result of her curiosity, she learned very quickly to use autohypnosis, but she fortunately did not try to prove things to her unconscious mind. She would get the question, *I wonder if I can change the pupils of my eyes,* and then set herself that task. But she didn't check up in the mirror. She just set herself the task when the question came up: Could she alter the size of her pupils in her eyes; could she dilate the right one and contract the left one at the same time? She finally got the feeling and the conviction that she could do it, and after she got that feeling, she checked up on it in the mirror.

Betty Alice needed an eye examination. The opthalmologist was examining her eyes: he looked in her right eye and measured the pupil—it was widely dilated, and he recorded it. He examined the retina, and then he shifted over to the left eye. He was utterly astonished: the left pupil was contracted way down. So he looked back at the right pupil, and now that was contracted way down! He checked on his measurements, and looked back at the left one and that was dilated! Betty Alice was just entertaining herself. But you don't check up on it first. You wait, Betty Alice says, until you get the feeling.

You wait until you get the feeling of things—many another experimental subject has told me that. With your patients you need to emphasize:

> **"With your high blood pressure [or whatever], you ought to be willing to learn to get the feeling. Don't try to check up right away with a test of your blood pressure. Relax and get all those general feelings; give your body a chance to learn, because otherwise you are going to interfere with yourself. If you want to learn to target shoot, you aim at the target and you pull the trigger. Then you reload, you aim comfortably at the target, and you shoot again. You reload, aim comfortably at the target, and shoot again. But if you load and dart down to the target, come back disappointed, load, and desperately shoot again, and dash down to the target, then you are going to interfere with the learning process of hitting the target. You need to assume that you are getting closer and closer to the bull's-eye, and *that feeling of comfort that you have enables you to have increasing control of your physiological processes."***

I think it is important for you to impress upon your patients this need of a feeling of comfort about their control of their own physiological processes. It is astonishing to me the number of juvenile subjects I have worked with who were confronted with this matter of establishing physiological control and who had such a natural insight into this matter of giving themselves adequate time to develop a physiological control. Incidentally, that pupillary behavior comes in very handy in case any of you have nice, blond daughters who want to travel abroad. Last year Betty Alice was in Italy. She had some difficulty with her passport, so she stood there with her big blue eyes and dilated pupils, and she won their hearts. A blond in Italy is an object of delight, and a blue-eyed blond with great big pupils—remember the term *belladonna?* So Betty Alice dilated her pupils at the Italians. That worked every time, she said! You need a willingness on your part to recognize that time is required to alter physiological behavior. [Question from the audience apparently concerns Betty Alice's

162

internal sensory process of learning to control her pupillary dilation.]

Betty Alice started that eye business by thinking to herself: *I've got my eyes shut . . . Now, if I open one eye and look right at the sun, I would feel it in my eye but the other eye wouldn't feel it so much; then if I shut this eye and opened this eye and looked at the sun* [the reverse would happen]. And she practiced that over and over again until she began to get feelings of a certain sort in her eyes, and then she confirmed it by looking at the wall and then getting the feeling of this pupil dilated, this one contracted; and then she would alternately close her eyes to see the affect in looking at that wall over there. The contracted pupil gave one sensation and the dilated pupil gave another sensation. She wanted to see how differently her eyes behaved as visual organs, and her original thinking was one of looking at the sun or a bright electrical light.

She also approached it from another angle and that was: *The sun is far away. Suppose I thought about looking at a light on the other side of the room, and have the light come closer and closer to my eye.*

There are two different reactions. You may be able to get your reaction much more quickly—Betty Alice was doing it solely to entertain herself. Her sister, Carol, learned to lift the right eyebrow and depress the left eyebrow.

Time and Imagery in Healing

Now, consider this matter of giving time to physiological processes in your enuretic patient. You ask him to give his bladder sphincter enough time to grow stronger: "Don't try to do it all this week; there is next week, too, you know, and you are going to live a long time." You tell your colitis patient: "You know, your colon really ought to heal. You've got ulcerative colitis. I think it can heal fairly soon, but let us have a nice healing from the bottom of the ulcer upward so that you have a good healing." *Then perhaps you could draw a picture for the patient to show him what healing from the bottom up looks like in ulcerative colitis, or ulcers of any kind.* Then you point out why you don't want surface healing, so that your patient understands that you want a nice, slow, progressive, effectual healing of the ulcers.

163

Intensification of Emotion

Learning to Intensify Emotion In Accordance with Individual Patient Needs and Understandings: Quitting Smoking in a Case of Tuberculosis; "Saying The One Worst Possible Word" for a Hesitant Patient

I have listed here one particular topic that I think I will mention and that is, *specialized hypnotherapeutic techniques with intensification of emotion, age regression,* and so on. When do you want to use an intensification of emotion? First, stop to consider patients in general. One patient comes to see you in a state of utterly, completely intense emotion because, "There is a stain in my tooth," and you want to react violently in the other direction. It is so silly. Another patient comes in with two cavities per tooth and says, "I may possibly need a little dental attention," and you may want to react violently in the other direction. What is intense emotion for a patient, and under what circumstances? You intensify emotion for patients in a way that is befitting to individual patients.

You tell the patient: "You've got a problem here that you want to correct. You've got this problem of tuberculosis. You had one lung removed, and you are smoking and inhaling three packages of cigarettes a day. What kind of an emotional desire do you think you ought to have to quit smoking? You tell me you are not interested; you tell me your physician sent you here to stop you from smoking; you tell me that you are not interested in discontinuing smoking."

What are you going to do with a patient with one lung who smokes three packages of cigarettes a day, and inhales the last drag? He has a family to support. His wife has no particular skill—eighth grade education—but the patient isn't interested. Do you want to intensify his emotion? He is a nice, quiet, placid chap; he is working hard; he has had his lung removed. Do you want to intensify emotion in a man like that? He has had a lung removed. He's got TB. If you intensify his emotion, you are going to build up his blood pressure. What is the right thing, physiologically, for the patient? And yet he doesn't really want to smoke. His family physician is alarmed and distressed. Therefore, you ask the patient in a trance state whether or not it is all right for a person to feel strongly on one point, just one small minor point. You offer the statement that in some families it is very much taboo, under any and all circumstances, ever to swear. You know that in some families the ultimate in swearing is to say "Darn." They feel awfully strongly about the subject, on the use of profanity, and they feel very, very strongly on the point of saying "Darn." It is an inconsequential thing in many another person's life, utterly inconsequential, whether or not you swear in another home situation. Then you ask the patient: "Do you understand what I mean about emotional intensity of one small point?

"Maybe you consider it small to be intense about swearing; maybe you consider it small to be intense about saying 'Darn.' And in some peoples' lives it can be considered small to feel intensely about smoking. But if you do feel intensely about something, I think that you—as the TB patient with only one lung—with a family, a wife (unskilled), and your own precarious health—*that you can afford to feel strongly about the wastefulness of cigarettes.* The wastefulness. You have a family to support; you have a limited physical ability; you are not a white-collar man; you work at manual labor; you have lost one lung; you are handicapped. I think you can afford to feel strongly about any kind of waste.

"You'd rather object to your wife throwing away 25 cents worth of butter a day. You would object to her throwing away 50 cents worth of meat. You would really object to her throwing away 75 cents worth of food supplies a day. I think you can feel rather strongly on the subject of wasting 75 cents by blowing 75 cents of smoke away. I don't know how you want to do that—whether you want to start with 1/60 of 75 cents and save 1/60 of 75 cents by cutting down your cigarettes from three packages a day—but I think you could feel strongly about that waste of one plus cents a day; that you could really feel strongly about the waste of 2 cents a day, of 3 cents, of 4 cents, of 8 cents, of 16 cents, 32 cents, 64 cents, 75 cents a day."

So you have approached the intensification of emotion in terms that are acceptable to this particular patient. You haven't alarmed him as a physical creature, but you have built up a highly specific intensification of emotion. Sometimes you need to intensify a patient's emotions by asking him to do certain things. In taking psychiatric histories, I know that patients will withhold information from me. I can think of a woman who came to me and said: "I have been dropping in to see you, at regular intervals, for four years. I come in, I spend the hour. I always come in and say, 'Now, please, Dr. Erickson, I came here. I am going to pay you your fee, and I must ask you to let me sit here quietly. I'm not going to talk to you. I just want to be here. Now, please, Dr. Erickson, do not talk to me.'"

The patient had come in on those terms, at very irregular intervals, for the past four years. The last time she was in she said: "I am beginning to feel some courage about coming into your office. I am awfully slow about it. There is something I wish I could say to you, but I just haven't the courage to say anything about it. I would like to talk to you about it but I can't." I recognized that as an opening:

"All right, may I say a few things to you? I would like to offer you some suggestions. I would like to have you listen to the clock so you can't see my face. I would like to have you listen to the clock so you can feel you are not listening to me, and now as you look at the clock, and as you listen to the clock, this is what I am going to say. You want to talk to me about something that seems awfuly, awfully important to you. You just can't bring yourself to talk on that subject to me, but I can tell you what you can do. You can think it over, as freely as possible, in your mind. It won't be too free, but select the one word—the worst word that you know—the worst possible word that you know connected with that subject—and just say that word to me. Having said it, you don't have to say a single other thing. It will be just the one word. It is the worst possible word, and then the next time you come in you will feel that the worst has been said."

166

Trance Without Asking For It

Reducing Ritual and Procedure By Inducing Trance Via Indirect,
"Conversational" Techniques: Recalling Headache Sensations;
Handshake Induction for Catalepsy; Synthesizing Your Own
Hypnotic Techniques: The Dentist's Gentle Touch: Pupillary
Dilation

During the intermission Dr. Brody mentioned one particular
issue to me: what to do about a patient who came in complaining
about a headache. I suggested that he say to the patient: "Now, tell
me about that headache. Perhaps, in order to recall it, you can
close your eyes and really remember all of the sensations." You
have asked the patient to remember the sensations. As he starts
remembering the sensations, he is going to start contrasting them,
comparing them, with present time and with future experiences.
As surely as he does that, he is going to alter his state of conscious
awareness—and the first thing you know, you have a trance state
and you haven't really asked for it.

There has been far too much ritual and traditional setup in the
practice of medicine. I agree with you that we should have a certain
amount of ritual and tradition, let us say, in the practice of surgery.
Yet, what have been the results of the controlled studies investigating the amount of scrubbing that should really take place in order to
do an operation? Has not the 20-minute scrubbing been substituted
for a much more intelligent way? What is the bacterial count in the
operating room? I think that penicillin taught us much more about
bacterial count in the operating room and in the hospital than all
previous studies of hospital bacteria. There has been too much
ritual and procedure.

Everyone who begins the use of hypnosis has to begin it, and
should begin it, by learning a certain technique—not only a
certain technique but a *variety* of techniques. Having learned a
variety of techniques, and having applied them on a variety of
patients, I think the practitioner ought to bear in mind that the time
has then come to examine those techniques for the effectiveness of

the various elements. I know that I can walk into a crowd of total strangers who do not know me, and in talking to them casually about weather conditions or something of that sort, I can shake hands with them, tell them my name is Jones, that I come from Wisconsin, that I am interested in psychology. And I can keep on talking and shaking hands with them to discover whether or not they are good hypnotic subjects. How do I do it? When you shake hands with people, there is a certain general pattern you follow, but I shake hands in a way that allows me to test them for catalepsy. I can shake hands with a person in just an ordinary handshake, and then I start letting loose. I had some experienced friends analyze how I could let loose of the hand. I start letting loose at the little finger here, then the thumb, little finger, the third finger. *All I am doing is redirecting the person's attention from one part of his hand to another, and he does not know exactly when I do let loose of his hand.* He doesn't know whether the last touch was on the little finger, or whether the last touch was on his thumb or my thumb, or whether the last touch was by my middle finger. He holds his hand there waiting, waiting, waiting. Then if I want to induce a trance, I can gently reach over and touch the other hand and lift it up, and I have my trance state induced by the technique of catalepsy. All I did was shake hands with somebody who didn't know who I was.[3]

I have always been interested in this matter of catalepsy and this matter of the individual phenomenon. I have asked various of my friends who say, "Yes, you can do it, but I can't do it." I remember Frank Patty, President of the American Society of Clinical Hypnosis, saying a few years ago, "Yes, Erickson can do that, but nobody else can do it." I had quite a set-to with Frank, pointing out to him that I was certain he could do it. About a year later Frank said, "Anything Erickson can do, I can do better—which was a nice discovery for Frank Patty. Yes, Frank Patty does it differently than I do, but Frank Patty is a different kind of a person. He behaves differently and thinks differently, so he does it differently, but he does the same thing. He doesn't handle a hand the way I do, but he can certainly employ the hand very, very nicely to induce a profound amnesia—and he does it so thoroughly and so easily and in such a conversational way. You must have a willingness to study each technique and then *find out what elements of the various techniques fit you as a person.* When you discover that, then you are not going to have to say: "Now sit down in a chair; put your feet flat on the floor; now look at a spot; now rest your hand on your thighs; now take a deep breath; and now begin to relax a little here, a little there, and work at that induction for half an hour."

I know of a dentist who says to his patient sitting in the chair (a new patient), "Do you mind if I arrange your hand and arm on the arm of the chair the way I would like to arrange it? I want relaxation in your arms." While he is speaking he is reaching out very gently; he is taking the patient's arm and lifting it over and resting it on the arm of the dental chair; and he touches it so gently. Then he says: "I know you are going to feel increasingly comfortable as I work with you." He usually spends that much time in inducing a trance state—thirty seconds is adequate time, but, as you see, he practiced that technique over and over again.

I watched this dentist in a social situation in which he was sitting beside a friend of his and carrying on a social conversation. He reached over and said to the young lady, "May I look at your ring?" And he picked up her hand, took her wrist, looked at that ring, and did it so gently—and it was a delight for me to watch the expression on his friend's face. The dentist was practicing in that social setting. The young lady didn't know what was going on in the matter of hypnotic trance induction. Her eyes would turn glassy and then the dentist would speak up and say, "It is a very pretty ring." And her eyes would lose that dilated pupil, that glassy look; and she would be very pleased and happy. Then he would say, "I suppose I ought to put your hand back." Then he would take her hand and put it back in its original position. *Her pupils would dilate and her facial features would become fixed and rigid.* Then he would make another appropriate comment. He got a lot of practice at that particular party, and nobody knew it except me!

The dentist tried to practice on my daughter-in-law but she has had a couple of babies by hypnosis, and she immediately recognized that there was something going on that shouldn't be going on. So she said, "Excuse me, I am going to sit on the other side of the room." And the dentist was embarrassed. Then my daughter-in-law asked me what he was up to. I told her and she said, "Oh, why didn't you tell me so that I could let him practice." She was sophisticated, but that give you the idea of how easily you can practice if you are willing to single out the individual elements of the various techniques.

Two-Level Communication[4]

Body Response in Romance; Communicating Opposite
Messages to Conscious and Unconscious Minds

Now, I was talking about body compensatory abilities. In hypnosis when you approach a patient on any topic, I think you ought to be aware of the fact that your patient has both a conscious mind and an unconscious mind; that the patient doesn't really know what is going on in his unconscious mind, and that he isn't likely to. You ought to be aware of the fact that when you talk to a patient, *you ought to talk for the benefit of his conscious mind but also talk for the benefit of his unconscious mind.* Earlier I mentioned the young lady in the place, and the young man sitting here by the young lady. The young man was handsome. I noticed them looking at each other. Why shouldn't they look at each other? I found out later that the young lady was 23 years old and a widow, and the young man was unmarried. She was a good-looking girl. Well, that sideways glancing of the eyes, total strangers, told me that there was this question of romance and that involved body responses of various sorts. Therefore, why shouldn't I be aware of the fact that there was, undoubtedly, some unconscious thinking going on despite the well-bred, conscious thinking that was talking place? Then I mentioned that pinching of certain spots. I was speaking to their conscious minds but I was also speaking to their unconscious minds and appealing to whatever thinking the young lady was doing about the young man, and appealing to whatever thinking the young man was doing about the young lady. She was unconsciously aware too, and so I simply made use of remarks that could appeal to both the conscious mind and the unconscious mind.

Consider this matter of carrying on a *double-barrelled conversation or a two-level conversation*.

> *"You know you honestly believe—you really do to the best of your knowledge—you honestly believe that you cannot lose this headache."*

What am I doing? I am saying, "You honestly believe on the conscious level that you cannot lose this headache." That is all I am saying, but I am also saying at another level, "Unconsciously, you know that you can lose this headache. You don't know when, though." That is what I am saying at an unconscious level. So when I talk to patients I keep in mind the fact that there is a conscious mind listening and an unconscious mind listening, and *I phrase my remarks to the conscious mind by using words that the unconscious mind is going to take the opposite meaning of, or take the special meaning that I want to convey.*

The unconscious mind is very acute, very alert, very understanding, and very, very primitive. You ought to bear that in mind. So you can talk very carefully at the conscious level with the knowledge that the unconscious mind is going to listen to you. My children all have the attitude of, "When Daddy talks, you had better stop and think it over and see what half-dozen other things are underneath that simple sentence." And they are right. You want your patients to be aware of the fact that they can listen to you consciously, they can listen to you unconsciously. *There is too much superstition about making the unconscious conscious.* Bear in mind that the conscious mind and the unconscious mind have been biologically separated since the beginning of the human race 1,700,000 years ago, according to today's headlines. We haven't gotten any factual proof the unconscious exists, but then most things human have a long history.

Permissive Hypnosis

Hypnotic Anesthesia Via Sense Memories: Interpreting
Suggestions According to Unique Life Experience; Reducing
Headache Indirectly by Accessing Unconscious Train of
Thought: "Have the Kitten Stomp Lighter"

Now, you look upon hypnosis not as something that you *do*. Too often the beginner starts out using hypnosis and thinking: "This is what I do because the patient does such and such; because I say: 'Let your hand become numb', the patient lets his hand become numb." The actuality is quite different. You do certain things. You tell the patient: "Let your hand become numb," and what does the patient do? The patient says: "Now, let's see. I was six years old, and I was sitting in the rocking chair. I was reading a book and I crossed my legs and my leg went to sleep. Then, when I found out it was asleep, I felt it and it was so different." *What is our patient doing? Actually, nothing but recovering some memories and understandings; and you didn't tell the patient to do that.* You told the patient, "Turn the switch on in your brain and turn off that sense of feeling." Bear in mind that *you offer suggestions, and that patients interpret the suggestions according to their own unique experiences, and they carry out the suggestions in their own particular ways. That is why you use a permissive approach.* The authoritarian approach can be effective, but for lasting results it is much less effective. *You want the permissive approach because it enlists the activity of the patient, and the patient is stimulated into developing an awareness of simething that fits in with your suggestions.*

Going back to the example of the hangover, and the kitten stomping on the Persian rug making the headache worse—What is the actual approach to that? Should you tell the patient, "Have your headache stop"? That is one approach. I don't think it is a good approach, because the reality of the patient's headache is very firm, very significant, to the patient. Therefore, I would approach the problem by asking the patient: "Have that kitten stomp light, lighter, and lighter," so that the patient then would begin to attach less and less and less painful significances to the headache. That is what you want. When you say, "Have your headache stop," the patient says: "You are speaking about by headache. You are telling my headache to stop. My headache can't stop." But when you say, "Have the kitten stomp lighter, lighter, and lighter," *the patient has to think about the decreasing significance of those auditory stimuli and, therefore, the patient is thinking about decreasing sensations.* You have asked the patient to think about decreasing sensations, which includes the headaches, and so you have offered your suggestion for decrease in the headache. In other words, *you have said something to the conscious mind about making the kitten quit stomping the feet, but to the unconscious mind you have said: "Revivify your understandings of decreasing stimuli, of decreasing sensations, of lessening experience." The unconscious mind then goes down that train of thought, with the resulting decrease in the headache.*

Symptom Utilization—Not Removal!

Letting the Patient Determine the Degree of Symptom Correction: Keeping the Symptom Only for Unusual Circumstances: Convenient Dysmenorrhea: Minor Seasickness

Then there is always the question, how much of any illness should a patient keep? There is that perfectionist attitude that too many doctors have of curing patients. "I will give you a perfect set of teeth ... I will give you complete relief of your headache ... I will really straighten your nose so that it is absolutely perfect." What is the attitude you should take? How do you know that the patient wants to lose all of that headache? Let us take the example of a 30-year-old woman with lifelong dysmenorrhea. She was disabled for three days every 28 days with her dysmenorrhea (painful menstruation). When she sought therapy from me my point was:

"Let's be reasonable about this. Under all ordinary circumstances you ought to be free of dysmenorrhea—under all ordinary circumstances." Now, what are *ordinary circumstances?* They have to be defined by her, not be me.

But there are possibly some other situations in which you might want some dysmenorrhea. You may have a quarrel with your husband and want to punish him by having dysmenorrhea. To me that seems ridiculous because you would be suffering the pain, but then he would be suffering the discomfort, too. So you might want dysmenorrhea under those circumstances. You might get involved in some social invitation and feel you just have to break the invitation and you need a good excuse. All of your friends know about your dysmenorrhea. You could really get out of the social situation by developing dysmenorrhea, so why lose your capacity for dysmenorrhea? You might want to employ it. You might want a new car or a mink stole. I don't know what, but I think under all ordinary circumstances you can be free of dysmenorrhea. And in those unusual circumstances that may develop, I think you should be free to have dysmenorrhea. The only question that come to my mind is:

"Do you want a large amount of dysmenorrhea, or will you settle for three hours instead of three days? How much do you really want? I think you want just enough dysmenorrhea to meet your needs, but not one bit more.

"I think on this Carribbean cruise that you ought to have all of the seasickness you want, but it does seem to me that parting with one meal is sufficient experience for anybody. You might want to separate from two meals; you might want to have seasickness for a whole forenoon. You might want it for a whole day. I don't know, but if you have to have seasickness, go ahead and have it as a legitimate part of your life experience."

What happened on the Carribbean cruise when you took that approach to a goodly number of the passengers? They settled for a minor amount of seasickness. Well, why shouldn't they settle for a minor amount? Why should you ask your patient to be completely free of his illness, his pain, his difficulty, because as a psychological being he may want a part of it for purely unconscious reasons. Let him have that part, but don't let him handicap himself.

Obsessional Thinking

Questions Facilitating Conscious and Unconscious Exploration:
Moving An Obsessional Focus Into a "Wealth of Other Ideas":
The Knife Stabbing Obsession

One mother who came to me was miserable because she was having an obsessional thinking: "I'll get a knife and I'll stab my son, and I don't want to get a knife and I don't want to stab my son." Life was very, very miserable for her, and she had seen a number of psychiatrists who had offered her various kinds of therapy. She didn't want shock, she didn't want insulin, and she didn't want to keep thinking: "I want to get a knife. I want to stab my son." When she came to me she told me flatly that she didn't want hypnosis either, but she did want treatment. I told her I thought that, first of all, she wanted understanding of what she had said. Did she know what a knife was? Did she really know what a knife was and what a knife could do? And did she know what her son was? Did she really know that her son was. Did she really know how old he was? Well, that was a silly question and she needed to say immediately: "Of course I know who my son is, and I know how old he is." And she felt very pleased with her special knowledge that she did know who her son was, and how old he was, and how tall he was.

What was she really doing? She was justifying my question—"Do you know what a knife is? Do you really know what a knife is?" She had to give the same, full answer to that question that she gave to the question, "Do you know who your son is? Do you know how tall he is?" Then the legitimacy of the question about her son made the first question about the knife also a legitimate question. "Well, what do you mean, do I know what a knife is?" I said:

"There are various kinds of knives. There are kitchen knives, there are butcher knives, there are Bowie knives; and great big long knives, and little short knives, pen-

knives, and jackknives. Oh, lots of different kinds of knives, like the surgeon's knives. Do you know what a stab is? How can you stab? Can you stab with an upward movement? A downward movement? A lateral movement."

What was I doing with this woman's obsessional compulsive thinking? I was really taking in every kind of territory imaginable. Then the question was raised: "How deep a stab? Does it have to be on your son's chest? Could it be on the back of his chest? Could it be on the neck or the wrist? Could it be on the elbow, or the shoulder, or the calf of the leg, or the ankle? Really, could it? How deep is the stab, or how deep does it have to be? With a penknife it can't be very deep; with a Bowie knife it would really be deep; with a sword—my heavens—much deeper than it needs to be; *and certainly you don't need a stab wound any deeper than it needs to be."*

What happened to all of that patient's serious, obsessional, compulsive thinking? I had thrown in so may related, pertinent, relevant ideas that the question came up: "Do I need to stab him?" That was a question she needed to answer. I said: "I don't know. Sometimes he is upstairs; sometimes he is downstairs; sometimes he is in the basement; sometimes he is in the frontyard; sometimes in the backyard; and sometimes he is on the streetcar. I really don't know. Now the question is, where would you stab him? In the wrist, the chest, the back, the elbow? Where? The backyard, the frontyard, the street, upstairs, downstairs, all around the town?" What had happened to the word *where* will you stab him? And without the patient realizing it, I had expanded that word *where* so extensively that the question no longer was simply that frightening, horrible idea: "Get a knife; stab my son!"

Now it became a problem with many ramifications—interesting—not really pleasant—but really interesting. What are the ramifications? "On a streetcar there are people whom you know and there are people whom you don't know." And I enlarged upon that point so that the patient could then settle down with me to examine all the ramifications. It only took a couple of hours of intensive questioning to extend that obsessional focus and relieve the woman's absolute terror so that she could go home and get a night's sleep; so that she could come out to see me the next day and look at this question of her son, look at this question of her feeling toward her son and her feeling toward her husband. And it wasn't very long before the woman gained insight into her obsessional thinking about her son.

What do you do with patients? You accept their statement and then you offer them ideas. *You offer them ideas at the conscious level, but you also offer them ideas at the unconscious level.* When I raised those questions—what kind of a stab? What kind of a knife? What is a knife? How tall is your son? How old is he?—*I compelled that woman to explore and investigate a whole wealth of other ideas at the unconscious level.*

Depotentiating Dental Phobias

Utilizing Suggestion to "Break Down" Unreasonable Fears and "Build Up" New Perspectives

I can think of the girl who neglected her teeth horribly. She needed upper and lower dentures. She was afraid of the dentist. I have seen quite a number of young people in their twenties who have mouths with horrible pathology, and who have fears and anxieties—they can't stand to go to the dentist—from their childhood experiences. They come in to the psychiatrist to see what he can do about it and they tell you, "I have an unreasoning fear of a dentist, and I can't bring myself to see a dentist." Well that is right. They can't.

"Let's see, you live on such-and-such a street. You know your street address, do you not? You know where your street is in Phoenix? You know which way your house faces, and who else is living there? Your mother is living there, and do you happen to know her dentist's name?"

She does know the dentist's name. She knows that the whole family goes to that particular dentist, or that the family has a couple of dentists. Then I point out to her that she doesn't know the dentist who took care of me when I was a small boy and she agrees with that. She can't see the pertinency of that fact, however. "So you can't have an unreasoning fear about *that* dentist, can you?" And she thinks that is a ridiculous and silly thing for me to mention, but she doesn't have an unreasoning fear of the dentist who took care of *me* when I was a boy. *I have just simply broken her statement that she has an unreasoning fear of dentists.*

Now, I can bring it down, and down, and down. She's not got an unreasoning fear of a dentist she doesn't know who lives in Phoenix; she doesn't have an unreasoning fear of a dentist she never even met or thought of, and whose name she doesn't know, but "you do have an unreasoning fear of the dentist you might want to go to." Well, let us admit that she does have that fear—that unreasoning fear of the dentist she might want to go to. She can agree. When she agrees that she does have an unreasoning fear of that dentist "who you might want to go to," *she is agreeing that she might want to go to that dentist.*

"And if you should want to go to that dentist, you know there are only seven days in the week. Would you prefer to go on Monday, Tuesday, Wednesday, Thursday, Friday, Saturday? You can't go on Sunday." Let's name the day she *can't* go. That means there are six days on which she can go. So her *can't going* is cut down to 1/7th of the total possibility. Now, let's magnify the total possibility. "You could go in the forenoon; you could go in the afternoon. That is, on six forenoons you could go, or on six afternoons you could go. That is twelve possibilities of going—on Sunday, you can't go. That is twelve possibilities of going, and only one possibility of not going." So you have built up the possibility.

"Now, where would you be most likely to have that unreasoning fear of the dentist? It seems to me you really ought to have it when you are sitting in the dental chair. You certainly would not need to have it when you were leaving his office." She really wouldn't need to have an unreasoning fear of the dentist when she leaves the office. That is something she can agree to most emphatically, so you can build it up. She need not have an unreasoning fear of the dentist when she leaves his office. And you build it up. "You don't need to have a fear, an unreasoning fear of the dentist, when he is not going to work on your teeth." You build that up. The patient can agree with you, and so you send her up to make an appointment with the dentist for some future date, and she walks out without an unreasoning fear of the dentist. So she has walked *in* without an unreasoning fear and she has walked *out* without an unreasoning fear. She comes and tells you, "You know, it wasn't half bad at all, and I think I am going to get along all right." You see, she didn't even know what you were doing with her in presenting those ideas.

The Art of Therapeutic Suggestion

Engaging Positive Participation in Reframing Unreasonable Fears of Pregnancy into Realistic Concerns

You take the young woman who says, "I want to get pregnant. I want to have a baby. My husband wants a baby. In fact, we are going to have a divorce if we don't have a baby. I want a baby, my husband wants a baby, but I have an unreasoning fear of pregancy."

What do you do about it? Do you tell her:

"Pregnancy is a fairly common thing. There is no real difficulty in achieving a pregnancy. You wouldn't have an unreasoning fear of pregnancy if you knew you were pregnant. Le't see, it would take you a whole month, at least, to find out that you were pregnant. You could be pregnant a whole month without an unreasoning fear. In fact, you could postpone the rabbit and frog tests for six weeks. That is, for six weeks you could be pregnant without any unreasoning fear. Now, that just tells me that you would not have an unreasoning fear for all of the pregnancy, but you do have an unreasoning fear. Just where is that unreasoning fear located? Fear that you might have twins? You know that you might. Triplets have happened too. This is your first baby, and I suspect you don't want to double, triple, or quadruple your difficulties. You know you are going to handle that baby as if it's made of very delicate china; you will be afraid it will come apart if you pick it up; you will try to bathe it with the gentlest of touches."

What am I doing? I am talking about the baby that she has already had. She doesn't know it, but I am throwing at her every possible idea, so that I extend the issue and I'm still measuring. "But certainly you will have an unreasoning fear, and I don't know about what. In fact, I don't know how long you are going to keep it." She has to admit the truth of the statement that I just don't know how long she is going to keep her unreasoning fear. Why should I sit down with her and say, "Now, you have an unreasoning fear and I want you to lose it?" There is a gentler yet more forceful way of telling her that she has an unreasoning fear that she is going to lose.

Do you see what I mean by suggesting that you write out your conversation with the patient, your therapeutic suggestions, and then you look for their meaning and you look to see how you could restate the suggestions so that your patient accepts them? *It is the art of suggestion, the art of getting your patient to listen to you, to understand you.* You talk about bathing the baby. "I expect that with this unreasoning fear of yours"—you certainly as the physician ought not to be afraid of your patient's fear. Therefore, you ought to be able to name it and call it *unreasoning fear* comfortably. "It is going to make you rather thoughtful in selecting your obstetrician and, of course, you will choose a good hospital." Let us cut out the obstetrician as a fearful object. Let us cut out the hospital as a fearful object. There are more and more acceptable objects coming into that situation, and that unreasoning fear is being cut down, cut down, and cut down, and cut down without my saying: "Now, let that unreasoning fear get smaller and smaller and smaller," because that is something that can be resisted. But the patient can't resist the idea that she will select a good obstetrician and a good hospital. "And, of course, in making the layette, or buying one, you see to it that it is a reasonably good layette." Just reasonably good, but the patient can think: "But this is going to be my first one, and it is going to be an *unusually good* layette." Let the patient do the thinking. I don't need to do that, but *I am having the patient participate.*

"Now, of course, you don't know which month you are going to get pregnant, which means you are going to get pregnant. You don't know which month." So the patient is thinking, *I don't know which month I am going to get pregnant*. The patient is not thinking: *I am going to get pregnant, but which month?* That is a complete reversal for the patient. She is going to get pregnant with a pregnancy she won't know anything about for six weeks—and, therefore, a pregnancy of which she cannot have an unreasoning fear.

"As your pregnancy develops, I wonder what sort of an attitude you are going to take about the changes in your breasts? And I really wonder. What kind of an attitude are you going to take about the changes in your breasts? What does that mean? You are the kind of a person who takes an unreasoning attitude on some things. Are you going to take an unreasoning attitude about your breasts?"

The patient is going to be mildly defensive and say, "Well, I will take good care of my breasts." She will be a little bit on the defensive. Then, of course, there is this question of her teeth, and "you certainly don't want the calcium to be depleted, so you will see your dentist and you will watch your diet." If there is anything to be feared, let us make it depletion of calcium in the teeth. Let us make it this question of diet—faulty diet. *Let us give her something really to fear, reasonably, and so you are giving her reasonable fear. You are decreasing the unreasonable fear.*

Then you discuss: "You know this question of a girdle, and just exactly what are you going to do about maternity clothes? About cutting down your athletic activities? You know that horseback riding—you are going to cut that out. You will miss it, but then you will comfort yourself after the delivery by returning to horseback riding." If she needs any comfort, let's have her comforting herself that she has had a baby and can go horseback riding after the baby has reached a certain age. You haven't denied that she may need comforting. *You are decreasing the unreasoning fear and you are increasing her understanding of pregnancy as a total experience. You are not shying away from this matter of unreasoning fear and you are presenting a wealth of ideas.* Now, have I emphasized that in sufficient detail?

Time Elements in the Experience of Pain

Past, Present, and Future Components of Pain and Problems:
Transforming Current Pain by Confining It to Immediate Present

Another thing that you ought to bear in mind about patients' ills, worries, fears, and distresses: very seldom do you see a patient who comes to you with his very, very first experience with illness or distress or injuries. Literally impossible. Now, let us take pain, for example. What is pain? "My headache is very painful. It feels like the time I was horseback riding and bumped my head against the branch of a tree." Pain, as your patient tells you about it, is made up of more than one component. It is a pain he is experiencing as of the moment, but it is also the pain that he remembers of a similar kind in the past. So pain in that regard is a complex of two components: the pain of the moment and pain as he remembers it; and so the memory of previous pain is added to the current pain.

Then the patient says, "You know, that pain I had when I bumped my head against the branch of the tree when I was horseback riding ten years ago lasted three days. Today's headache is like that pain of ten years ago." So he is looking forward to having today's headache last three days. His pain complex is comprised of *remembered pain*, the *pain being experienced*, and the *anticipated pain* of the next three days. He has magnified his pain by those attitudes of the past and the future.

The patient comes to you and says: "I am sick to my stomach, as sick as a dog, as sick as I was three years ago. That time I was sick for a week, and the way it feels now I will be sick longer than a week." He is telling you about past nausea, present nausea, future nausea, and all of his thinking is done in that regard. The cancer patient treats pain in exactly the same way. *Your task is to get the patient to think about his pain or his illness as his immediate current experience.*

"This pain you had, this headache, is similar to the one you got after you bumped your head against the branch of a tree years ago. Do you mind closing your eyes, leaning back in your chair, and trying to describe the exact feelings you have in your head right now?" I don't care about that headache of three years ago. I want

182

my patient to be thinking about the headache right now, and when the patient thinks of the headache right now, what is he going to do? He is going to measure the pain by contrasting it with his memories of a good feeling.

"How cold is your hand?"

"It is cold, very cold—not like when it was nice and warm."

That is right, the patient is thinking about *warm* and how it doesn't feel when it is cold. He has some pleasant memories. He is going to think about immediate pain, and he is going to try to contrast it in order to define it for you; and as he defines that pain he is thinking about it as belonging right now. He has come into your office so that one hour from now he is not going to have the problem, and so you have him think about it *right now*. You have him locate it in the immediate present. He doesn't know it, but as Dr. Brody mentioned to me this morning, the patient is suddenly surprised because his headache has departed. Yes, he is located in the immediate present and, unnoticeably, he has stepped into the future of five minutes from now. *Immediate present* disappeared into the *past* so rapidly—that has been his experience. And so he examines his headache in the immediate present against a background: *I will not have a headache in the future.*

I can think of a companion aboard a plane who was reading and all of a sudden made a grab for that horrible bag and proceeded to use it, saying, "Excuse me" between heaves. I said, "That was only a slight dip in the plane right then, and now it seems to be smoothing out. Maybe another dip will occur in the plane, but it seems to be smoothing out."

My companion looked around and began sensing his other feelings of the plane; and the plane had lurched a little bit before. He was waiting for another *lurch*; he wasn't waiting for another *heave*. Why should he wait for another heave? His natural tendency would be to wait for another heave, but my simple remark was all that was necessary to direct is attention. I justified his heaving. *Then I put it into a question of the future, which was entirely different. It seemed to be smoothing out now, and* [*the implication was that the*] *heaving belonged immediately to the rapidly growing remote past.*

He was so apologetic and couldn't understand how suddenly his nausea and vomiting had developed, and how suddenly it had disappeared. But I used that removal from the immediate present into the immediate past, and then the more and more remote past, and separated the immediate present from the impending future. *In dealing with patients and in getting ideas across to them, you ought to recognize this matter of the past, the present, and the future so far as their complaints are concerned.*

Learning Hypnotic Experience

Focusing Attention on Body Sensations; Schizophrenic Dissolutions

[Question from the audience] Is it possible to induce a [trance] state if the patient has had no prior experience?

E: You don't have to have prior experience, but you can study it. In certain neurological diseases you can lose that sense of weight and your patient can experience it right then and there. But he still has his weight—gravity is still acting on him. He doesn't know what's happened to him, and he can have a violent reaction to it as a first-time experience. How did your wife, yesterday, alter the size of her body, expecially her arms? Did you know about that? How did she do it? I have had quite a number of hypnotic subjects do that for me very, very nicely as an original experience. You see, we have the capacity to give our attention to a certain narrow span. We start thinking about one thing, and then another thought comes in our mind. In our attentiveness to our body sensations, we fixate briefly on this sensation and then on another, and then another—but not necessarily in an orderly fashion of one, two, three, four, five. We may have the experience of fixating on one, then 17, 24, 82, 83. We get a totally different picture. In schizophrenia you will find the patient suddenly losing various body sensations; losing the body sensation of a right buttock and then recovering it; losing the sensation of the left arm. So you can have it *de novo* ... by virtue of the ordinary processes of arranging of attention.

Discussing the Worst Possible Word

[Question from the audience concerns the woman who was told to say the worst possible word.]

E: I told that woman, "Say the worst possible word that you know connected with that subject, and just say that one word to me. And having said it, you won't have to say a single other thing, only just the one word. It is the worst possible word, and then the next time you come in, you can feel that the worst has been said."

She thought a while and then she said, "Sex."

I said, "That is the worst possible word you can say to me. You really ought to be able to talk freely next time on a number of things."

She said, "I am going to start right now."

The worst had been said. *All I wanted to do was to intensify her reaction, to make it very very specific. And the worst had been said: "Sex," and she was then free to talk.* I didn't want to give her any explanation. [I wanted] . . . to give her freedom to talk, if not this time then next time. She had control over the next time she came in, and she might talk on a *number of subjects*, because I had said "a number of subjects." You need to protect your patients in every possible regard. I wouldn't want to tell her to talk freely on *that* subject—only a number of subjects.

DEMONSTRATION

Preparing the New Hypnotic Subject for Trance

Changing the Total Psychological Situation by Changing Chairs for Comfort

The best thing to do in presenting before a group is to come up with the unexpected. When you come up with the unexpected, you attract everybody's attention: you have it, and you can deal with it, and then you have the possibility of illustrating a goodly number of points.

One of the topics I have here reads: "Preparation of the Subject for Hypnosis; Induction Procedures; Dealing with the Totally New Subject."

E: During the intermission I got acquainted with you, didn't I? Will you come up please? Now, as I recall it, you said you were a little bit afraid of hypnosis, and that you haven't been in a trance before. You lack confidence in your husband's ability.

S: No, that isn't it at all.

E: That isn't it at all.

S: No.

E: Something else?

S: I don't know what, but it is not his ability. It is not that at all.

E: Do you think I ought to provide a more comfortable chair for you?

S: I don't know. My heart is racing.

E: Let's try the other chair.

Now, the first thing I did was go into the preamble of the introduction. I have her up here. I had her bring out the fact that her heart was racing, and then I introduced the idea of a more comfortable chair. And, of course, by telling her about it now she recognizes what I did and it is much less effective measure. But in the office if I change chairs for patients they find the situation changed psychologically into a much more comfortable chair. The total situation would be so much more comfortable [by simply changing chairs], and that could be communicated to the subject so easily and gently, and without the subject having any awareness of it.

Inducing Comfort Paradoxically

Utilizing "Stay Very Wide Awake" as an Indirect Induction Technique for New Patients; Observing Minimal Behavioral Cues of Trance

186

E: How do you think I ought to go about putting you in a trance?

S: You will have to get me more relaxed than I am right now.

E: I will have to get you more relaxed than you are right now. Don't you think it is nice to be tense once in a while?

S: Perhaps so.

E: Perhaps so, but suppose you tense up this hand. That is it. Now keep it tense even if it does get tired. Do you notice any tension in the other hand?

S: Yes.

E: In your legs?

S: Yes.

E: In your legs. All right. Let's take the other hand. Keep that hand tense, and slowly relax this hand. And now this arm is comfortable, and your shoulders are comfortable, too. Are your shoulders comfortable?

S: Yes.

E: I think your legs are getting more comfortable.

S: Yes.

E: Do you want to make your right arm comfortable?

S: It is up to you.

E: It is up to me. How much resistance is there now? It is all up to me. Relax this one. That is it. Now, what would be the best way of going into a trance?

S: For me? I don't know.

E: You really don't know, so I am going to suggest that you stay very, very wide awake—very, very wide awake, and you would like comfort about those contact lenses. Would you not?

S: Yes, I would.

E: All right. Now, speak about those contact lenses. Think about those contact lenses, and stay wide awake. Very, very wide awake, and think about those contact lenses. Now keep on thinking about the contact lenses, and keep right on thinking about the contact lenses. That is right, that is right. Now your eyes will be closed, and you can feel them under the eyelids, underneath. Just close your eyes and keep them closed.

I let the fluttering of the eyelids continue for some time after she showed catalepsy of the arm. She has never been in trance before. She probably doesn't know that she is in a trance now; there is immobility of the face and a certain rigidity of her body; there is an alteration in the rhythm of her breathing; there is a loss of the ordinary normal responses of self-consciousness, and so on. In the office you have enlisted this sort of a trance by asking the patient to stay very widely awake, attentive, alert to certain stimuli.

When you get a new patient in the office who doesn't know that you know anything at all about hypnosis—someone who has looked you up in the Classified Directory—and you don't know how to introduce the subject of hypnosis, you say instead: "Stay very alert to look at the clock, to listen to it, just to hear what I say while you are hearing the clock." And you notice that the patient's eyelids begin to blink a certain way and that you are beginning to get a nice hypnotic response as he is narrowing down his attention, as he is paying less and less attention to his surroundings. You notice the alteration in the breathing; you notice that he is cataleptic; and so you go right on with your therapeutic problem without trying to investigate the hypnotic state.

Now, I had the subject close her eyes so that you could watch. I first had you notice the blinking of her eyes, which she did very nicely and in a pattern quite different from the ordinary blinking pattern. *What is important is your willingness to observe all of these individual patterns of breathing, of holding the face, of holding the head, of holding the hand, and all of the body postural responses that are ordinarily made but which the hypnotic subject promptly ceases to make.*

Awakening From Trance

Ratifying Trance Via Amnesia, Emotional Changes, and "The Quieting Down"

How do you arouse patients from the trance after you have done it? I usually leave them with their eyes wide open so as to make it less difficult. Or I tell them that they can close their eyes, because their eyes might smart from continued looking at the clock and holding their eyeballs still. And with the eyes shut, they can save themselves the smarting.

E: Now that the end of the hour is approaching, you can open your eyes. And how do you feel?

S: Fine.

E: What have you been doing?

S: I know I had my hand up here. I hear everything that is going on.

E: That is right.

S: That my husband was telling me something about people feeling they haven't been in a trance, so I could swear I haven't been in one.

E: You'd swear that you haven't, and do you ordinarily sit that quietly?

S: No, but I notice I am very calm. I'm not usually.

E: Where did the calmness come from?

S: [Inaudible]

E: "Maybe my heart was going pitter patter." The calmness had to come from you, didn't it? The rate of your heart beat . . .

S: Yes.

E: And the quieting down. And by the way, how much attention did you pay to the audience?

S: I don't remember. I can't recall.

E: Maybe you weren't in a trance.

S: I really did. I was paying attention to what you were saying. Then you said something about my arm.

E: [To audience] I was talking about her too, and when you talk about a woman and she doesn't remember what you had to say—! *So, you could develop an amnesia that quickly?*

S: Maybe in this situation.

E: Maybe in this situation.

S: I'm not used to being in front of . . .

E: How did they look?

S: [Inaudible]

E: Look intelligent, alert? Have you ever before looked so appraisingly at a group of men?

S: I have never been on stage before.

E: Did you expect to be as calm, poised? You see, I am deliberately rocking you off balance again and again.

S: I guess I knew I would calm down.

Unconscious Ideomotor Signaling

Eliciting Answers from the Unconscious; Perseveration of Unconscious Responses; Deepening Trance Without Awareness of It; Facilitating Hypnotic Amnesia

E: All right. I am going to ask you a question. I don't want you to answer it consciously. You know, a long time ago you learned to nod your head when you meant yes; shake your head when you meant no. That is right. Now I am going to ask your unconscious mind a question. Consciously, you don't know the answer that is the answer of your unconscious mind. You know your conscious answer. That isn't what I want, so I am going to ask your unconscious mind a certain question, and you will wait, and I will wait, for your unconscious mind to answer it. And your unconscious mind will answer it by nodding your head or shaking it. Now the question that I am going to put to your unconscious mind is this: Were you in a trance?

S: [S makes an abrupt conscious movement of her head.]

E: No, that was your conscious mind that answered. Now, you wait. Were you in a trance? Slowly. That is right. What was the feeling?

S: There I was, but I couldn't shake my head. And I was waiting for it but it wouldn't do it by itself.

E: That is right. You had the feeling. Isn't that right? Now this time let your head nod slowly in answer to that question. Have you been in a trance? Slowly, let your head nod.

All I wanted to do was to elicit, unconsciously, directed and motivated behavior. As surely as you get that, you get a trance state.

190

How often do you have a patient sitting in the office who says: "When I was first married I wanted a child so much." You heard the words, you know what the patient is telling you, and you pay attention to what the patient is telling you.

Now, of course, I didn't tell the subject to stop, did I? And that is continuing. How did she know, unconsciously, that she was to continue and continue that which is contrary to every other ordinary understanding? You see, we have a tremendous number of learnings within ourselves—a tremendous number of body learnings that allow us to do things. Subjects who have never even heard about a trance, never seen it, never experienced it, will go into a trance and demonstrate to you a great number of utterly commonplace patterns of behavior—and do it with no awareness that they are doing it. My subject doesn't really have any idea of what she is doing, and yet she is doing it perfectly. *I set it up knowing her unconscious mind ought to respond, and her unconscious mind's understanding was in accordance with the understanding that I gave her—and that can go on, and on, and on.* And, of course, it tells me another thing: she is in a much, much deeper trance than she was before, and *she, herself, is deepening the trance.*

It rather surprised my subject to find out that she had an amnesia. She remembered that I had talked to the audience; she remembered one item, but she developed an amnesia. How did she develop that amnesia? I think if you play back the record you will find out that I had given instructions to develop the amnesia by the very wording of my remarks.

A patient comes in to my office and I want him to have an amnesia. As he comes into the office I say: "Is it very hot outside today?" And the patient answers: "Yes, it is." The patient sits down; I induce the trance. I want the patient to have an amnesia for the full hour of the trance, so when he awakens I say, "It is usually hot outside in Phoenix in the summertime." Now, remember, I had asked the patient, "Is it hot outside?"—that casual remark upon coming into the office. After the patient is awake I revert back to the remark as if there had been no interruption in that conversational chain. Therefore, the patient has an amnesia for all the intervening events. I have merely hooked back onto the original train of conversation, and that is usually how I induce an amnesia: by starting a train of thought and then reestablishing it.

Awakening from Trance

Trance Ratification Via Amnesia and Body Dissociation; the Slight Startle Reaction of Reassociation; Adjusting to Contact Lenses

All right. I haven't asked the subject to develop a trance, really, either time that she has developed one. Should I ask her to come out of the trance? What is the best way? There are any number of best ways.

E: You are really enjoying that trance. I would like to have you people [the audience] learn every conceivable thing of value to you. As a hypnotic subject, you are interested in contact lenses and you are interested in wearing them to a greater extent. You are not quite certain of the feeling in your eyeballs. You really don't want to injure your eyeballs when you don't know what feelings are really harmful; what feelings aren't just a little bit different. Actually, of course, I think your unconscious mind will be able to make that analysis for you, and I think your unconscious mind can accustom you to the sensation of contact lenses. And I am very certain that your unconscious mind will detect any little change or something bad in the feel. You think that might be comfortable? All right. Now take it easily and gradually. I would like to have you feel exceedingly rested and comfortable and at ease and happy as you awaken. And continue, when you are awake, to have that feeling.

E: Hi. How do you feel?

S: Fine.

E: We were talking about what I said to the audience. You remembered your arms.

S: Not as much this time as I did the last time.

E: What is it not as much this time?

192

S: [What do you mean?]

E: You remembered your arm, not as much this time as you did last time. [To audience] *That is, I raised the question of the memory of the arm and she said, "Not as much this time as last time."* What additional [information] has she told me? Plenty. [Back to subject] By the way, how do you feel about wearing contact lenses?

S: I had something under one of them right now, but other than that I don't . . .

E: What do you suppose you have under them? Maybe you are getting acquainted with the feeling. That is, if you had a numbness of your hand and couldn't really feel adequately, completely with your hand, and then I were to touch you, you might feel it before you felt this. And you would feel this and this before you felt this. And you would feel this and this before you felt this; and not until you had located all parts of your hand would you feel complete touch. Do you understand? And I rather imagine that you have quite a bit to learn about the feeling of your eyeball under the contact lenses. It ought to be interesting, and I think you will just automatically learn to recognize ordinary new different feelings, and feelings that indicate adverse or wrong conditions; and your husband can explain that to you more fully. *By the way, how does it feel to you when you forget the presence of the audience?*

S: It makes me feel much more at ease.

E: *It does, and how much have you forgotten the presence of the audience? How many times?*

S: I guess the majority of the time.

E: *You mean after looking over that handsome group you can forget them? But you can, can't you?*

S: Yes.

E: How do you think you do that?

S: Concentrating on something else, I guess.

E: You guess?

S: On what you were saying.

E: On what I was saying. And it is perfectly possible to forget them even with your eyes wide open. How is your right arm?

S: [Inaudible]

E: Had you forgotten that?

S: Yes.

E: Yes. Was it much of a jar to get reconnected with it?

S: Yes. I guess it it true.

E: *Because you gave quite a startled reaction as you reassociated your right arm.* Now tell me, how did you learn to go into a trance?

Trance Reinduction Via Not Knowing[6]

Shifting Attention in Obsessive Fears; Time Distortion

S: I don't know how I learned. I guess I wanted to please you.

E: But how do you know all the right ways to please me?

S: I don't know.

E: All right. Did you go into a trance without knowing you were going to go?

S: I don't think I can answer that.

E: *You don't know how to answer that, and you really don't, do you? Not at all. You really don't, do you? That is right, and you really don't. Just close your eyes.*

And all you do [to reinduce trance] is just say, *you really don't,''* and you hold the attention. In hypnosis it is a matter of communicating ideas and understandings. You ask your patient to give attention to this area or to that area. Where do you want the patient giving his attention if you are sewing up a suture? Do you want him giving his attention here? Or do you want him giving his attention somewhere else? If I want the subject to give her attention to an idea, do I want her paying attention to the audience? No. I speak to her in such a way that she is going to give her attention to me and to the idea I am expressing.

The patient says, "I don't like that obsessive fear." When a patient is overwhelmed by an obsessive fear, it is your obligation to do somthing about it. So you tell the patient: "And you really don't like that obsessive fear, and you really don't, and you really want to get rid of it; you'd really like to understand it." The patient becomes completely absorbed in understanding that obsessive fear and isn't thinking about other things. *The patient is going to be absorbed in the idea of understanding this obsessive fear, and because her attention is so absorbed, she is open to any discussion of that fear.*

I asked the subject something that was of no particular importance to her to demonstrate that the fixation of attention and the development of a trance state can occur just as soon as the patient develops a good state of attentiveness to an idea.

Teaching Time Distoration

Utilizing Posthypnotic Suggestion to Evoke An Altered Sense of Time; A Spontaneous Source Amnesia; Studying Time Distortion In Children

[Question from the audience concerns inducing the phenomenon of time distortion.]

E: [Addresses subject] And do you know, time is passing and you have been sitting here a whole hour? A long, long time. Long enough to feel awfully tired, and you sat here somewhere around 3:15, and then 3:30 came, and 3:45, 4:00; and you really ought to be home by 6:00. And it is getting pretty close to that time, and I don't want you to worry too much about it. You won't leave, but you really have to be home at 7:00, or somewhere else but not here, and it must be pretty close to 6:00 already. *Now, I want you to wake up with the feeling you have been here too darned long.*

S: I am indebted to you.

E: Where do you think you will go now?

S: Home.

E: Why?

S: It is getting close to dinner time.

E: You've got to cook dinner?

S: Yes.

E: Are you a good cook?

S: [Inaudible]

E: He [presumably, the subject's husband] looks well nourished. Besides, it is getting dark outside. How do you feel about me taking so long? It really wasn't thoughtful, was it? Was it?

S: You had your purpose.

E: I had my purpose. What time do you cook, really?

S: I don't know.

E: Make a guess.

S: 4:30 or 5:00.

E: 4:30 or 5:00. What makes you think it is 4:30 or 5:00?

S: *I feel as though I have been here a long time.* [S is following E's posthypnotic suggestion.]

E: You feel like you have been here a long time. Am I that boresome?

S: No.

E: Haven't you been learning a lot?

S: Yes.

E: Well, why does it seem so long?

S: I don't know. [S is demonstrating a source amnesia for E's posthypnotic suggestion that she awaken "feeling you have been here too darned long."

E: Do you know the opposite of time feeling long? The opposite is, time feeling short. You know time passes so rapdily that a whole afternoon can pass and it still feels as if it is the beginning of the afternoon. And that is such a nice feeling, isn't it? It really does feel as if it is the beginning of the afternoon. About what time is it?

S: Seven minutes to four.

E: Seven minutes to four. All right. Now I want you to feel as if it were 2:30. We've done an awful lot of work in that time haven't we?

S: I have?

E: Haven't you?

S: Washed the car.

E: You have washed the car. What else have you done?

S: I have been lazy.

E: What else?

S: That is all.

E: And you got down here.

S: My husband drove me down.

E: And you got down here. What time is it?

S: About six minutes to four.

E: About six minutes to four.

What I have been trying to do is quickly jump without giving her much in the way of cues. Usually time distortion requires very, very little suggestion if you are willing to recognize what time values are. Every little child can teach us an awful lot about time. The morrow is an endless eternity for a child. You observe the behavior of a child and ask him to wait a minute; he looks at you and he waits a minute. It is a lifetime he has waited, and he doesn't want to wait another lifetime. He just can't stand it. You tell the child: "Here are two pieces of candy. There is the short one and there is this long one. If you wait until tomorrow you can have the long one. If you insist on having candy today, you can have only the short one and we will throw away the big piece." The child says, "Can I have both?" You say, "No, you can have just one piece. You can have the big piece tomorrow, the little piece right now." The child can't possibly wait that eternity until tomorrow, and then one day the child looks and says, "If I wait until tomorrow, can I have *both* pieces?" You tell him again, "No. You can have the small piece today and the big piece tomorrow, but if you wait until tomorrow you can have the big piece and we'll throw away the little piece today." The child responds. "I'll wait until tomorrow." The child has gotten older and has developed a new concept of time. There is your willingness to investigate that concept of time—all children can teach you something about time distortion—and all of us have had plenty of experience in time distortion.

197

Establishing Two Trains of Thought

Utilizing Talking and Hand Movement to Facilitate Unconscious Response of Trance

    E: What have I been talking about?
    S: Time distortion.
    E: What does that mean? [E begins to move S's hand.]
    S: You've got me on the spot.
    E: Got you on the spot?
    S: Considering time to be longer than it is, or shorter than it is.
    E: Keep on talking. Explain about time.
    S: What is your stand with little children? They think of time as being...
    E: All right. You can wake up now.

I wanted to show you how to establish two trains of thought in your subjects by asking them to talk to you and keep right on talking, and then you start moving their hand, back and forth. They are trying to explain to you about time distortion and little children, and here is this disturbing thing about you moving their hand around; and yet *they feel obligated to keep right on talking because they know it is a medical situation. But their hand is being manipulated. They need to understand, so the unconscious mind takes over and a trance state supervenes.*

    E: What am I talking about?
    S: I was going to say my subconscious didn't take over very well, did it?
    E: Didn't it?
    S: I didn't feel that it did.
    E: Why did you wake up?
    S: Because you told me to.
    E: How could you wake up if your unconscious hadn't taken over?

S: You have me there.

E: I have you there. That is right. [To the audience] There is no reason why the patient should notice what is happening. Now, she didn't know anything at all about what behavior could be expected of her. Some of you didn't know, but she manifested it in expert fashion. [Back to subject] How are your eyes?

S: Fine.

E: They are fine. I think they are, too. They are delightful. I would like to give you a posthypnotic suggestion. I am labeling it as a posthypnotic suggestion, not for you as the subject, but for them [as the audience] so that they will know I am giving you a posthypnotic suggestion. You know, there is a tomorrow coming, a next week, a next month, a next year. There are a lot of things of interest in the coming days, months, and years. Various things will happen. I want you to have every rightful pleasure and satisfaction; I want you to have every rightful freedom from distress. I would like to have you enjoy everything of value. Now close your eyes and think that over and apply it to yourself in all the ways that are needful, and when you have thought it over, just take a breath or two and wake up feeling rested and refreshed and energetic.

E: Hi!

S: Hi!

E: It didn't take us long to get on an informal basis, did it?

S: No.

E: What is your first name?

S: Ingrid.

E: Ingrid—of what descent?

S: My father was Swedish.

E: That is too bad.

S: Swedish, Scotch, Irish, and English.

E: You know, 10,000 Swedes ran through the weeds pursued by one Norwegian!

S: By one Norwegian?

E: I started that first. I think us squareheads should stick together, Don't you?

S: I do.

Thinking Things Through in Hypnosis

How much effort should you really put into working with a new naive subject? How much effort should you put into thinking over, in the privacy of your office, how you would approach a new or different subject? What would you say and how you would say it? *I think this is where the greater amount of labor comes in the use of hypnosis: thinking through how to say things, how to present ideas.* You should expect to be awkward and clumsy, but then we are all awkward and clumsy. Sometimes you misspeak, yourself. Well, why not? We never always speak perfectly, and your subjects are going to correct you automatically because they will know your exemptions. I noticed that I misspoke, myself, a couple of times, but it didn't disturb the subject—it didn't distress her in any way.

Everyday Examples of Time Distortion

Concerning suggestion for time distortion: I usually like to give the illustration that if you are waiting for a bus on a cold, wet, rainy, windy day, and you have an urgent appointment downtown and the bus is two minutes late, it seems to you as if it takes forever for that bus to get there. Then it seems to you as if the bus just pokes along so slowly, and the driver takes his time at each stop, and you get more and more anxious about your urgent appointment. And then on a nice sunny day when it is warm and comfortable and you are in no hurry at all, you are waiting for a bus and a pretty girl comes along and talks to you, and you would swear that the bus arrived ten minutes *ahead* of schedule. That is time distortion. Friends can come and visit you and stay all afternoon. It seems to you as if it is only 1:30, but the clock says otherwise. You go and listen to a lecturer and you wonder, will he never, never run down? He seems to take so awfully, awfully long. There are plenty of time distortion experiences in everybody's daily life. I have taught some patients time distortion by asking them to take the stopwatch, look at it, hold their nose shut, and hold their breath. They really find out how long a minute is, and they watch that second hand! It is a miserable experience watching that second hand on the stopwatch slow down. They learn something about time distortion!

Ideomotor Signaling and Trance

Direct Communication with the Unconscious Via Catalepsy;
Facilitating Trance by Asking a Question the Conscious Mind
Cannot Answer; Final Trance Ratification

I suppose I ought to mention this head nodding. *Whenever you establish a direct communication with the unconscious mind, you have elicited a trance.* Your experienced subject is likely to recognize that fact and to decide whether or not to remain in the trance. My daughter, Betty Alice, will say: "Daddy, you caught me unaware there. It took me about one-tenth of a second to realize it." And she will come out of the trance state. Mrs. Erickson will do the same thing. Various other experimental subjects will do the same thing. In your office you ought to be willing to induce a trance by direct communication with the unconscious mind and then to offer subjects in the trance state enough distraction so that they remain in that trance.

When I asked Ingrid to talk about time distortion [while I moved her hand], it was awkward for me because I was in the wrong position. I should have twisted around in the chair and used my left arm. But *in maneuvering her arm while she was trying to talk about time distortion, I literally forced her unconscious mind to step to the foreground, forming a direct communication.* When you ask patients to answer a question which they do not know consciously, their unconscious answers. *They wait for their unconscious answer; they have to go into a trance.*

"Now, do you think you could go into a trance? If you think you can, your right hand will lift up. If you think you can't go into a trance, your left hand will go up."

So the subject thinks: "Oh, I can't go into a trance . . . No, I can't go into a trance . . . I can't go into a trance." The left hand goes up.

It goes up unconsciously, so you reach over and demonstrate the catalepsy in the right hand.[7] They had to go into a trance in order to get the hand levitation to say, "No, I can't go into a trance." Your ordinary subject, the ordinary doctor, doesn't know about that separate functioning of the conscious mind. Now, I think I had better tell Ingrid what she has been doing this afternoon.

E: You have been demonstrating how to go into a trance and out of a trance; how to make time very, very long; how to gain poise and comfort; how to blot out the audience and pay no attention to them; how to go deeply into a trance; how to develop amnesia, anesthesia, and dissociation from the audience; how to develop poise and comfort. How do your eyes feel? You weren't even thinking about them. You have learned a great deal. Do you suppose you could use hypnosis for anything else?

S: Use it for anything else?

E: Yes.

S: [Inaudible]

E: And you can use hypnosis with a great deal of comfort and satisfaction. All right. I am very much indebted to you for helping me out.

PART III

THE STATE-DEPENDENT MEMORY AND LEARNING THEORY OF THERAPEUTIC HYPNOSIS

Ernest Lawrence Rossi

Introduction: An Information Theory of Mind-Body Healing and Therapeutic Hypnosis

Every age imposes the limits of its current world view on the way it defines hypnosis and we, of course, are no different. In the broadest sense, hypnosis is a touchstone for all the mysteries of the psyche—for all the ways man has sought to relate constructively to his own mind and body. In this Part, we will update Erickson's concepts of the "neuro-psycho-physiological" basis of therapeutic hypnosis and outline how his naturalistic approach can be applied to a variety of mind-body disorders that traditionally have been called "psychosomatic."

We will begin by suggesting how today's therapists can most usefully conceptualize the mind-body problem that has been a basic issue in Western philosophy for over 2,000 years. We will then reformulate our understanding of how hypnosis accesses and facilitates mind-body communication for therapeutic purposes by exploring the implications of the following three propositions.

203

1. From a psychotherapeutic perspective, the mind/body problem reduces itself to the process of information transduction: how does information transform or translate itself between mind and body?

The process of transduction has been described as the central problem of neurobiology (Delbruck, 1970) and as the basic issue of psychosomatic medicine (Weiner, 1977). From a practical hypnotherapeutic point of view, the mind/body problem becomes a question about the flow of information within the person: How does information at the level of words, meaning and beliefs become transduced into information on the somatic level of sickness and health (Bowers, 1977; Dafter, 1978; Cunningham, 1986)?

2. Failures of transduction result in statebound information: information in one state of being is no longer freely transformable into other states when it is needed. This leads to stress and its consequent, psychosomatic illness.

All human problems can be conceptualized as blocks in the free flow of information between and within mind, body, and society. When there is a lack of information, our coping capacities fail and we fall into stress. Aggravated and accumulated stress (Selye, 1976) is associated with the psychophysiological breakdowns we typically call "psychosomatic." Forty years of experimental studies on the psychobiology of state-dependent memory and learning is the research base for this pivotal concept of "statebound information" as the basis of psychosomatic problems (Fischer, 1971a & b; Overton, 1978).

3. Therapeutic hypnosis is a process of accessing statebound information and utilizing it for problem solving.

We hypothesize that the basic processes and phenomena of hypnosis such as dissociation and reversible amnesia can be most cogently conceptualized today as manifestations of state-dependent memory and learning. During many ordinary and extraordinary life situations, our constantly shifting psychophysiological states can encapsulate memory so that it is not available to our usual, conscious frames of reference. The naturalistic approaches of Ericksonian hypnotherapy are all means of accessing and utilizing this statebound information for problem solving (Erickson, 1959/1980; Erickson & Rossi, 1974/1980, 1976/1980; Rossi, 1986a & b).

Simple as these three propositions may appear, we will need to integrate a vast array of concepts and data to explore them in a manner that is scientifically verifiable and therapeutically useful. All too often medical and psychological researchers pursue their scientific, experimental work in a manner that is independent of the needs of clinicians. Since clinicians (particularly those dealing with mind-body relations) often have access to phenomenological facts that are unknown to researchers, they develop *ad hoc* theories and practices independently of ongoing research. Unfortunately, these clinical theories frequently conceptualize *experiential "facts"* in ways that simply are not verifiable by the standard practices of science.

This has been the situation with hypnosis for over two centuries. Since its inception, hypnosis has been the stepchild of medicine and psychology. It has never been fully accepted because no common framework existed that could conceptualize both the clinical phenomena of hypnosis and the experimentally verifiable data of scientific physiology and psychology. The formulations of these pages are but a step in the direction of assembling a conceptual framework that can integrate the major lines of scientific data about hypnosis with the clinical practice of it.

Therapeutic Hypnosis and State-Dependent Memory, and Learning Behavior

In this section we will present the following lines of evidence to support the concept of *therapeutic hypnosis as a special case of state-dependent memory and learning:*

1. James Braid originally defined hypnosis in terms that we recognize today as equivalent to the concept of state-dependent memory and learning.

2. The phenomena of hypnosis and state-dependent memory and learning are manifestations of the same basic psychological process of *dissociation* and its natural consequent, *statebound information and behavior.*

3. The acquisition conditions that generate hypnosis and state-dependent memory and learning are essentially identical.

4. The psychobiology of (a) drug induced state-dependent memory and learning, (b) the neurobiolgy of "endogenous state-dependent learning," (c) therapeutic hypnosis, and (d) psychosomatic problems are all the same class of mind-body phenomena mediated by the limbic-hypothalamic systems that encode memory and learning.

1. James Braid's Original Definition of Hypnosis

James Braid (1795–1860), a Scottish physician generally regarded as one of the founders of hypnotism, recommended that it be defined as follows (Tinterow, 1970, pp. 370–372):

> Let the term *hypnotism* be restricted to those cases alone in which . . . the subject has no rememberance on awakening of what occurred during his sleep, but of which he shall have the most perfect recollection on passing into a similar stage of hypnotism thereafter. In this mode, *hypnotism* will comprise those cases only in which what has hitherto been called the double-conscious state occurs.
>
> And, finally, as a generic term, comprising the whole of these phenomena which result from the reciprocal actions of mind and matter upon each other, I think no term could be more appropriate than *psychophysiology.*

In the first part of the quotation Braid defines hypnotism as a process that modern researchers would term "state-dependent memory and learning": what is learned and remembered is dependent on one's psychophysiological state at the time of the experience. Memories acquired during the state of hypnosis are forgotten in the awake state, but are available once more when hypnosis is reinduced. Since memory is dependent upon and limited to the state in which it was acquired, we say it is "state-bound information."

In the second part of the quotation, Braid's use of the generic term *psychophysiological* to denote all the phenomena of "the reciprocal actions of mind and matter upon each other" was another prescience of current thinking in the fields of medicine and psychology.

The appendix contains an outline of some of the major theories of historical and modern hypnosis which traces the evolution of the concepts of *statebound information* and the *psychophysiological* as explanatory principles.

2. Hypnosis and Statebound Information and Behavior

After a long period of abeyance, Pierre Janet's (1889–1907) concept of dissociation has found new life in Ernest Hilgard's *neodissociation* theory of hypnosis (1977). Hilgard integrates historical and modern experimental and clinical data to document how the major classical phenomena of hypnosis can be conceptualized as aspects of "divided consciousness." Hilgard was one of the first to recognize a possible relationship between dissociation and state-dependent learning as follows (Hilgard & Hilgard, 1975, p. 183):

> Another approach to dissociated experiences is the peculiar action of certain drugs upon the retention and reinstatement of learned experiences, leading to what is called state-dependent learning. If learning takes place under the influence of an appropriate drug, the memory for that learning may be unavailable in the nondrugged state, but return when the person is again under the influence of the drug. This occasionally happens with alcohol: the drinker forgets what he said or did while intoxicated, only to remember it again when next intoxicated. Because the memory is stored, but unavailable except under special circumstances, this phe-

nomenon has some characteristics of hypnotic amnesia. Presumably, when the site and nature of these effects become known, they may have some bearing on the physiological substratum for hypnosis.

In his neodissociation theory of hypnosis, Hilgard classified the major hypnotic phenomona as forms of "divided consciousness" (Hilgard, 1977, pp. 244–245):

> If information acquired in one state, as under the influence of a drug, is forgotten in the nondrugged state but recalled again in the drug state, that is an experimental illustration of a reversible amnesia. This arrangement is of course the paradigm of *state-dependent learning*. The literature has been reviewed by Overton, who is also one of the leading investigators in the field (Overton, 1972, 1973) .... According to Overton (1973), drug discrimination ... may be based "on the dissociative barrier which impairs a transfer of training between the drug and no-drug condition." *The concept of dissociation employed by Overton is consonant with neodissociation theory. That is, two types of behavior may be isolated from each other because of differently available information.* [Italics added]

The theoretical integration of the concepts of therapeutic hypnosis and state-dependent learning that is being explored in this section is an extension of these intimations by Hilgard and earlier formulations by Erickson and Rossi (1974/1980).

Table 1 matches the basic terms and processes of hypnosis with those of state-dependent memory and learning to demonstrate their hypnothesized identity. Both hypnosis and state-dependent learning have *special acquisition or induction conditions* that mark them as distinctive from the ordinary situations of life. Because of this they both are encoded by distinctive *mind/body communication processes* from which they generate a variety of statebound behaviors. These *statebound behaviors* typically involve patterns of memory and life experience that are dissociated—that is, they are not available to the person's ordinary awareness. However, these patterns can be *recalled* by either reactivating the conditions

208

Table 1: A matching of the basic terms and processes of hypnosis and state-dependent memory and learning.

Acquisition/ Induction	Mind-Body Connection	Dissociated/ Statebound Behavior	Access/ Recall
Distinctive conditions for state-dependent memory & learning	Distinctive mind-body connections	Statebound learning; amnesia	Similar acquisition conditions
Distinctive conditions for hypnotic induction	Distinctive mind-body connections	Hypnotic behaviors; amnesia	Similar hypnotic induction conditions

during which they were acquired or by *accessing* these conditions vicariously via hypnosis.

3. Identical Acquisition Conditions for Hypnosis and State-Dependent Memory and Learning

The appendix outlines how both historical and modern methods of facilitating (inducing) the experience of hypnosis are essentially identical with the acquisition conditions for state-dependent memory and learning. In this section we will review modern experimental data that support this view.

Tables 2 and 3 match the basic processes of state-dependent memory and learning with those of hypnosis on the many independent but corresponding lines of research between them. We will discuss each of these lines of research (the rows in Tables 2 and 3) to demonstrate how therapeutic hypnosis can be conceptualized today as a special case of state-dependent memory and learning.

Drugs

The most obvious identity match between state-dependent learning and hypnosis occurs in the use of drugs as an acquisition condition to produce both phenomena. As we have seen, the effect of drugs on learning has provided the major paradigm for demonstrating state-dependent learning over the past forty years. It is probably no coincidence that it was also forty years ago, after World War II, that "hypnotic" drugs such as amytal were used together with hypnosis to access dissociated memories considered to be the basis of traumatic war neuroses (Grinker & Spiegel, 1945; Kubie, 1943; Watkins, 1949). The traumatic situations of battle experience encoded memories under psychophysiological conditions so different from those of ordinary civilian life that the war memories become dissociated and statebound: the memories would manifest themselves by nightmares and nervousness, for example, but not via the typical associations of everyday memory. Drugs such as amytal, together with hypnosis, enabled therapists

210

to access memories of the original battle situation with appropriate questions and then reassociate them with the patients' more typical patterns of consciousness so that the memories were no longer statebound and symptomatic. Freudian psychoanalytic concepts such as "lifting repressions" were used to describe this early approach to treating war neuroses. Today we give the same approach a more specific and operational focus by describing it as "accessing statebound information."

One of the clearest demonstrations of the way in which drugs and hypnosis can both access the same state-dependent memories was originally done by Erickson in 1932 and finally published in 1963 (Erickson, 1963/1980). The subject of this demonstration was Dr. A, a Ph.D., who had been analyzed by Freud and consequently believed he had uncovered all his past memories. In a series of carefully recorded experiments, Erickson questioned Dr. A while under ether anesthesia to recall a traumatic memory from the age of three that had not been uncovered in the previous analysis with Freud. Upon awakening from the ether anesthesia, however, Dr. A was again amnesic for the memory. When ether was administered at a later session, he again recovered the memory. This state-dependent memory was recovered under anesthesia several times and lost again, even after being discussed in the normal awake state. It became a permanent part of Dr. A's normal awake memory system only when he was allowed to access the memory under hypnosis and work through the emotions associated with it. Hypnosis accessed the state-dependent memory and enabled Dr. A to integrate it therapeutically into waking consciousness in a way that the drug, ether, alone could not do.

Biological Rhythms

A much less obvious similarity between the acquisition conditions for state-dependent learning and hypnosis is the influence of biological rhythms on both. Rossi (1982, 1986a) found a striking resemblance in the behavioral characteristics of what Erickson described as the "common everyday trance" and the behaviors manifested in the rest phase of the ultradian rhythms that take place every 90 to 120 minutes throughout the day. Holloway (1978) has

211

Table 2: The areas of research outlining the acquisition conditions, mind-body connections, and statebound behaviors associated with state-dependent memory, learning, and behavior (SDMLB).

Acquisition/ Induction	Mind-Body Connection	Dissociated/ Statebound Behavior	Access/ Recall	Reference
Drugs with psychoactive effects	Sensory-perceptual processing	Dissociated memory and learning; neuro-transmitters	Same drugs	Fischer, 1971a, b & c; Fischer & Landon, 1972; Overton, 1968, 1978
Biological rhythms	Neuroendocrinal hormones	Conditioned response	Same time of day	Evans, 1972; Holloway, 1978
Early life experience	ACTH and brain protein synthesis	Infantile amnesia, hypnoidal states	Hypnosis	Bower, 1981; Cheek, 1960; Rosenzweig, 1984; Hilgard, 1972
Motivation, mood, expectancy and emotion	Peripheral hormones modulating central storage of memory, neurotransmitters, neuroendocrines	Differential T-maze learning, emotional memory, ego states, multiple personality, mood states	Same organismic state	Bower, 1981; Gage, 1983; Izquierdo, 1984; Izquierdo & Dias, 1983a, b & c; McGaugh, 1983; Overton, 1978; Swanson & Kinsbourne, 1979; Weingartner, 1977

Physical and semantic contexts	Distinctive cues	Context bound and episodic memory	Similar involvement	Bowers, 1977; Erickson & Rossi, 1974/1980; Gage, 1983; E. Hilgard & Bower, 1975; Pribram, 1969; Tulving, 1972, 1985
Social and cultural contexts	Distinctive cues	Natural memory and amnesia	Similar context	Erickson & Rossi, 1974/1980; Fischer, 1971a & b; Neisser, 1982
Imaginative involvement, belief system	Distinctive associations of psychological and physiological factors	Statebound experience, state specific consciousness	Similar psychological or physiological arousal	Fischer, 1971a & b; Tart, 1972, 1983; Hilgard, 1979
"As if" phenomena	Cognitive and somatic cues epinepherine	"As if" experience	Uniting cognitive and somatic cues	Hohmann, 1966; Maranon, 1924; Schachter & Singer, 1962; Vaihinger, 1911
Psychotherapy	Altered cues, contexts, and arousal levels	Amnesia, defense symptoms	Hypnosis, matching cues, and arousal levels	Peak et al, 1979; Reus et al, 1979; Meier, 1974

Table 3: The areas of research outlining the acquisition/induction conditions, mind-body connections, and statebound behaviors that can be accessed via modern hypnosis.

Acquisition/ Induction	Mind-Body Connection	Dissociated/ Statebound Behavior	Access/ Recall	Reference
Drugs with psychoactive effects	Encoding of distinctive sensory-perceptual cues	War neuroses, dissociated memories	Drugs and hypnosis	Grinker & Spiegel, 1945; Kubie, 1943; Watkins, 1949
Biological rhythms	Circadian, ultradian, and REM rhythms	Psychosomatic, everyday trance	Ultradian rhythms	Evans, 1972; Kripke, 1982; Rossi, 1972/1985, 1982, 1986a
Early life experience	Distinctive encoding of early life experience, eidetic memory	Multiple personality, hypnotic susceptibility	Similar situation, hypnosis	Cheek, 1957, 1960, 1969, 1975; J. Hilgard, 1972, 1979; Nash et al, 1984
Motivation, mood, expectancy, emotion	Cerebral hemispheric processing	Task motivational instructions, etc.	Similar situation, hypnosis	Barber, 1972; Cheek, 1957; Erickson, 1937/1980; Reyher, 1977

214

Physical and semantic contexts	Hyper- and hypo-arousal levels, minimal cues	Hypnotic experience	Similar contexts, hypnosis	Blum, 1967; Erickson, & Rossi, 1974/1980
Social and cultural contexts	Hyper- and hypo-arousal levels	Statebound experience	Similar contexts	Erickson & Rossi, 1974/1980; Fischer, 1971a, b & c; Tart, 1972, 1983
Imaginative involvement, belief system	Right hemispheric arousal	Hypnotic experience and skills	Hypnosis	Fischer, 1971a, b & c; Kroger & Fezler, 1976; Tart, 1972, 1983
"As if" and reality sense	Cognitive and sensory experience	"As if" experience	Cognitive and/or sensory input	Erickson & Rossi, 1979; Orne, 1972; Sarbin, 1950
Psychotherapy	Altered cues, contexts, and arousal levels	Amnesias, defenses, symptoms	Hypnosis, matching cues and arousal levels	Erickson & Rossi, 1979; Gage, 1983; Reus et al, 1979

demonstrated how circadian (24-hour) and ultradian rhythms generate continually changing acquisition conditions for state-dependent learning. Learning takes place more easily at certain times of the day, and memories are better when they are tested at the same time of day as when they were acquired. Experimental animals can utilize their internal biological rhythms as a kind of circadian clock to help them recall a learned task. Holloway attributes many of these interesting state-dependent effects to the fluctuating concentrations of neuroendocrinal hormones that regulate memory and learning. These fluctuations, in turn, are governed by ultradian rhythms in the release of hormones by the suprachiasmatic nucleus of the hypothalamus.

Rapid Eye Movement (REM) sleep is a 90-minute ultradian rhythm that can also function as an acquisition condition for both state-dependent learning and hypnosis. In a series of studies, Evans (1972) found evidence for state-dependent memory and learning in subjects who were given verbal suggestions during their REM phases of sleep. These studies also demonstrated that while the brain-wave patterns of sleep and hypnosis are distinctly different, good hypnotic subjects could respond to suggestions during REM sleep. Overton finds that this evidence for the existence of state-dependent learning during REM sleep "provides an attractive alternative to repression as an explanation for the rather universally observed difficulty in recalling dreams" (Overton, 1978, p. 298). This supports the view that "lifting repressions" is better conceptualized as "accessing statebound information." In a later section we will provide additional examples of how the concepts of dynamic psychotherapy can be more adequately conceptualized by the experimentally verifiable data of state-dependent memory and learning.

The menstrual cycle is another biological rhythm that apparently generates statebound information and behavior. Individual life experiences, attitudes, and beliefs can modulate a woman's mood and comfort level during these periods even when she is not consciously aware of how she learned these effects. In Part I of this volume, Erickson reported several cases which leave little doubt that the learned aspect of menstrual distress (PMS, premenstrual syndrome) can be ameliorated hypnotherapeutically.

Other investigators (Chiba, Chiba, Halberg & Cutkomp, 1977) have found circadian and circasptan (7-day) rhythms that influenced the behavior of a normal couple along a variety of dimensions (e.g., temperature, pulse, strength, eye-hand skills). It has been my clinical observation that couples with good relationships tend to integrate spontaneously their circadian and ultradian rhythms so that their general activity levels, appetite, and sexual rhythms are in synchrony; unhappy couples invariably report conflict and desynchrony on all these rhythms. Since these biological rhythms are frequently regulated by the same hormones that modulate memory and learning (McGaugh, 1983), we can assume that state-dependent effects underlie many more family relationship issues than we are currently aware of (Ritterman, 1983).

Early Life Experience

The intense experiences and special contexts of childhood readily lend themselves to dissociation and its natural consequents, statebound information and amnesia. The work of Bower (1981) suggests how such dissociations could account for infantile amnesia. The analysis of the origins of multiple personality in the dissociated experiences of early life support this view (Gruenwald, 1984). Lienhart (1984), whose work will be presented in more detail elsewhere (Rossi, 1986b), has vividly documented the relation between traumatic statebound experiences of childhood and the generation of multiple personalities, and between an accessing of this condition via hypnosis and its resolution.

Josephine Hilgard (1972) has summarized evidence for a developmental-interactive theory of hypnotic susceptibility as follows (pp. 396–397):

> Two developmental strands have been shown to provide a background for hypnotizability of young adults. The first was maintenance into young adulthood of the imaginative involvements prevalent in childhood; the second is an after-effect of rather severe punishment in early childhood.... When either or both of these strands are present, the young

217

adult is a good candidate for hypnosis. The hypnotic experience itself is an interactive one, in which the stage is set for the hypnotist to capitalize on the readiness that the developmental experiences have provided.

Nash, Lynn, and Givens (1984) have confirmed Hilgard's findings on the relation between childhood punishment and adult hypnotic susceptibility. Hilgard advances the view that children faced with punishment seek to escape by developing "skills" in using dissociative mechanisms which then become the basis of their adult hypnotic susceptibility. This indicates once again how dissociative mechanisms are a common denominator in the acquisition conditions generative of both hypnosis and state-dependent learning. Children with a high expectation of punishment also have altered levels of psychophysiological arousal. As we shall see in the next section, these altered arousal levels are involved in mediating state-dependent learning that is particularly available to being accessed by hypnosis.

On the basis of extensive clinical experience, Cheek (1960) has postulated that traumatic life events (particularly those in childhood) lead to the spontaneous experience of hypnoidal states and hypnotic dissociation as a form of self-protection—much as some animals, particularly when young and defenseless, will "freeze" in the presence of danger. The amnesias usually associated with these early traumas attest to their statebound nature. Cheek has found that resistance to hypnosis is often due to the painful affect of these early traumas which is reactivated in adults when they try to enter trance. In a study of 60 clinical patients who showed conscious cooperation but unconscious resistance to entering hypnosis, Cheek (1960) found that almost 75 percent had had an unpleasant childhood experience with inhalation anesthesia. These patients report that the similarity of the hypnotic "sleep" with the anesthetic "sleep" reactivated their negative feelings. This supports the view that some forms of resistance to hypnosis are due to those experiences of state-dependent learning associated with unpleasant feelings and memories. Cheek (1957, 1960, 1969, 1975) has carefully described and illustrated the hypnotic approaches that can be used to access these negative statebound effects for the resolution of many psychosomatic problems.

218

Experimental research on the effects of early life experience in relation to the formation of memory and the growth of brain tissues may be of increasing relevance for understanding these clinical issues. Rosenzweig (1984), for example, has recently reviewed several decades of innovative experiments that demonstrate how enriching life experience (particularly early life experience) increases protein synthesis in the brain. Rosenzweig outlines the process as follows (1984, p. 371):

> Some of the findings on rapid structural changes in neurons come from research on long-term potentiation, and work on this effect is showing some interesting convergences with our own. In several parts of the brain, and especially parts of the limbic system, stimulating with a burst of impulses results in potentiation of the responses to subsequent stimuli. A component of the potentiation has a half-life of about a week, whence the designation long-term potentiation (LTP). Some consider LTP to be a model system for investigation of the biological bases of memory, and others consider it to be a process that probably enters into consolidation of memory. The hypothesis that LTP is closely related to learning and memory is supported by the facts that it is elicited by brief physiological events yet is long-lasting and that it is strengthened by repetition . . . . Experience in an enriched environment leads to an increase in numbers of dendritic spines (Globus *et al.*, 1973). Appropriate stimulation of brain tracts that enter the hippocampus leads to long-term potentiation, and *such stimulation has been shown to increase within minutes* the diameter of dendritic spines on the hippocampal alb (Fifkova & Van Harrweld, 1977). [Italics added]

The finding that appropriate stimulation can "within minutes" increase the physical size of the fine dendritic association areas of the brain cannot but make us pause with wonder about the possibility that this might be the neurobiological basis of the highly focused attentional effects of hypnotic intervention. Erickson (1937/1980) and Cheek used procedures of reviewing a sought-for traumatic memory repeatedly before expecting a fuller recall to become available. Is it possible that they were thereby tapping into the neurobiological basis of the long-term potentiation (LTP) of memory? How could we devise experiments to test such a hypothesis?

Motivation, Mood, Expectancy, and Emotion

According to Overton (1978), any significant change in arousal level, motivation, expectancy, and emotion can alter one's internal psychophysiological state enough to generate an acquisition condition for state-dependent learning. In humans, for example, Bower (1981) has demonstrated how happy and sad moods can generate a variety of state-dependent learnings that could account for a wide range of phenomena from infantile amnesia, to multiple personality, to the ego states of everyday life. Gage (1983) has found that such state-dependent learning based on mood is related to the greater lateralization of emotion in the right cerebral hemisphere. Weingartner (1977) has found that the more extreme mood changes of manic-depressive episodes can generate specific acquisition conditions for state-dependent learning as well. Attitudes and memories during the manic stage, for example, are not always available during the depressed periods, and vice versa. Overton has summarized how state-dependent studies on "affect-specific recall" are contributing to our basic understanding of how internal cues and contexts generate "feelings."

In a recent review of experimental research concerning hormonal influences on memory storage, McGaugh (1983) demonstrated how feelings associated with highly motivating life experiences can generate "peripheral" epinephrine (from the adrenal medulla) that strengthens the consolidation of long-term memory in the hippocampus and amygdala structures of the limbic system.

Izquierdo and Dias (1983b) reported how a number of hormones associated with motivation and stress (such as adrenocorticotropic hormone [ACTH] and B-endorphin) are involved in "endogenous state dependency" memory regulation. Izquierdo (1984) has recently summarized the origin of the concept of "endogenous state dependency" memory regulation by neurophysiologists as follows (p. 646):

This chapter deals primarily with data from this laboratory that suggest that learning and memory depend on the relationship between the endogenous state that develops after training and the one that develops during retention testing; or, in other words, that there is endogenous state dependency.

The origin of this idea is difficult to trace. Kety (1967, 1970, 1976) suggested that biogenic amines and hormones released in the peculiar "affective states" that accompany learning "might modulate trophic processes occurring at recently activated synapses in order to promote the persistence of those circuits that have led to reward to the relief of discomfort." Implicit in that suggestion is the notion that a repetition of the neurochemical change(s) caused by the substances released will repeat the conditions appropriate for a facilitated operation of the circuits involved in the emission or omission of a given response. Spear (1973, 1978) and later Riccio and Concannon (1981) considered that "interoceptive cues experienced in a given drug (or hormonal) state might serve as contextual cues for retrieval" and that drug (or hormone)-induced memory reactivation might "depend on the reinstatement of a sufficient number (or kind) of retrieval attributes that were present at, or immediately following, original learning."

The first formal and explicit statement of the endogenous state dependency hypothesis was made by Zornetzer (1978):

"In normal memory formation the specific pattern of arousal present in the brain at the time of training may become an integral component of the stored information. The neural representation of this specific pattern of arousal might depend on the pattern of activity generated by brainstem acetylcholine, catecholamine and serotonin systems. It is this ideosyncratic and unique patterned brain state, present at the time of memory formation, that might need to be reproduced, or at least approximated, at the time of retrieval in order for the stored information to be elaborated."

221

It is difficult to resist the conjecture that this hormonal activity is the psychophysiological basis of the kinds of state-dependent memory and learning that are of concern for the clinician who is usually dealing with the effects of highly motivating life experiences. I have reviewed a variety of clinical cases which demonstrate how the psychophysiology of memory consolidation described by McGaugh, Zornetzer, and Izquierdo is the common denominator in the state-dependent learning and hypnotherapy of traumatic and/or significant life-shaping events (Rossi, 1986b).

Studies relating motivation, mood, expectancy, and emotion to hypnotic induction are almost too numerous to mention. They range from carefully quantified research by experimentalists such as T.X. Barber (1978, 1984) who uses "task-motivational instructions," and Blum (1972) who evokes cognitive and affective arousal to facilitate hypnotic responsiveness; to the case presentations of clinicians such as Erickson (Rossi, 1973/1980) and Cheek (1957), who have illustrated how personal motivation can be a critical factor in hypnotic induction and the experiencing of deep hypnotic phenomena. The work of Erickson and Cheek is particularly striking in this regard when they demonstrated how the same individual would respond very differently when highly meaningful motivational factors were changed. Erickson sometimes alarmed his colleagues by using psychological shock in intimidating and embarrassing contexts in order to stimulate different levels of psychophysiological arousal in his patients and thereby facilitate hypnotherapeutic responsiveness.*

*The Context of Experience: Physical & Semantic,
Social & Cultural*

A preoccupation with the concept of context is perhaps the major common denominator of theory and experiment in the areas of hypnosis and state-dependent learning. Blum, for example,

---

*In particular, see Section 5 in Volume 4 of *The Collected Papers*. Rossi (1973/1980) has outlined some of the ethical and professional guidelines for such unconventional hypnotherapeutic approaches.

concluded from his "experimental observations on *the contextual nature of hypnosis*" (1967, pp. 169–170):

Contents of the mind are inevitably embedded in the contexts of their occurrence. The important role of context in retrieving information from memory is well accepted. In hypnosis the contextual role is even more pronounced because of its uniqueness. When the hypnotic context is sustained or reintegrated either by a later return to the hypnotic state or by partial contact, at least in the case of a posthypnotic signal, the content [originally] registered and reverberated in that context becomes exceptionally salient. Having that cognitive field virtually to itself, the hypnotic instruction comes to dominate thought, feeling and action to an unusual degree.

In his "Notes on Minimal Cues in Vocal Dynamics and Memory," Erickson reported on how *physical and social contexts in everyday life* can generate what we would call today *statebound memory* (1980b, p. 373):

Following Clark L. Hull's example, I made notes on a lot of observations on things that interested me and that I thought might some day be useful. A couple of weeks ago I happened to pull a folder out of my filing cabinet and found sheets of yellow and white paper bearing the enclosed material which I put together as a continuum. The first part was discussed with Larry Kubie and with Dave Rappaport when he was engrossed in writing his book on "Memory."

It is all material that helped shape my thinking about hypnosis and the importance of factors seemingly totally unrelated.

One of my favorite recollections is an incident that occurred when I was standing in the barn doorway when I was about ten years old. A "brilliant" idea occurred to me, now long forgotten. I knew to execute that brilliant idea I would need a hammer and a hatchet. But those things were on the back porch. I rushed to get the tools, but in some way, by the time I reached the porch, I had completely forgotten what I

223

was after. Following a long, fruitless mental search, I returned to the barn door and recalled my brilliant idea and what was needed to execute it. My brilliant idea was associated with the barn door where I happened to get it.

That led to climbing trees and learning poems from an old magazine of my grandmother's. I picked trees at random, short poems at random, and noted the connection between individual trees and the poems I learned while sitting in those trees. Three years later I went on an exploration tour and found that when I climbed the right tree, my memory of the poem associated with it was greatly improved.

In later life Erickson conducted many "field experiments" investigating this relationship between context and memory. He found that, for example, regional accents returned spontaneously when one returned home to that part of the country where they were originally acquired; and he found that a doctor's memory of his patients' names was affected by location as well as by social context: recall was better nearer the hospital and in the presence of other doctors who also knew the patients (Erickson, 1985). Neisser (1982) has admirably assembled a rich collection of examples and data about this kind of "remembering in natural contexts."

The incredible variety of stimuli, contexts, and conditions that lead to the acquisition of state-dependent learning justifies the generalization that anything which influences the way an experience is perceived, organized and stored will of necessity result in some degree of state-dependent memory and learning. Whatever is learned during the acquisition condition will be remembered better when that state is reexperienced later. If the acquisition condition is an extremely unusual situation or traumatic life incident, the memory of it may become so isolated from the normal associative networks of everyday consciousness that it becomes totally statebound; it is completely dissociated and unavailable in the normal waking state so that one is amnesic for it.

A number of the studies listed in Table 2 reveal important features about state-dependent memory and learning that make it particularly suitable as a conceptual bridge between the fundamental learning theories of experimental psychology and those of therapeutic hypnosis. Swanson and Kinsbourne (1979) have discussed the relationship between the basic learning processes of stimulus-response generalization and state-dependent learning, together with their adaptive value as follows (pp. 294–295):

> The state-dependence of learning, if viewed in isolation, seems like an arbitrary limitation on memory, the adaptive advantage of which is difficult to discern. But its biological origins become comprehensible if it is viewed within the broader context of human memory. Regardless of the details of the mechanisms and theories discussed above, we can regard state-dependence as one of the range of phenomena that reveal the effect of context on remembering. . . .
>
> Essentially, this equates the mechanism responsible for state-dependent learning with the mechanism that established "response set," and it differs little from the usual discussion of similarity effects and the concepts of stimulus and response generalization (E. Hilgard & Bower, 1975).
>
> What is the adaptive significance of "response set" and of stimulus and response generalization? Since the total capacity of any organism is limited, these processes are important for biasing the probabilities of particular responses at a particular point in time. Utilization of context is one way that the "appropriate" response may be chosen, and the "inappropriate" response may be suppressed. This effect of context may occur automatically, leaving the full processing capacity of the organism available for processing of more specific environmental stimuli. If this type of response selection is automatic, it would have a profound biological significance. It would allow complete attention to the here-and-now, and thus minimize the chance of the organism falling prey due to its lack of vigilance, while at the same time providing use of prior experience.
>
> What memory mechanisms are responsible for making responses readily available? Pribram (1969) has suggested a distinction between context-free and context-bound memories, which is related to Tulving's (1972) distinction between episodic (context bound) and semantic (context free) mem-

225

ory. One way that episodic memory and other memory systems differ is that the former represents unique personal experiences and the latter represents general rules. Precisely because general rules may be called upon to guide behavior at virtually any time and place, they have to be readily accessible by a mechanism that is automatic and context-free (Pribram, 1969). Therefore, information in semantic memory is rehearsed until it is highly overlearned. On the other hand, precisely because particular events (episodic memories) are characterized by their distinctiveness, their recovery has to be context-bound (Pribram, 1969). It is confined to settings which bear a sufficiently striking "family resemblance" to the original episode to provide the contextual cues that trigger recall of the event. The rarely experienced situation, by virtue of its uniqueness and non-recurrent nature, is not learned through repetition. Furthermore, it would be pointless to keep recollecting such a unique event which would not render the individual's general pattern of responding more adaptive. Episodic memories apparently are readily accessible only at times when they are likely to be utilized to direct response selection. In terms of infrequent events, this utilization is directed by the context which recurs and is shared with a previous event.

It is clear from the several theories of coding in memory (Martin, 1972; Tulving, 1972; Keppel & Zubrzycki, 1977) that remembering a prior event is not cost free. As [E.] Hilgard and Bower (1975, p. 547) point out, the reinstatement of the original context is important because it "isolates interpolated material and prevents interference at the time of recall of some originally learned material."

In these paragraphs Swanson and Kinsbourne use the concept of state-dependent learning to build a bridge between fundamental concepts of learning theory (such as stimulus and response generalization) and the contextual determinants of memory in normal as well as extraordinary life experience. The concept of *episodic* or *context-bound memory* may be an appropriate experimental analogue of the types of traumatic/clinical situations that typically generate statebound amnesias, which traditionally have been accessed by hypnosis.

Imaginative Involvement and Belief Systems

Fischer (1971a, b & c; 1986) has reviewed a vast collection of data from experimental, clinical, and cultural sources to create his interesting concept of *statebound experience,* which is related to state-dependent learning but may not be entirely identical with it. The acquisition condition for statebound experience is a distinctive association between a specific psychological (symbolic) belief system and a specific level of physiological arousal. Because of the uniqueness of its acquisition condition, statebound experience is not available to the typical association networks of a person's usual awareness, but it can be accessed by either the psychological or physiological component that originally generated it. Fischer describes his concept as follows (1971a, pp. 373–374):

> Inasmuch as meaningful experience arises from the binding or coupling of *(1) a particular state or level of arousal with (2) a particular symbolic interpretation of that arousal, experience is statebound and can thus be evoked either by inducing—'naturally,' hypnotically or with the aid of drugs—*the particular level of arousal, or by presenting some symbol of its interpretation such as an image, melody or taste. The following passage from Juan Luis Vives (1538) is perhaps the oldest description of stateboundness:
>
> "When I was a boy at Valencia, I was ill of a fever; while my taste was deranged I ate cherries; for many years afterwards, whenever I tasted the fruit I not only recalled the fever, but also seemed to experience it again."
>
> Another, a contemporary example of stateboundness, is from Marcel Proust's *Swann's Way:*
>
> "And soon, mechanically, weary after a dull day with the prospect of a dull morrow, I raised to my lips a spoonful of the tea in which I had soaked a morsel of the cake. No sooner had

the warm liquid, and the crumbs in it, touched my palate then a shudder ran through my whole body, and I stopped, intent upon the extraordinary changes that were taking place.

"Undoubtedly what is thus palpitating in the depths of my being must be the image, the visual memory which, being linked to that taste, has tried to follow it into my conscious mind."

But state-bound recall can be evoked not only by imagery, melodies and other symbols of the content of an experience, but also by simply inducing that particular level of arousal which prevailed during the initial experience, as in this next example. A young man complaining of unpleasant "flashbacks" from a previous LSD experience remembered on questioning that they seemed to occur each time he took some pills prescribed for him (in the emergency room of a university hospital) "to drain his sinuses." The tablets were soon identified as amphetamine, which apparently produced the level of arousal necessary for recall of his previous (statebound) drug experience. This, then, is the very nature of a flashback: the coupling of an experience to a level of drug-induced arousal which may then be re-induced at a later time. In our opinion, "LSD flashbacks" are only a special case of the general phenomenon of stateboundness, and their unpleasant nature is likely due to the anxiety associated with a seemingly unprovoked experience....

We submit, however, that—while remembering from one state to another is usually called "state-dependent learning," implying that the individual was confronted with a learning task—extended practice, learning or conditioning is not necessary for "stateboundness" to occur. On the contrary, the examples by Vives and Proust (above) illustrate that a *single experience may be sufficient to establish stateboundness.* Note also that "state-dependent learning" could just as well be termed "state-dependent adaptation," since learning and adaptation are as indistinguishable from each other as hallucinations and dreams. [Italics added]

The work of J. Hilgard (1979) on *imaginative involvement* as a major variable in hypnotic experience, the work of Bowers and

Bowers (1972) on creativity and hypnosis, and Sheehan's (1972) research on "hypnosis and the manifestations of imagination," all overlap and provide further support for the "family resemblance" between current conceptions of the nature of hypnosis and of "statebound experience" as formulated by Fischer. The work of Tart (1972) demonstrates how the subjective experiences reported on his self-report scales of deep hypnotic phenomena exhibit the type of discontinuities that are typical of statebound experience and suggests how the concept may be fundamental to formulating a general theory of consciousness (Tart, 1983).

Erickson and Rossi have outlined how therapeutic trance and, indeed, all phenomenological life experience can be conceptualized as statebound (Erickson, Rossi, & Rossi, 1976, p. 299):

> Fischer generalizes these results into a theory of "how multiple existence became possible by living from waking state to another waking state; from one dream to the next; from LSD to LSD; from one creative, artistic, religious or psychotic inspiration or possession to another; from trance to trance; and from reverie to reverie."
>
> We would submit that therapeutic trance itself can be most usefully conceptualized as but one vivid example of the fundamental nature of all phenomenological experience as "statebound." The apparent continuity of consciousness that exists in everyday normal awareness is in fact a precarious illusion that is only made possible by the associative connections that exist between related bits of conversation, task orientation, and so on. We have all experienced the instant amnesias that occur when we go too far on some tangent so we "lose the thread of thought" or "forget just what we were going to do." Without the bridging associative connections, consciousness would break down into a series of discrete states with as little contiguity as is apparent in our dream life.

The "As-If" Phenomenon and the "Sense of Reality"

Closely related to imaginative involvement and belief systems is

229

the "as-if" experience. The accumulated observations by philosophers, psychologists, psychophysiologists, and clinicians over the past 200 years on the subjective experience of "as-if" may be used as a kind of phenomenological X-ray into the actual structure and composition of our "sense of reality." Vaihinger (1852-1933) built his *Philosophy of the "As-If"* (1911) on Immanual Kant's *Critique of Pure Reason* (1781) which proposed the basic thesis that we cannot know "reality" in itself. Our so-called sense of reality is actually a fiction—an artificial construction of the human mind that creates a subjective world (Watzlawick, 1984). We then act *as-if* this subjective creation had an objective existence apart from us. This, of course, is an illusion.

It is perhaps more than a coincidence that in this same time period, the Benjamin Franklin Commission of 1784 had established that Mesmerism, the forerunner of hypnosis, was caused by subjective "imagination" rather than by any objective magnetic fluid. There was a *zeitgeist* 200 years ago that recognized the essentially subjective nature of mind, reality, and psychophysiological healing. This *zeitgeist* gave rise to the field of psychology as something quite different from philosophy. Hypnosis and suggestion was the first form of mind-body healing to use this new concept of psychology. All our current forms of psychotherapy evolved from this source in Mesmerism and hypnosis (Ellenberger, 1970).

In modern hypnosis the as-if position has been expressed by the psychologist Sarbin, who described the role-taking aspect of trance behavior as follows (1950, p. 267): "The *as-if* formulation may be seen not only in drama, in hypnosis, but in fantasy, play, and in fact, all imaginative behavior. Imaginative behavior is *as-if* behavior." Orne (1972) has developed experimental designs using as-if simulation of trance behavior as control groups in an effort to determine whether or not any given behavior is due to hypnosis or artifact. Erickson (Erickson & Rossi, 1979, 1981; Erickson, Rossi, & Rossi, 1976) took great pains to "ratify" the subjective experience of therapeutic trance so that it would be accepted as real or valid by the patient's personal belief system. Hypnosis could be well defined as the science of what is experienced as real and how these realities influence our mentation and behavior in sickness and health.

230

The most recent contributions to the phenomenon of as-if have been made independently by a number of clinicians and psychophysiologists. Marañon (1924) explored the then mysterious effects of epinepherine by injecting it into patients and asking them about their experience. About one-third reported that they felt something similar to an emotional state, and the remainder reported that they experienced a physiological state of arousal. Those who reported an emotional state recognized it was not real but rather *"as-if"* they were excited, afraid, or anticipating that something was about to happen. When Marañon talked to some of these patients about a recent and important event in their lives (i.e., a wedding, a death, etc.), however, their *as-if* emotion became converted into a real experience of full emotion.

Schachter and Singer (1962) later confirmed these results in more controlled laboratory experiments. They concluded that both physiological arousal (epinephrine injection) and a psychological belief were needed to experience an emotion. When either was missing, the experience had an as-if quality. This theory was further confirmed in another way by Hohmann (1966), who questioned patients with spinal cord injuries about the differences in their emotional experiences before and after their injury. He found that the higher the location of their injury in their spinal cords (thus eliminating progressively more of their bodies' sensory experience), the more frequently did they describe their emotions in terms of an "as-if" quality (Bloom, Lazerson, & Hofstadter, 1985).

The results of Marañon and Hohmann are complementary and supportive of a two-factor theory of real emotional experience. Marañon's patients experienced the as-if phenomenon when they had no appropriate cognitive cues to shape their physiological arousal. Hohmann's patients had the reverse situation: they reported the as-if experience when the right cognitive cues were present but lacked the possibility of actual physiological mediation. Thus both cognitive and physiological components are needed for a real emotion. This two-factor theory elucidates what is needed for a "sense of reality." *Our sense of reality is a state-dependent phenomenon based on the coordination of a certain level of physiological arousal with a specific cognitive label* (which can be a frame of reference or belief system). When either

231

is missing, we experience the as-if phenomenon. This state-dependent coordination of cognition and physiological arousal is important for the success of hypnotherapy in particular and psychotherapy in general, as we shall see in the next section.

Psychotherpy and State-Dependent Learning and Memory

The clinical implications of state-dependent learning in psychotherapy and hypnosis have been explored recently by many workers (Reus, Weingartner, & Post, 1979). These effects are to be expected and have been postulated when patients in psychotherapy are administered psychoactive drugs. The actual evidence for such state-dependent drug effects is still only marginal, however (Overton, 1978). Other workers (Peake, Van Noord, & Abbott, 1979) have focused on the psychotherapeutic process itself as being generative of an altered state of awareness because of the special context of the relationship with the therapist, the approach to the subject matter discussed, and the special setting of the therapeutic situation. These workers have found an equivalence between the concepts of state-dependent learning, Tart's state-specific knowledge, meditation, biofeedback, and hypnosis.

The limited scope of this section does not allow us to do anything more than merely suggest how many of the fundamental concepts of psychoanalysis and psychotherapy can be more adequately conceptualized in terms of state-dependent memory and learning and its natural consequent, statebound information and behavior. Terms such as ego, id, superego, creative unconscious, complex, archetype, attitude, role, state of development, personality trait, habits, sets, imprinting, fantasy, obsession, compulsion and transference can all be understood as statebound forms of information, behavior, and phenomenological experience that have heuristic value from a psychotherapeutic point of view. The classical psychoanalytical mechanisms of defense such as "regression, repression, reaction-formation, isolation, undoing, projection, introjection, turning against the self, [sublimation], and reversal" (Freud, 1946, p. 47) are all cognitive strategies for coping with the basic processes of statebound information in their relationships to the associative structures competing for conscious

232

awareness. From this point of view, we would hypothesize that so-called "psychological conflict" is a metaphor for competing patterns of state-dependent memory and learning. Reframing therapeutic concepts in terms of statebound patterns of information and behavior renders them immediately (1) more amenable to operational definition for experimental study in the laboratory, and (2) more available for active, therapeutic utilization than the traditional process of "analysis" and "understanding"—which unfortunately does not always lead to the desired goals of problem solving and behavior change (Erickson & Rossi, 1979; Rossi & Ryan, 1985).

What all the focal psychotherapeutic concepts have in common are processes of emotionality, dissociation, and amnesia. This can be illustrated with the concept of the "complex" as it was originally studied experimentally by C. G. Jung in the "association experiments," and as it was used by Sigmund Freud to describe the content of emotional conflicts. Jung described his view as follows (In Meier, 1984, pp. 112–112):

> At the end of the [association] experiment, the subject is questioned as to whether he correctly recalls the reaction he gave previously to each single stimulus-word; it then becomes apparent that forgetting normally takes place at or immediately after disturbances caused by a complex. We are in fact dealing with a kind of "Freudian forgetting." This procedure provides us with complex indicators which have proved to be of practical value.

Meier, who was one of Jung's closest associates, goes on to outline the experimental criteria for "complex indicators" as follows (Meier, 1984, p. 120):

> These take the form of "failures," lapses of memory reminiscent of the well-known phenomenon of "persistent amnesia," prolonged reaction-times, reactions in the form of sentences accompanied by intense feeling-tones, etc. In cases where a sexual complex is involved, what are known as screen-reactions tend to appear—i.e., contents are produced which are calculated to distract the experimenter from the

complex. This phenomenon, like the equally common "distraction by the environment," is interpreted in terms of Freud's mechanisms of repression and displacement. "The complex," again, is seen as the common denominator of all hysterical symptoms. The patients were treated mainly by hypnosis, as was still customary at that time owing to the influence of Auguste Forel. At the same time, Freud's discoveries were taken into account and in fact confirmed, since "free association" was employed to elucidate the complex reactions.

Meier continues (1984, p. 126):

Emotion, as the dynamic component of the complex, is responsible for the effects of the complex in the association experiment (the complex indicators) and also for the symptoms thrown up by complexes in psychiatric disorders. It is for this reason that "feeling-toned complexes" are so constantly mentioned in the literature of the period.

The entire edifice of depth psychology and modern psychotherapy could be said to rest upon this effort to explain the nature of emotional problems by these "feeling-toned complexes." The original therapeutic approach to resolving emotional problems was to access these complexes by hypnosis and its derivatives (free association, active imagination, guided imagery, etc.) in order to recover forgotten life experiences that were at the source of psychological disturbances. The accessing and recall of these forgotten sources of problems was a way of making available the statebound information that was expressed in the form of symptoms. The therapeutic ideal was to help the patient use the now conscious information to facilitate the transformation and maturation of the total personality while eradicating the need for symptomatic behavior.

When we shift from these original sources of depth psychology to the ideas of modern workers, we find the same state-dependent phenomena as the essential though generally unrecognized basis for their concepts. For example, the idea of the "creative unconscious" could be conceptualized as the repertory of state-dependent patterns of memory and learning that can be made available for problem solving. Erickson termed this inner repertory "experiential learnings." His suggestions were usually designed to access the memories of past experience and utilize them for current therapeutic needs (Erickson, 1985). For example, in one case in which he was attempting to relieve a woman of terminal cancer pain no longer responsive to morphine, Erickson proceeded as follows (Erickson & Rossi, 1979, pp. 133–134):

> I didn't want to try to struggle with her and tell her she should go into a trance, because that would be a rather futile thing. Therefore I asked her to do something that she could understand in her own reality orientations. I asked her to stay wide awake from the neck up. That was something she could understand. I told her to let her body go to sleep. In her past understandings as a child, as a youth, as a young woman, she had had the experience of a leg going to sleep, of an arm going to sleep. She had had the feeling of her body being asleep in that hypnagogic state of arousing in the morning when you are half awake, half asleep. I was very very certain the woman had some understanding of her body being asleep. Thus the woman could use her own past learnings. Just what that meant to her, I don't know. *All I wanted to do was to start a train of thinking and understanding that would allow the woman to call upon the past experiential learnings of her body.*

In this case Erickson used the state-dependent nature of comfort associated with the body being asleep to relieve the woman of her pain. Researchers (E. Hilgard, 1984) have wondered just exactly what Erickson meant by the term "creative unconscious." I believe that *state-dependent memory and learning* is an adequate experimental analogue to his use of "experiential learnings" of the creative unconscious for hypnotherapeutic problem solving.

When psychotherapists are unaware of the state-dependent nature of the learning taking place in the special context of therapy, the new insight and knowledge gained may not generalize to the rest of their patients' life situations. Patients can acquire a great

235

deal of understanding that is not used in real life because it is statebound to the therapy situation. Care must be taken to build associative connections between therapy and real-life contexts so that understanding can generalize. Hypnotherapists usually deal with this issue by using posthypnotic suggestions that associate a therapeutic process with a behavioral inevitability (Erickson & Rossi, 1979). Erickson's routine use of context (usually called "frames of reference" in Erickson & Rossi, 1979) and specific cuing of statebound information (Gage, 1983) will be described in a later section.

Reus *et al* (1979) has outlined three practical implications of state-dependent learning for psychotherapy. These are (1) *controlling the context* in which information is presented and generated; (2) *manipulation of arousal level;* and (3) *specific cuing* for evoking statebound information. The researchers base the "manipulation of arousal level" factor on studies that demonstrated how the pituitary peptides (especially vasopressin and adrenocorticotropic hormone) are of importance in emotional and contextual memory. As mentioned earlier, many of Erickson's highly unconventional hypnotherapeutic approaches have involved great reliance on this "manipulation of arousal level" factor.

4. The Psychology of State-Dependent Memory and Learning, Therapeutic Hypnosis, and Psychosomatic Problems

The main purpose in organizing the rows of Tables 2 and 3 was to outline the similarities and differences in the more or less independent lines of experimental research in hypnosis and SDLMB to determine what their common factors might be. A careful study of Tables 2 and 3 suggests at least two common factors:

(1) *External sensory cues and contexts generate distinctive acquisition conditions for both hypnosis and state-dependent learning (SDMLB).* This is especially evident in the last five rows of Tables 2 and 3 dealing with the lines of research in

physical and social contexts, belief systems, and psychotherapy.

(2) *Internal cues, often generated by distinctive levels of
biological arousal, mediate between the psychological and
physiological in both hypnosis and state-dependent learning
(SDMLB).* This is especially evident in the first four rows of
Tables 2 and 3 dealing with the lines of research on drugs,
biological rhythms, early life experience, and motivation,
mood, expectancy, and emotion.

In any real-life situation, of course, both of these factors—
external cues and contexts, and internal psychophysiological
processes—are parts of the same process. I would hypothesize that
the "new psychobiology" of dissociation, therapeutic hypnosis,
and SDMLB can be found in this common psychophysiological
denominator of Tables 2 and 3 (Rossi, 1986b). Recent research in
the neurobiology of memory and learning as represented by
McGaugh (1983) and his colleagues (McGaugh, Liang, Bennett,
& Sternberg, 1984) provides significant insights into the biochemistry (hormones and neurotransmitters) and anatomical locus
(midbrain reticular formation and limbic system) of these mind-
body connections. They summarized research on the effects of the
release of stress-related hormones on memory and learning as
follows (Gold & McGaugh, 1975, p. 375):

If the physiological consequences of an experience are
considerable, the organism would best retain that experience
for long periods of time. If the consequences are trivial, the
experience is best forgotten quickly. *Thus time-dependent
memory processes may be the result of the development of a
mechanism with which organisms select from recent experiences those that should be permanently stored.* [Italics
added]

McGaugh continues (1983, p. 163):

It is well known that sensory stimulation activates nonspecific brain systems. Several studies have shown that retention is influenced by electrical stimulation of the midbrain reticular formation. . . . *There is evidence that consolidation may involve activation of the amygdala and hippocampus [of the limbic system].* . . . Sensory stimulation also results in the release of hormones, including ACTH, epinephrine, vasopressin, and the opioid peptides, enkephalin and endorphin. A great deal of recent research has shown that learning and memory are affected by these hormones. . . . The convergence of these two lines of research has provided evidence strongly supporting the view that hormones released by experiences act to modulate the strength of the memory of the experience and suggest that central modulating influences on memory interact with influences of peripheral hormones [from the adrenals of the body]. [Italics added]

McGaugh's concept of *"time-dependent* memory processes," whose consolidation are a function of the "consequences of an experience" encoded under the influence of hormones, is typical of recent research on "endogenous state dependency" (Izquierdo, 1984) in the neurobiology of memory and learning. The essential identity between this neurobiology model of memory and learning and Overton's state-dependent model of memory and learning is outlined in the first two rows of Table 4. The *drugs* used to generate distinctive internal psychophysiological conditions associated with memory consolidation in Overton's experimental model of SDMLB correspond to the *hormones* that generate the correspondingly distinctive internal conditions for the consolidation of memory and learning discussed by McGaugh. I believe this correspondence is a paradigm for most of the mind-body connections postulated and validated to varying degrees by the lines of research summarized in Tables 1, 2, and 3—as well as those to be presented in Tables 4, 5, and 6.

The last two rows of Table 4 are an integration and matching of Erickson's concepts of the psychoneurophysiological basis of hypnotic phenomena and psychosomatic medicine, Selye's theory of psychosomatic problems, and the concepts of drug and endogenous state-dependent memory, learning, and behavior. This matching suggests how state-dependent learning, therapeutic hypnosis, and psychosomatic problems are all aspects of the same class of psychobiological phenomena. The central role of the limbic-hypothalamic system in all these phenomena indicates that it is the core of what Selye (1976) called the "General Adaptation Syndrome" (GAS), and what Erickson (1944/1980) called the "psycho-neuro-physiological" basis of hypnotherapy. Selye and Erickson both contributed profoundly original observations to our understanding of psychosomatic phenomena—Selye primarily from physiological experimentation; Erickson primarily from empirical psychological investigations. Integrating their work leads to a more comprehensive understanding of *psychophysiological dysfunctions,* which may be expressed as follows: *Psychosomatic symptoms are acquired by a process of experiential learning, specifically the state-dependent learning of response patterns of the General Adaptation Syndrome. Enduring psychosomatic problems are manifestations of statebound patterns of the GAS. Therapeutic hypnosis resolves psychosomatic problems by accessing, utilizing, and reframing these statebound patterns of the GAS.*

The first stages of Selye's General Adaptation Syndrome—the alarm reaction, the stage of resistance, and the stage of exhaustion—take on a profoundly new significance in the light of the more recent research in state-dependent memory and learning. The initial alarm reaction is characterized by the activation of the sympathetic branch of the autonomic nervous system which stimulates the release of epinephrine and norepinephrine from the adrenal medullae. As we saw earlier in McGaugh's and Izquierdo's research, these are the same hormones that modulated the retention of memory. *Learning and memory acquired during Selye's alarm reaction therefore tends to be state-dependent!* A person in a traumatic car accident experiences an intense rush of the alarm reaction hormones. His detailed memories of the accident are now intertwined with the complex psychophysiological state associated with these hormones. When he returns to his "normal" psychophysiological state of awareness a few hours or days later, the memories of the accident become fuzzy or, in severe cases, the victim may become completely amnesic: the memories of the accident have become statebound, and they are bound to the precise psychophysiological stated encoded by the hormones of

Table 4: A matching of the basic terms and processes of SDMLB, the neurobiology of memory and learning, hypnotic phenomena, and stress-induced psychosomatic problems. The mind-body communication is mediated by the limbic-hypothalamic system in all four situations.

Acquisition/ Induction	Mind-Body Connection	Dissociated/ Statebound Behavior	Access/ Recall	Reference
Distinctive cues associated with *state-dependent memory and learning experiences*	*Drugs* generate distinctive internal psychophysiological conditions associated with memory	Drug state-dependent memory and learning	Similar internal and external cues	Overton, 1968, 1978
Distinctive cues associated with the *neurobiology of memory and learning experiments*	*Hormones* generate distinctive internal psychophysiological conditions associated with memory	Endogenous state-dependent memory and learning	Similar internal and external cues	Izquierdo, 1984; McGaugh, 1983

| Distinctive cues associated with *hypnotic induction* | *Psycho-neuro-physiological* basis of hypnosis | Hypnotic phenomena; coincidental phenomena; encode state-bound psychosomatic symptoms | Hypnotic accessing of statebound memory; shock | Erickson, 1943a, b, c, & d/1980 |
| Distinctive cues associated with *stress* | *Stress-released hormones* of the GAS encodes symptoms | Statebound GAS expressed as psychosomatic symptoms | Shock; nonspecific therapies; autohypnosis | Selye, 1974, 1976, 1982; Benson, 1983a & b |

the alarm reaction, together with its associated sensory impressions.

Selye's next stage, the *stage of resistance,* is the period during which psychosomatic symptoms become particularly evident and troublesome. In our car accident example, the psychosomatic response could be any part of the alarm reaction that was originally experienced—anxiety, pain, hysterical paralysis, headaches, ulcers, etc. The victim is stuck with a subtle "problem of adaptation" which traditional physical medicine does not know how to deal with. This is especially the case when the initial cause of the stress (such as the car accident) has disappeared and yet the mind-body, having learned a new defensive (psychosomatic) mode of adaptation, continues with it. *The psychosomatic mode of adaptation was learned under state-dependent conditions; it continues because it remains statebound and prevents the normal psychophysiological pattern from reinstating itself.*

Selye had a number of solutions for the psychosomatic problems manifested during this *stage of resistance.* Most typically, medication could be used to counteract the stressor hormones or, in extreme cases, surgery could remove the adrenals that produced the hormones. Selye frequently described this stage of resistance as being "stuck in a groove." That was his way of describing what we now recognize as statebound psychophysiological behavior. Selye reasoned that if a shock could get one stuck in a groove, perhaps another shock could get one out again so that the person could "snap out of disease" (Selye, 1976, p. 9). Selye believed that the various forms of shock (electroconvulsive and insulin shock treatment for the mentally ill, psychological shock, etc.) were types of *nonspecific therapies* that counteracted many of the *nonspecific aspects* of the GAS. This relationship between shock and the nonspecific approach to psychosomatic problems has an almost exact though previously unrecognized correspondence to Erickson's use of psychological shock as a general (nonspecific) approach to evoking a variety of hypnotic phenomena and dealing with a variety of emotional problems (Rossi, 1973/1980).

Erickson's original contributions to the field of psychosomatic medicine are contained in four papers that were published together in the January 1943 issue *Psychosomatic Medicine* (1943a,b,c,d/ 1980). These papers on the *psychological* components of psychosomatic phenomena summarized the results of a decade of wide-ranging experimental and clinical hypnotic work that took place during the same period when Selye was making his fundamental discovery of the *physiological* components. In a sense, their research was both complementary and reciprocal: Selye discovered the same physiological response to different stressors in what he termed the "General Adaptation Syndrome"; Erickson discovered psychologically different responses to the same stressor in what he termed "coincidental phenomena." Taken together, their work provides a comprehensive picture of the genesis and methods of resolving psychosomatic problems.

From the point of view developed here, we would characterize Erickson's "coincidental phenomena" as manifestations of the individual statebound patterns of information and behavior that each person acquires as a result of his or her particular life history of experiential learning. These individual patterns are the basis of each person's unique repertory of hypnotic responsiveness that can be utilized therapeutically. This retrospective analysis also enables us to understand that all of the classical hypnotic phenomena (amnesia, age regression, automatic writing, hallucination), which are described as manifestations of "mental dissociation," are actually partial aspects of that type of state-dependent memory and learning that Erickson called "coincidental phenomena." When a person is subjected to undue stress over a period of time, however, these "coincidental phenomena" become the psychobiological "raw material" out of which the person unconsciously can create one or more psychosomatic symptoms. Tables 5 and 6 outline a variety of traumatic and stressful life conditions that activate the autonomic, endocrine, immune, and neuropeptide systems to encode endogenous state-dependent memory, learning, and behavior that may be experienced as coincidental phenomena, hypnotic phenomena, or psychosomatic symptoms. All of these conditions are resolvable by therapeutic hypnosis, which can access statebound information and make it available for problem solving (Rossi, 1986b).

Table 5: A variety of traumatic/clinical acquisition conditions that evoke the alarm response via the autonomic and endocrine systems, to encode statebound information, behavior, and symptoms that are resolvable by therapeutic hypnosis.

Acquisition/ Induction	Mind-Body Connection	Dissociated/ Statebound Behavior	Access/ Recall	Reference
Traumatic war experiences	Emotional distress	War neuroses; nightmares	Drug-facilitated hypnosis	Grinker & Spiegel, 1945; Kubie, 1943; Watkins, 1949
Murder in public	"Greatly agitated state"; hormonal and neuroendocrine modulation of memory	Amnesia	Hypnosis	Sirhan-Sirhan in 1968 (Bower, 1981)
Homicidal assault	Unconsciousness via poison and blow to head	Amnesia, unconsciousness	Hypnosis	Erickson, 1937/1980

Surgical anesthesia	Chemical anesthesia	Amnesia and problematic healing	Ideomotor signaling	Bennett *et al*, 1986; Cheek, 1959, 1981; Levinson, 1965
Childbirth	Heightened emotions, chemical anesthesia	Amnesia	Ideomotor signaling	Barnett, 1984; Bowers, 1981; Cheek, 1975, 1976; Erickson & Rossi, 1979
Critical Illness	Psychophysiological distress	Amnesia	Ideomotor signaling	Cheek, 1969
Accidents	Psychophysiological trauma	Hemorrhage	Ideomotor signaling	Cheek, 1965; Selye, 1976
Dreams (traumatic)	REM state	Amnesia	Ideomotor signaling, hypnosis	Cheek, 1965; Evans, 1972

Table 6: A variety of typical life stress situations that generate statebound information, behavior, and problems, encoded by the autonomic and endocrine systems, and resolvable by therapeutic hypnosis.

Acquisition/ Induction	Mind-Body Connection	Dissociated/ Statebound Behavior	Access/ Recall	Reference
Early life deprivation	State-dependent identity flux	Memory and identity creation	Hypnosis	J. Hilgard, 1972; J. Hilgard & LeBaron, 1984
Sexual assault	"Hypnotically stunned"	Multiple personality	Hypnosis	Braun, 1983a & b; Lienhart, 1983
Double bind communication in families	State-dependent family consensus	Behavioral problems and symptoms	Hypnosis	Ritterman, 1983

Work and performance	Autonomic/endocrine arousal for performance optimization	Arousal levels	Hypnosis	Blum, 1972; Sarbin & Coe, 1972
Witness situations	Psychophysiological shock & arousal	Pseudomemories, confabulation	Hypnosis	Orne, 1979
Demonstration hypnosis	Stage arousal	Potent therapeutic effects	Hypnosis	Rogers, 1985
Deep hypnosis	State-dependent identity shifts	Life reframing	Hypnosis	Erickson & Rossi, 1979

Summary

In the final Part of this volume, we have reviewed an unusually rich and complex fabric of ideas about mind-body communication and healing. We began by outlining an information theory of modern hypnotherapy that brings us closer to understanding the core of Erickson's utilization or naturalistic approaches. Evidence was presented for the view that *state-dependent memory and learning* is the basic process that makes up the repertory of each individual's life learnings that are utilized in hypnotherapy. We have integrated the pioneering work of Hans Selye and Milton Erickson to conceptualize psychosomatic problems as state-bound patterns of information and behavior that become functionally autonomous. This state-dependent memory and learning theory of therapeutic hypnosis enables us to more adequately understand and facilitate the resolution of many forms of psychosomatic and personality problems caused by stress and traumatic life circumstances. The key to mind-body communication and healing is to access and reframe the state-dependent memory and learning systems that encode symptoms and life problems.

APPENDIX

STATEBOUND INFORMATION AND
BEHAVIOR IN THE HISTORY OF HYPNOSIS

Acquisition Conditions of Historical Hypnosis

Table 7 lists a wide range of acquisition conditions used in historical hypnosis. The common denominator between these historical approaches to hypnosis, those of modern hypnosis (listed in Table 3), and the acquisition conditions of statebound memory and learning (listed in Table 2) is that they all utilize special cues, conditions, motivations, belief systems, and expectations to place the hypnotic experience outside the context of ordinary life and normal relationships. Here we will survey briefly the variety of acquisition conditions developed in both historical and modern hypnosis.

Father Johann Gassner (1727–1779) was a Catholic priest who utilized the belief system of the Church to fixate the attention of his parishioner-patients. He would begin by asking whether they were ready to do anything he commanded. If they agreed, he would proceed with mysterious, thunderous demands in Latin such as, "If there be anything preternatural about this disease, I order in the name of Jesus that it manifest itself immediately!" When his parishioner-patients responded with frightened convulsions, Gassner took it as proof that the illness was due to spirits. He then demonstrated his power to control the spirits by directing the convulsions to different parts of the body, and finally ordering them expelled from the fingertips and toes. He then sometimes offered practical advice on preventing the recurrence of the symptom. The fact that some of Gassner's patients had only vague

Table 7: Acquisition/induction conditions and proposed mind-body connections for the phenomena of historical hypnosis.

Acquisition/ Induction	Mind-Body Connection	Statebound Behavior	Access/ Recall	Reference
Religious command	Healing by exorcism of evil spirits	Convulsive crisis, symptom, displacement, amnesia	Religious command	Gassner, 1770 (Ellenberger, 1970)
"Passes" transferring magnetic influence operating through Mesmerist	Animal magnetism and body fluids in disequilibrium	Convulsive crisis, rapport, amnesia	Magnetic influence	Mesmer, 1779 (Tinterow, 1970; Sheehan & Perry, 1976)
Touch and mental transference	Magnetism	Artificial and lucid somnambulism, auto-suggestion, amnesia, hypersensitivity	Mental transference	Puysegur, 1784 (Tinterow, 1970)

Eye fixation on hand with direct suggestion, "Sleep"	Concentration, thin blood	Lucid sleep, taste hallucinations, individual differences, posthypnotic suggestion, placebo	Direct suggestion	Faria, 1819, (Perry, 1978)
Mesmeric passes	"Mesmeric torpor of the brain"	Anesthesia	Reverse passes	Esdaile, 1850/1957
Physical and magnetic suggestion	Hysterical neurosis	Lethargy, catalepsy, somnambulism; posttraumatic and hysterical paralyses	Posthypnotic suggestion	Charcot, 1878 (Tinterow, 1970)
Eye fixation on luminous object and suggestion	"Psychophysiology"	Amnesia, hallucinations	Eye fixation and suggestion	Braid, 1855 (Tinterow, 1970)
Eye fixation and direct suggestion	Exaltation of ideomotor and sensory reflexes	Ideodynamic behavior	Direct suggestion, "psychotherapeutics"	Bernheim, 1886/1957

memories of the dramatic exorcism they had experienced (Ellenberger, 1970) indicates that an amnesia (a condition of statebound information) was unwittingly generated by these unusual contexts—just as we would expect from current experiments on state-dependent learning and memory.

Quaint as this exorcism procedure may seem, it remains, remarkably enough, an adequate four-stage model for the way many "sophisticated" modern practitioners operate today. Most practitioners access the patient's belief system and seek to utilize it to inspire faith in the practitioner's methods. They then frequently "prescribe the symptom" (Zeig, 1980a, b, 1985), seeking to turn it on and off and/or altering and transforming its expression in some way (Rossi, 1986b). Having thus demonstrated their control over it (the symptom's compliance with therapeutic belief system), the modern practitioner then "suggests it gone" either directly or more indirectly by asking the patient's "unconscious" to resolve it. The successful work is usually terminated by helping the patient correct the errors of a past belief system and by providing ways of reframing an understanding in a therapeutic manner. This process is well exemplified by Erickson's work (Erickson & Rossi, 1979; in particular, see the cases cited in Chapters 6 through 8).

Mesmer (1734–1815) changed the belief system and context of such healings from the realm of religion to a primitive, psychophysiological view by conceptualizing a type of energy which he called "animal magnetism," that realigned the source of illness in the imbalance of bodily fluids. Here again, however, acquisition conditions for the "mesmeric state" were generated by "mysterious passes" with magnets over the subject's body, and by dramatic proceedings that included placing 30 people tightly packed together in a baquet—a circular oak cask with powdered glass, iron fillings, and bottles of "magnetized" water. Under such unusual conditions of heightened expectations, patients fell into convulsive fits that apparently relieved or reframed some of their psychosomatic symptoms into health. The spontaneous amnesias that followed many of these convulsive catharses were again an indication of dissociation and a realignment of the patient's associative patterns of statebound information as an intrinsic part of the healing process.

Essentially the same situation continues with the other major figures in the history of hypnosis. Marquis de Puysequr (1751–1825), who was Mesmer's follower, developed less flambouyant approaches yet his position as a nobleman was one that gave his touch and presence a special influence which transported his peasant-patients out of the normal context of their ordinary lives. Here we see a special acquisition condition in the form of a role relationship, together with a belief system that supported the idea of healing through "mental transference." This was sufficient to generate the intense rapport and posthypnotic amnesia so characteristic of therapeutic trance.

Puysequr's discovery of artificial somnambulism was characteristic of the way most hypnotic phenomena were discovered: The subject taught the hypnotist. Puysequr's subject, Victor Race, effected greater intelligence and sensitivity in trance (thus the term "lucid somnambulism") than he did in his normal awake state. So hypersensitive was Victor when in trance that he began to sing aloud tunes which Puysequr was singing to himself only in his mind! In his apparent eagerness to please, *Victor took to reading Puysequr's lips!* Puysequr unfortunately misinterpreted such hypersensitivities as clairvoyance. Erickson (1932/1980) recognized this hypersensitive responsiveness to minimal cues and nuances of the hypnotist's verbal and nonverbal communications to be a more adequate interpretation of what the hypnotic subject actually experiences than to attribute it to "hypersuggestibility."

Esdaile (1808–1859) used essentially the same theory of mesmeric influence when he had his assistants make mysterious "passes" with their hands over the patient's body for hours, until an adequate surgical anesthesia was obtained by dissociating sensation from its normal context. In the days prior to the discovery of ether, there certainly was a heightened motivation to learn such dissociations: It was the only way of escaping the horrible fate of crude surgery! In addition, Esdaille was living in India at the time; perhaps the strangeness of the Western man's procedures placed the Indian patient into a state of psychological shock which was easily converted into an obedient state of dissociative anesthesia and amnesia (or state-dependent memory and learning).

Abbe Faria (1775–1856) took an important step in the development of hypnosis by freeing it from erroneous ideas about magnetic influence and recognizing the vital role of direct suggestion by the therapist and "concentration" by the subject. He was mistaken in believing that the essential mind/body connection was mediated by the thickness or thinness of the blood, but he rightly recognized the importance of the placebo effect and of individual differences in the subjective experience of hypnosis. He disagreed with the findings of the Benjamin Franklin Commission of 1784 by maintaining that the essence of hypnosis was not imagination and suggestion but rather the subject's "superior powers of concentration" (Perry, 1978). In this sense, Faria was very close to our modern views of focused thinking, feeling, and imagination as the basis of hypnotic experience. Many current theorists are exploring the possibility that this focus or "concentration" has something to do with the specialized abilities of the right hemisphere. Part III of this volume outlined evidence for the view that the right hemisphere's closer association with the statebound patterns of information filtered through the limbic-hypothalamic system may account for many of the mind/body effects of modern hypnotherapy.

Charcot (1835–1893) of the Nancy school was called "the Napoleon of the neurosis." He was a very important figure who used the clinical demonstrations, mysterious jargon, and belief systems of the medical world of his day to generate the special acquisition conditions for the states he attributed to hysterical neurosis.

Bernheim (1837–1919) opposed Charcot's psychopathological theories of the origins of hypnosis. He was closer to our modern view in believing that direct suggestion was sufficient to provoke an "exaltation of the ideomotor and ideosensory reflexes" for therapeutic purposes, even without the need for any elaborate induction procedure (Weitzenhoffer, 1978). Our popular current-day methods of using minimal cues and ideomotor head and finger signaling also derive directly from his work. The involuntary or autonomous nature of these responses was part of the acquisition condition that placed his healing procedures outside normal contexts and thus generated what we now term *state-dependent memory and learning.*

Outrageous and comical as many of these methods of historical hypnosis may seem, they all share the same four essential processes that define current-day studies on state-dependent memory and learning as outlined in Table 1:

1) unusual cue conditions during the original acquisition or induction experience;
2) distinctive or "altered" psychophysiological states;
3) the encoding of statebound information and behavior; and
4) retrieval of statebound information and behavior via the reinstatement of the distinctive cues or acquisition conditions under which they were first acquired.

In this broader context, *dissociation may be understood as one aspect of the more general four-stage process of state-dependent memory, learning and behavior (SDMLB) which more completely defines the class of phenomena usually described as "therapeutic hypnosis."* We will continue to use this four-stage paradigm of hypnosis or SDMLB to outline the acquisition conditions used in modern hypnosis.

Acquisition Conditions of Modern Hypnosis

How shall we make sense of the fact that current-day experts maintain that the acquisition conditions for hypnotic induction and trance can range from "nothing" to "everything"? T.X. Barber (1972) and Reyher (1977) have both marshalled experimental data to demonstrate their view that no induction is needed and no special state of hypnosis or trance is required for the experience of so-called hypnotic behavior. Erickson (1959/1980), on the other hand, maintained and demonstrated that any behavior manifested by the subject could be utilized as a hypnotic induction.

The apparent contradiction between the "nothing and everything" conceptions of hypnotic induction is easily resolved if we look at what each actually means operationally. In a "Historical Note on the Hand Levitation and Other Ideomotor Techniques,"

Erickson summarized his approach to trance induction with these words (1961/1980, p. 138):

> The essential consideration in the use of ideomotor techniques lies not in their elaborateness or novelty but simply in the initiation of motor activity, either real or hallucinated, as *a means of fixing and focusing the subject's attention upon inner experiential learnings and capacities.*

The entire panorama of Erickson's approaches to trance induction and therapy have this single purpose: focusing attention inward to access and utilize inner resources for problem solving (Erickson & Rossi, 1976/1980).

Reyher apparently took the reverse point of view when he stated (1977, p. 69):

> The seemingly inexhaustible techniques of inducing hypnosis implies [sic] that the induction of hypnosis has nothing to do with the induction procedure *per se,* and that the gradual development of an alleged state of hypnosis is an illusion, an artifact of the induction procedure.

Yet, incredibly, Reyher recommends the following approach which seems no different from the early authoritarian acquisition conditions that were so characteristic of historical hypnosis (1977, p. 84):

> In order to induce hypersuggestibility, level II, the practitioner is advised to adopt a paternalistic or maternalistic demeanor and to reinforce his/her image as an authoritative, helpful professional by displaying impressive credentials in a setting reinforcing these connotative meanings.

What Reyher hopes to motivate by this authoritarian stance, however, is the very same inward focusing of attention that is the essence of Erickson's approach. Reyher hopes thereby to "foster the adoption of a passive-receptive attitude" by the subject so that "expressive semantic-syntactic modes of the left cerebral hemisphere are suspended . . . and the analogic synthetic mode [of the

256

right hemisphere] incorporates the instructions [of the therapist]" (Reyher, 1977, p. 80). Thus while Reyher may protest that no hypnotic induction or special state is required, the operations he recommends to facilitate "hypersuggestibility II" are similar to the authoritative acquisition conditions of historical hypnosis; and the psychophysiological processes he proposes to evoke right- versus left-hemispheric processing are identical with those utilized by modern state theorists.*

T.X. Barber has organized an incisive body of experimental data to support what he calls "an alternative paradigm" in contrast to the traditional historical model of hypnosis. He formulated it as follows (Barber, 1972, pp. 119–120):

> There is another way of viewing responsiveness to test suggestions that does not involve special state constructs such as "hypnosis," "hypnotized," "hypnotic state," or "trance." This alternative paradigm does not see a qualitative difference in the "state" of the person who is and the one who is not responsive to test suggestions. Although the alternative paradigm has many historical roots (discussed by Sarbin, 1962), it derives primarily from my more recent theoretical endeavors and those of Sarbin (Barber, 1964a, 1967, 1969b, 1970a; Sarbin, 1950; Sarbin & Andersen, 1967; Sarbin & Coe, in press). An analogy to members of an audience watching a motion picture or a stage play may clarify the paradigm . . . .
>
> Although the member of the audience who is responding to the words of the actors and the experimental subject who is responding to the test suggestions of the experimenter have similar attitudes, motivations, and expectancies toward the communications and are similarly "thinking with" the communications, *they are being exposed to different types of communications.* . . .

*See Erickson, Rossi, & Rossi, 1976, and Erickson & Rossi, 1979, for clinical approaches to depotentiating the left hemisphere while enhancing right-hemispheric processing.

257

From this viewpoint, the member of the audience and the subject who is responding to test suggestions are having different experiences, *not because they are in different "states" but because they are receiving different communications.*

The purpose of these task-motivational instructions was to produce favorable motivations, attitudes, and expectancies toward the test situation and to heighten the subject's willingness to imagine and think about those things that would be suggested. They were worded as follows (Barber, 1972, pp. 124–125):

In this experiment I'm going to test your ability to imagine and to visualize. How well you do on the tests which I will give you depends entirely upon your willingness to try to imagine and to visualize the things I will ask you to imagine. . . . What I ask is your cooperation in helping this experiment by trying to imagine vividly what I describe to you. I want you to score as high as you can because we're trying to measure the maximum ability of people to imagine. If you don't try to the best of your ability, this experiment will be worthless and I'll tend to feel silly.

While these "task-motivational instructions" are less flamboyant than the command to "Sleep!" of historical hypnosis, they are nonetheless wonderfully appropriate for modern students (on whom Barber does most of his work) who are cognitively oriented and anxious to please their instructor in this special acquisition condition which is now called an "experiment" rather than a "hypnotic induction." The object of these task motivational instructions is to turn the subject's attention inward in order to access inner resources, just as it is with modern state theorists. Further, Barber's view that subjects "are receiving different communications" is entirely in keeping with Bernheim who originally described hypnotic communications as "ideodynamic." Erickson and Rossi also focused on ideodynamic communication as the essence of the art of therapeutic suggestion in their paper on "The Indirect Forms of Suggestion" (1980), in which they outlined over two dozen approaches for facilitating a patient's associative processes for problem solving.

Thus, while there has been much controversy and many different models and theories of hypnosis proposed by modern investigators, the actual procedures used are essentially similar to those of historical hypnosis. Both state and nonstate theorists today have special acquisition conditions that they use to facilitate dissociation which we now call "state-dependent learning and memory." Like the practitioners of historical hypnosis, modern investigators all propose some form of altered psychophysiological functioning in their subjects. This theorized functioning typically ranges from the special arousal conditions of emotionally motivating instructions, to the processing of information differently in the right and left cerebral hemispheres. Another common denominator of the modern approaches is to be found in the way they access statebound information. Historical hypnosis has called this accessing "ideodynamic communication." Whereas the typical communication of everyday life deals with some specific content about the outside world, ideodynamic or hypnotic communication is designed solely to evoke and facilitate specific processes and experiences within the subject. Ideodynamic communication does not give the subject new cognitions but rather seeks to motivate and facilitate the subject's own inner resources in accessing experiences that are not usually available to voluntary ego control.

We are now in a better position to understand the significance of the three basic propositions with which we began Part III of this volume. Mind/body problems are breakdowns in communication that lead to the formation of statebound information. Therapeutic hypnosis is a process designed to access and utilize this statebound information for therapeutic purposes.

Footnotes: Part I

1. This presentation served as the original source material for Erickson's later paper on the "Control of Physiologic Functions by Hypnosis," which was published by *The American Journal of Clinical Hypnosis* in 1977. (See Erickson, 1977/1980).

2. Erickson thus recommends the use of indirect suggestion to avoid the problem of simulating or faking hypnotic responses. His efforts to avoid the subject's conscious cooperation and complaisance are detailed in Erickson, 1967/1980.

3. See Erickson, 1980a.

4. See Bateson, Jackson, Haley, and Weakland, 1956; see also Erickson, 1960c/1980.

5. See Volume II of Erickson 1980c for detailed presentations of his experiments with hypnotic deafness.

6. See Sears, 1932.

7. Erickson's subtle exploration of the interrelationships between hypnotic phenomena and cues from apparently unrelated sensory modalities is detailed in Erickson 1943c/1980.

8. Erickson is actually inducing a temporary form of "experimental neurosis" or "therapeutic implant" to resolve a real neurosis in these cases. See Rossi's comments on "The Psychodynamics of Hypnotherapy with Experimental Neuroses: Hypothesis about 'Therapeutic Implants.'" In Volume IV of Erickson, 1980c, pp. 339–341.

9. Erickson is referring to *Experimental Hypnosis* (LeCron, 1948).

10. See Erickson, 1944/1980.

11. For a full survey of Erickson's writings on hypnotic deafness, see Section II of Volume II of Erickson, 1980c. In particular, see Erickson, 1938a & b.

12. See Locke and Hornig-Rohan, 1983.

13. See Erickson and Erickson, 1941/1980, wherein the Ericksons propose the novel idea that a very subtle posthypnotic trance accompanies the execution of posthypnotic suggestions. Often, therefore, there is an amnesia for the execution of the posthypnotic act.

14. See Erickson, 1941/1980.
15. See Bowers, 1981, and E. Hilgard, 1981a & b.
16. See LeCron, 1948.
17. See Section 7 in Volume III of Erickson, 1980c.
18. For a discussion of the pathological versus therapeutic uses of self-reflection, see Rossi, 1972/1985. See also Wilber, 1982, for a transpersonal approach to the use of self-reflection in many forms of psychotherapy.
19. Erickson later overcame his reluctance to use hypnosis with children and even wrote a paper on the subject (Erickson, 1958/1980).
20. See Erickson, 1939/1980.

Footnotes: Part II

1. See Erickson and Rossi, 1975.
2. See Erickson, Haley, and Weakland, 1959.
3. See Erickson and Rossi, 1981, and Erickson, Rossi, and Rossi, 1976, for detailed explications of the handshake induction.
4. See Erickson and Rossi, 1976/1980, for extensive discussion of the microdynamics of two-level communication in therapeutic work.
5. See Erickson and Rossi, 1974, and Erickson, Rossi, and Rossi, 1976, for discussions of structured amnesias.
6. See Erickson, Rossi, and Rossi, 1976, for an explication of "not knowing" in trance induction.
7. See Erickson and Rossi, 1981, for a discussion of catalepsy.
8. See Cooper and Erickson, 1959.

References

Barber, T.X. (1972). Suggested ("hypnotic") behavior: The trance paradigm versus an alternate paradigm. In E. Fromm & R. Shor (Eds.), *Hypnosis: Research development and perspectives*. New York: Aldine-Atherton, pp. 115–182.

Barber, T.X. (1978). Hypnosis, suggestions, and psychosomatic phenomena: A new look from the standpoint of recent experimental studies. *American Journal of Clinical Hypnosis, 21*(1), 13–27.

Barber, T.X. (1984). Changing unchangeable bodily processes by (hypnotic) suggestions: A new look at hypnosis, cognitions, imagining, and the mind-body problem. *Advances, 1*(2), 7–40.

Barnett, E. (1984). The role of prenatal trauma in the development of the negative birth experience. Paper presented at the American Society of Clinical Hypnosis Annual Meeting, San Francisco.

Bass, M. (1931). Differentiation of the hypnotic trance from normal sleep. *Journal of Experimental Psychology, 14*, 382–399.

Bateson, G., Jackson, D., Haley, J., & Weakland, J. (1956). Toward a theory of schizophrenia. *Behavior Science, 1*, 215–264.

Bennett, H., Hamilton, S., Giannini, J. (1986). Nonverbal response to intraoperative conversation. *British Journal of Anaesthesia.* (In press).

Benson, H. (1983a). The relaxation response and norepinephrine: A new study illuminates mechanisms. *Integrative Psychiatry, 1*, 15–18.

Benson, H. (1983b). The relaxation response: Its subjective and objective historical precedents and physiology. *Trends in Neuroscience,* July, 281–284.

Bernheim, H. (1886/1957). *Suggestive therapeutives: A treatise on the nature and uses of hypnotism.* Westport, Conn.: Associated Booksellers. Originally published by Putnam.

Bloom, F., Lazerson, A., & Hofstadter, L. (1985). *Brain, mind, and behavior.* New York: W. H. Freeman.

Blum, G. (1967). Experimental observations on the contextual nature of hypnosis. *International Journal of Clinical & Experimental Hypnosis, 15*(4), 160–171.

262

Blum, G. (1972). Hypnotic programming techniques in psychological experiments. In E. Fromm, & R. Shor (Eds.), *Hypnosis: Research developments & perspectives.* Chicago: Aldine-Atherton, pp. 359–385.

Bower, G. (1981). Mood and memory. *American Psychologist, 36* (2), 129–148.

Bowers, K. (1977). Hypnosis: An informational approach. *Annals of the New York Academy of Science, 296,* 222–237.

Bowers, K. (1981). Has the sun set on the Stanford Scales? *The American Journal of Clinical Hypnosis, 24*(2), 79–88.

Bowers, K., & Bowers, P. (1972). Hypnosis and creativity. In E. Fromm & R. Shor (Eds.), *Hypnosis: Research developments and perspectives.* Chicago: Aldine-Atherton.

Braun, B. (1983a). Neurophysiologic changes in multiple personality due to integration: A preliminary report. *The American Journal of Clinical Hypnosis, 26*(2), 84–92.

Braun, B. (1983b). Psychophysiological phenomena in multiple personality. *The American Journal of Clinical Hypnosis, 26*(2), 124–137.

Cheek, D. (1957). Effectiveness of incentive in clinical hypnosis. *Obstetrics & Gynecology, 9*(6), 720–724.

Cheek, D. (1959). Unconscious perception of meaningful sounds during surgical anesthesia as revealed under hypnosis. *The American Journal of Clinical Hypnosis, 1,* 101–113.

Cheek, D. (1960). Removal of subconscious resistance to hypnosis using ideomoter questioning techniques. *The American Journal of Clinical Hypnosis, 3*(2), 103–107.

Cheek, D. (1965). Some newer understandings of dreams in relation to threatened abortion and premature labor. *Pacific Medical & Surgical,* Nov-Dec, 379–384.

Cheek, D. (1969). Communication with the critically ill. *The American Journal of Clinical Hypnosis, 12*(2), 75–85.

Cheek, D. (1975). Maladjustment patterns apparently related to imprinting at birth. *The American Journal of Clinical Hypnosis, 18*(2), 75–82.

Cheek, D. (1976). Short-term hypnotherapy for fragility using exploration of early life attitudes. *The American Journal of Clinical Hypnosis, 19,*(1), 20–27.

Cheek, D. (1981). Awareness of meaningful sounds under general anesthesia: Considerations and a review of the literature, 1959–1979. *Theoretical and Clinical Aspects of Hypnosis.* Symposium Specialists, Miami, Florida.

Cheek, D., & LeCron, L. (1968). *Clinical hypnotherapy.* New York: Grune & Stratton.

Chiba, Y., Chiba, K., Halberg, F., & Cutkomp, L. (1977). Longitudinal evaluation of circadian rhythm characteristics and their circaseptan modulation in an apparently normal couple. In J. McGovern, M. Smolensky, & A. Reinberg (Eds.), *Chronobiology in allergy and immunology.* Springfield, Illinois: Thomas, pp. 17–35.

Cooper, L., & Erickson, M. (1959). Time distortion in hypnosis (2nd ed.). Baltimore: Williams & Wilkins.

Cunningham, A. (1986). Information and health in the many levels of man. *Advances, 3*(1), 32–45.

Dafter, R. (1978). From sunbeam to brain: Communication potential in an expanding complexity. Unpublished paper: New York University.

Delbruck, M. (1970). A physicist's renewed look at biology: Twenty years later. *Science, 168*, 1312–1314.

Ellengerger, H. (1970). The discovery of the unconscious. New York: Basic Books.

Erickson, M. (1932/1980). Possible detrimental effects of experimental hypnosis. In E. Rossi (Ed.), *The collected papers of Milton H. Erickson on Hypnosis. I. The nature of hypnosis and suggestion.* New York: Irvington, pp. 493–497.

Erickson, M. (1937/1980). Development of apparent unconsciousness during hypnotic reliving of a traumatic experience. In E. Rossi (Ed.), *The collected papers of Milton H. Erickson on hypnosis. III. Hypnotic investigation of psychodynamic processes.* New York: Irvington, pp. 45–52.

Erickson, M. (1938a/1980). A study of clinical and experimental findings on hypnotic deafness: I. Clinical experimentation and findings. In E. Rossi (Ed.), *The collected papers of Milton H. Erickson on hypnosis. II. Hypnotic alteration of sensory, perceptual and psychophysical processes.* New York: Irvington, pp. 81–99.

Erickson, M. (1938b/1980). A study of clinical and experimental findings on hypnotic deafness: II. Conditioned response technique. In E. Rossi (Ed.), *The collected papers of Milton H. Erickson on hypnosis. II. Hypnotic alteration of sensory, perceptual, and psychophysical processes.* New York: Irvington, pp. 100–113.

Erickson, M. (1939/1980). An experimental investigation of the possible antisocial use of hypnosis. In E. Rossi (Ed.), *The collected papers of Milton H. Erickson on hypnosis. I. The nature of hypnosis and suggestion.* New York: Irvington, pp. 498–530.

Erickson, M. (1940/1980). The translation of the cryptic automatic writing of one hypnotic subject by another in a trancelike dissociated state. In E. Rossi (Ed.), *The collected papers of Milton H. Erickson on hypnosis. III. Hypnotic investigation of psychodynamic processes.* New York: Irvington, pp. 177–187.

Erickson, M. (1949/1980). The successful treatment of a case of acute hysterical depression by a return under hypnosis to a critical phase of childhood. In E. Rossi (Ed.), *The collected papers of Milton H. Erickson on hypnosis. III. Hypnotic investigation of psychodynamic processes.* New York: Irvington, pp. 122–144.

Erickson, M. (1943a/1980). Experimentally elicited salivary and related responses to hypnotic visual hallucinations confirmed by personality reactions. In E. Rossi (Ed.), *The collected papers of Milton H. Erickson on hypnosis. II. Hypnotic alteration of sensory, perceptual and psychophysical process.* New York: Irvington, pp. 175–178.

Erickson, M. (1943b/1980). Hypnotic investigation of psychosomatic phenomena: A controlled experimental use of hypnotic regression in the therapy of an acquired food intolerance. In E. Rossi (Ed.), *The collected papers of Milton H. Erickson on hypnosis. II. Hypnotic alteration of sensory, perceptual and psychophysical processes.* New York: Irvington, pp. 169–174.

Erickson, M. (1943c/1980). Hypnotic investigation of psychosomatic phenomena: Psychosomatic interrelationships studied by experimental hypnosis. In E. Rossi (Ed.), *The collected papers of Milton E. Erickson on hypnosis. II. Hypnotic alteration of sensory, perceptual and psychophysical processes.* New York: Irvington, pp. 145–156.

Erickson, M. (1943d/1980). Investigation of psychosomatic phenomena: The development of aphasialike reactions from hypnotically induced amnesia. In E. Rossi (Ed.), *The collected papers of Milton H. Erickson on hypnosis. II. Hypnotic alteration of sensory, perceptual and psychophysical processes.* New York: Irvington, pp. 157–168.

Erickson, M. (1944/1980). An experimental investigation of the hypnotic subjects' apparent ability to become unaware of stimuli. In E. Rossi (Ed.), *The collected papers of Milton H. Erickson on hypnosis. II. Hypnotic alteration of sensory, perceptual and psychophysical processes.* New York: Irvington, pp. 33–50.

Erickson, M. (1952). Deep hypnosis and its induction. In L. LeCron (Ed.), *Experimental hypnosis.* New York: Macmillan, pp. 70–114.

Erickson, M. (1958/1980). Pediatric hypnotherapy. In E. Rossi (Ed.), *The collected papers of Milton H. Erickson on hypnosis. IV. Innovative hypnotherapy.* New York: Irvington, pp. 174–180.

Erickson, M. (1959/1980). Further clinical techniques of hypnosis: Utilization techniques. In E. Rossi (Ed.), *The collected papers of Milton H. Erickson on hypnosis. I. The nature of hypnosis and suggestion.* New York: Irvington, pp. 177–205.

Erickson, M. (1960a/1980). Breast development possibly influenced by hypnosis: Two instances and the psychotherapeutic results. In E. Rossi (Ed.), *The collected papers of Milton H. Erickson on hypnosis. II. Hypnotic investigation of sensory, perceptual and psychophysical processes.* New York: Irvington, pp. 203–206.

Erickson, M. (1960b/1980). Psychogenic alteration of menstrual functioning: Three instances. In E. Rossi (Ed.), *The collected papers of Milton H. Erickson on hypnosis. II. Hypnotic investigation of sensory, perceptual and psychophysical processes.* New York: Irvington, pp. 207–212.

Erickson, M. (1961/1980). Historical note on the hand levitation and other ideomotor techniques. In E. Rossi (Ed.), *The collected papers of Milton H. Erickson on hypnosis. I. The nature of hypnosis and suggestion.* New York: Irvington, pp. 135–138.

Erickson, M. (1963/1980). Hypnotically oriented psychotherapy in organic brain damage. In E. Rossi (Ed.), *The collected papers of Milton H. Erickson on hypnosis. Vol. IV. Innovative hypnotherapy.* New York: Irvington, pp. 283–311.

Erickson, M. (1967/1980). Further experimental investigation of hypnosis: Hypnotic and nonhypnotic realities. In E. Rossi (Ed.), *The collected papers of Milton H. Erickson on hypnosis. I. The nature of hypnosis and suggestion.* New York: Irvington, pp. 18–82.

Erickson, M. (1973/1980). A field investigation by hypnosis of sound loci importance in human behavior. In E. Rossi (Ed.), *The collected papers of Milton H. Erickson on hypnosis. II. Hypnotic alteration of sensory, perceptual and psychophysical processes.* New York: Irvington, pp. 121–141.

Erickson, M. (1977/1980). Control of physiological functions by hypnosis. In E. Rossi (Ed.), *The collected papers of Milton H. Erickson on hypnosis. II. Hypnotic alteration of sensory, perceptual and psychophysical processes.* New York: Irvington, pp. 179–191.

Erickson, M. (1980a). Explorations in hypnosis research. In E. Rossi (Ed.), *The collected papers of Milton H. Erickson on hypnosis. II. Hypnotic alteration of sensory, perceptual, and psychophysical process.* New York: Irvington, pp. 313–336.

Erickson, M. (1980b). Notes on minimal cues in vocal dynamics and memory. In E. Rossi (Ed.), *The collected papers of Milton H. Erickson on hypnosis. I. The nature of hypnosis and suggestion.* New York: Irvington, pp. 373–377.

Erickson, M. (1980c). *The collected papers of Milton H. Erickson on hypnosis (4 vols.).* Edited by Ernest Rossi. New York: Irvington.

Erickson, M. (1985). Memory and hallucination, Part I: The utilization approach to hypnotic suggestion. Edited with commentaries by Ernest Rossi. *Ericksonian Monographs, 1,* 1–21.

Erickson, M., & Erickson, E. (1941/1980). Concerning the nature and character of posthypnotic suggestion. In E. Rossi (Ed.), *The collected papers of Milton H. Erickson on hypnosis. I. The nature of hypnosis and suggestion.* New York: Irvington, pp. 381–411.

Erickson, M., Haley, J., & Weakland, J. (1959). A transcript of a trance induction with commentary. *The American Journal of Clinical Hypnosis, 2,* 49–84. (Also in Erickson, 1980c, Vol. I., pp. 206–257).

Erickson, M., & Rossi, E. (1974/1980). Varieties of hypnotic amnesia. In E. Rossi (Ed.), *The collected papers of Milton H. Erickson on hypnosis. Vol. III. Hypnotic investigation of psychodynamic processes.* New York: Irvington, pp. 71–90.

Erickson, M., & Rossi, E. (1975/1980). Varieties of double bind. *The American Journal of Clinical Hypnosis, 17,* 143–147.

Erickson, M., & Rossi, E. (1976/1980). Two-level communication and the microdynamics of trance and suggestion. In E. Rossi (Ed.), *The collected papers of Milton H. Erickson on hypnosis. I. The nature of hypnosis and suggestion.* New York: Irvington, pp. 430–451.

Erickson, M., & Rossi, E. (1979). *Hypnotherapy: An exploratory casebook.* New York: Irvington.

Erickson, M., & Rossi, E. (1980). The indirect forms of suggestion. In E. Rossi (Ed.), *The collected papers of Milton H. Erickson on hypnosis. I. The nature of hypnosis and suggestion.*

Erickson, M., & Rossi, E. (1981). *Experiencing hypnosis: Therapeutic approaches to altered states.* New York: Irvington.

Erickson, M., Rossi, E., & Rossi, S. (1976). *Hypnotic realities.* New York: Irvington.

Esdaile, J. (1850). *Mesmerism in India and its practical application in surgery and medicine.* Hartford, Conn.: S. Andrus & Son. (Republished and retitled: *Hypnosis in medicine and surgery. An introduction and supplemental reports on hypnoanesthesia by W. Kroger.* New York: Julian Press, 1957.)

Estabrooks, G. (1943). *Hypnotism.* New York: Dutton.

Evans, F. (1972). Hypnosis and sleep: Techniques for exploring cognitive activity during sleep. In E. Fromm, & R., Shor (Eds.), *Hypnosis: Research developments and perspectives.* Chicago: Aldine-Atherton, pp. 43–83.

Fischer, R. (1971a). Arousal-statebound recall of experience. *Diseases of the Nervous System, 32,* 373–382.

Fischer, R. (1971b). The "flashback": Arousal-statebound recall of experience. *Journal of Psychedelic Drugs, 3,* 31–39.

Fischer, R. (1971c). A cartography of ecstatic and meditative states. *Science, 174,* 897–904.

Fischer R. (1986). Toward a neuroscience of self-experience and states of self awareness and interpreting interpretations. In B. Wolman and M. Ullman (Eds.) *Handbook of States of Consciousness.* New York: Van Nostrand Reinhold Co.

Fischer, R., & Landon, G. (1972). On the arousal state-dependent recall of "subconscious" experience: Stateboundness. *British Journal of Psychiatry, 120,* 159–172.

Freud, A. (1946). *The ego and the mechanisms of defense.* New York: International Universities Press.

Gage, D. (1983). Mood state-dependent memory and the lateralization of emotion. Doctoral dissertation, Catholic University of America.

Gold, P., & McGaugh, J. (1975). A single trace, two-process view of memory storage processes. In D. Deutsch & J. Deutsch (Eds.), *Short-term memory.* New York: Academic Press.

Grinker, R., & Spiegel, J. (1945). *Men under stress.* Philadelphia, Blakiston.

Gruenewald, D. (1984). On the nature of multiple personality: Comparisons with hypnosis. *International Journal of Clinical & Experimental Hypnosis, 32*(2), 170–190.

Hilgard, E. (1977). *Divided consciousness: Multiple controls in human thought and action.* New York: Wiley.

Hilgard, E. (1981a). Further discussion of the HIP and the Stanford Form C: A reply by Frischolz, Spiegel, Tryon & Fischer. *The American Journal of Clinical Hypnosis, 24*(2), 106–107.

Hilgard, E. (1981b). The eyeroll sign and other scores of the Hypnotic Induction Profile (HIP) as related to the Stanford Hypnotic Susceptibility Scales, Form C (SHSS:C). *The American Journal of Clinical Hypnosis, 24* (2), 89–97.

Hilgard, E. (1984). Book review of *The collected papers of Milton H. Erickson on hypnosis. The International Journal of Clinical & Experimental Hypnosis, 32* (2), 257–265.

Hilgard, E., & Bower, G. (1975). *Theories of learning?* (4th Edition). Englewood Cliffs, New Jersey: Prentice-Hall.

Hilgard, J. (1972). Evidence for a developmental-interactive theory of hypnotic susceptibility. In E. Fromm & R. Shor (Eds.), *Hypnosis: Research developments and perspectives.* Chicago: Aldine-Atherton, pp. 387–398.

Hilgard, J. (1979). *Personality and hypnosis: A study of involvement.* (Rev. Ed.) Chicago: University of Chicago Press.

Hilgard, E., & Hilgard J. (1975). *Hypnosis in the relief of pain.* Los Altos, Calif.: Kaufman.

Hilgard, J., & LeBaron, S. (1984). *Hypnotherapy of pain: In children with cancer.* Los Altos, Calif.: Kaufman Press.

Hohmann, G. (1966). Some effects of spinal cord lesions on experienced emotional feelings. *Psychophysiology, 3,* 143–156.

Holloway, F. (1978). State-dependent retrieval based on time of day. In B. Ho, D. Richards, & D. Chute (Eds.), *Drug discriminatin and state-dependent learning.* New York: Academic Press, 319–343.

Hull, C. (1933). *Hypnosis and suggestibility.* New York: Appleton-Century Crofts.

Izquierdo, I. (1984). Endogenous state-dependency: Memory depends on the relation between the neurohumoral and hormonal states present after training at the time of testing. In G. Lynch, J. McGaugh, & N. Weinberg (Eds.), *Neurobiology of learning and memory.* New York: Guilford Press, pp. 65–77.

Izquierdo, I., & Dias, R. (1983a). Effect of ACTH, epinephrine, β-endorphin, naloxone, and of the combination of naloxone or β-endorphin with ACTH or epinephrine on memory consolidation. *Psychoneuroendocrinology, 8,* 81–87.

Izquierdo, I., & Dias, R. (1983b). Endogenous state dependency: memory regulation by post-training and pretesting administration of ACTH, β-endorphin, adrenaline and tyramine. *Brazilian Journal of Medical and Biological Research, 16,* 55–64.

Izquierdo, I., & Dias, R. (1983c). The influence of adrenergic receptor antagonists on the amnestic and anti-amnestic actions of adrenaline and tyramine. *Psychopharmacology, 80,* 181–183.

Kant, I. (1781). *Critique of pure reason.* New York; Doubleday.

Kripke, D. (1982). Ultradian rhythms in behavior and physiology. In F. Brown & R. Graeber (Eds.), *Rhythmic aspects of Behavior.*

Hillsdale, New Jersey: Erlbaum & Associates, pp. 313–344.

Kroger, W., & Fezler, W. (1976). *Hypnosis and behavior modification: Imagery conditioning.* Philadelphia, Pa.: Lippincott.

Kubie, L. (1943). Manual of emergency treatment for acute war neuroses. *War Medicine, 4,* 582–598.

LeCron, L. (Ed.) (1948). *Experimental hypnosis.* New York: Citadel Press.

Levinson, B. (1965). States of awareness during general anesthesia. *British Journal of Anesthesiology, 37,* 544–546.

Lienhart, J. (1984). Multiple personality and state-dependent learning. Doctoral dissertation, U.S. International University, San Diego, California.

Locke, S., & Hornig-Rohan, M. (Eds.) (1983). *Mind and immunity: Behavioral immunology. An annotated bibliography.* Auburndale, Mass.: Elliot Press.

Marañon, G. (1924). Contribution a l'etude de l'action emotive de l'adrenaline. *Revue Francaise d' Endocrinologie, 2,* 301–325.

McGaugh, J. (1983). Preserving the presence of the past: Hormonal influences on memory storage. *American Psychologist, 38*(2), 161–173.

McGaugh, J., Liang, K., Bennett, C., & Sternberg, D. (1984). Adrenergic influences on memory storage: Interaction of peripheral and central systems. In G. Lynch, J. McGaugh, & N. Weinberger (Eds.), *Neurobiology of learning and memory.* New York: Guilford Press, 313–332.

Meier, C. (1984). *The psychology of C. G. Jung: The unconscious and its empirical manifestations.* Translated by E. Rolfe. Boston: Sigo Press.

Nash, M., Lynn, S., Givens, D. (1984). Adult hypnotic susceptibility, childhood punishment, and child abuse. *International Journal of Clinical & Experimental Hypnosis, 32*(1), 6–11.

Neisser, U. (1982). *Memory observed: Remembering in natural contexts.* San Francisco: Freeman & Co.

Orne, M. (1972). On the simulating subject as a quasi-control group in hypnosis research: What, why and how? In E. Fromm & R. Shor (Eds.), *Hypnosis: Research development and perspectives.* Chicago: Aldine-Atherton.

Orne, M. (1979). The use and misuse of hypnosis in court. *International Journal of Clinical & Experimental Hypnosis, 27* (4), 311–341.

Overton, D. (1968). Dissociated learning in drug states (state-dependent learning). In D. Effron, J. Cole, J. Levine, & R. Wittenborn (Eds.), *Psychopharmacology: A review of progress, 1957-1967.* Public Health Service Publications, 1836. U.S. Government Printing Office, Washington, D.C., pp. 918–930.

Overton, D. (1972). State-dependent learning produced by alcohol and its relevance to alcoholism. In B. Kissen & H. Begleiter (Eds.), *The biology of alcoholism. Vol. II. Physiology and behavior.* New York: Plenum, 193–217.

Overton, D. (1973). State-dependent learning produced by addicting drugs. In S. Fisher & A. Freedman (Eds.), *Opiate addiction: Origins and treatment.* Washington D.C.: Winston, 61–75.

Overton, D. (1978). Major theories of state-dependent learning. In B. Ho, D. Richards, & D. Chute (Eds.), *Drug discrimination and state-dependent learning.* New York: Academic Press, pp. 283–318.

Peake, T., Van Noord, W., Abbott, W. (1979). Psychotherapy as an altered state of awareness: A common element. *Journal of Contemporary Psychotherapy, 10*(2), 98–104.

Perry, C. (1978). The Abbe Faria: A neglected figure in the history of hypnosis. In F. Frankel & H. Zamansky, *Hypnosis at its bicentenial.* New York: Plenum Press, pp. 37–45.

Pribram, K. (1969). The amnestic syndromes: Disturbances in coding? In G. Talland & N. Waugh (Eds.), *The pathology of memory.* New York: Academic Press.

Reik, T. (1949). *Listening to the third ear: The inner experience of a psychoanalyst.* New York: Farrar & Straus.

Reus, V., Weingartner, H., & Post, R. (1979). Clinical implications of state-dependent learning. *American Journal of Psychiatry, 136*(7), 927–931.

Reyher, J. (1977). Clinical and experimental hypnosis: Implications for theory and methodology. *Annals of New York Academy of Sciences, 296,* 222–237.

Ritterman, M. (1983). *Using hypnosis in family therapy.* San

Francisco: Jossey-Bass.

Rogers, C. (1985). Personal communication on the value of demonstration therapy. La Jolla, California.

Rosenzweig, M. (1984). Experience, memory, and the brain. *American Psychologist, 39*(4), 365–376.

Rosenzweig, M., & Bennett, E. (1984). Basic processes and modulatory influences in the stages of memory formation. In G. Lynch, J. McGaugh, & N. Weinberger (Eds.), *Neurobiology of learning and memory.* New York: Guilford Press, pp. 263–288.

Rossi, E. (1972/1985). *Dreams and the grow of personality: Expanding awareness in psychotherapy.* (2nd Edition) New York: Brunner/Mazel.

Rossi, E. (1973/1980). Psychological shocks and creative moments in psychotherapy. In E. Rossi (Ed.), *The collected papers of Milton H. Erickson on hypnosis. Vol. IV. Innovative hypnotherapy.* New York: Irvington, pp. 447–463.

Rossi, E. (1982). Hypnosis and ultradian cycles: A new state(s) theory of hypnosis? *The American Journal of Clinical Hypnosis, 25,* 21–32.

Rossi, E. (1986a). Altered states of consciousness in everyday life: The ultradian rhythms. In B. Wolman (Ed.), *Handbook of states of consciousness.* New York: Van Nostrand, pp. 97–132.

Rossi, E. (1986b). *The psychobiology of mind-body healing: New concepts of therapeutic hypnosis.* New York: Norton.

Rossi, E., & Ryan, M. (Eds.) (1985). *Life reframing in hypnosis. Vol. II. The seminars, workshops and lectures of Milton H. Erickson.* New York: Irvington.

Rossi, E., Ryan, M., & Sharp, F. (Eds.) (1983). *Healing in hypnosis. Vol. I. The seminars, workshops and lectures of Milton H. Erickson.* New York: Irvington.

Sarbin, T. (1950). Contributions to role-taking theory: I. Hypnotic behavior. *Psychological Review, 57,* 255–270.

Sarbin, T., & Andersen, M. (1967). Role theoretical analysis of hypnotic behavior. In J. Gordon (Ed.), *Handbook of clinical & experimental hypnosis.* New York: MacMillan.

Sarbin, T., & Coe, W. (1972). Hypnosis: A social psychological analysis of influence communication. New York: Holt, Rinehart, & Winston.

Sarbin, T., & Coe, W. (In press). *Hypnotic behavior: The psychology of influence communication*. New York: Holt, Rinehart & Winston.

Schachter, S., & Singer, J. (1962). Cognitive, social, & physiological determinants of emotional states. *Psychological Review, 69,* 379–399.

Sears, R. (1932). An experimental study of hypnotic anesthesia. *Journal of Experimental Psychology, 15,* 1–22.

Selye, H. (1974). *Stress without distress*. New York: Signet.

Selye, H. (1976). *The stress of life*. New York: McGraw-Hill.

Selye, H. (1982). History and present status of the stress concept. In L. Goldberger, & S. Breznitz (Eds.), *Handbook of stress*. New York: MacMillan, pp. 7–20.

Sheehan, P. (1972). Hypnosis and manifestations of "imagination." In E. Fromm & R. Shor (Eds.), *Hypnosis: Research developments and perspectives*. Chicago: Aldine-Atherton.

Sheehan, P., & Perry, C. (1976). *Methodologies of hypnosis*. Hillsdale, New Jersey: Erlbaum.

Swanson, J., & Kinsbourne, M. (1979). State-dependent learning and retrieval. In J. Kihlstrom, & F. Evans (Eds.), *Functional disorders of memory*. Hillsdale, New Jersey: Erlbaum Publishers.

Tart, C. (1972). Measuring the depth of an altered state of consciousness with particular reference to self-report scales of hypnotic depth. In E. Fromm & R. Shor (Eds.), *Hypnosis: Research developments and perspectives*. Chicago: Aldine-Atherton, pp. 445–477.

Tart, C. (1983). *States of consciousness*. El Cerrito, Calif.: Psychological Processes.

Tinterow, M. (1970). *Foundations of hypnosis*. Springfield, Illinois: C. C. Thomas.

Tulving, E. (1972). Episodic and semantic memory. In E. Tulving & W. Donaldson (Eds.), *Organization of memory*. New York: Academic Press.

Tulving, E. (1985). How many memory systems are there? *American Psychologist, 40*(4), 385–398.

Vaihinger, H. (1911). *Philosophy of the as-if.* Translated by C. K. Ogden in 1924. London: Routledge.

274

Watkins, J. (1949). *Hypnotherapy of the war neurosis.* New York: Ronald.

Watzlawick, P. (Ed.) (1984). *The invented reality.* New York: W.W. Norton.

Weiner, H. (1977). *Psychobiology and human disease.* New York: Elsevier.

Weingartner, H. (1977). Human state-dependent learning. In B. Ho, D. Richards, & D. Chute (Eds.), *Drug discrimination and state-dependent learning.* New York: Academic Press.

Weitzenhoffer, A. (1957). *General techniques of hypnotism.* New York: Grune & Stratton.

Weitzenhoffer, A. (1978). What did he (Bernheim) say? In F. Frankel & H. Zamansky (Eds.), *Hypnosis at its bicentennial.* New York: Plenum Press.

White, R. (1941). A preface to the theory of hypnotism. *Journal of Abnormal and Social Psychology, 36,* 477–505.

Wilber, K. (1982). *The spectrum of consciousness.* Wheaton, Illinois: Quest Books.

Zeig, J. (1980a). Symptom prescription and Ericksonian principles of hypnosis and psychotherapy. *The American Journal of Clinical Hypnosis, 23*(1), 16–22.

Zeig, J. (1980b). Symptom prescription techniques: Clinical applications using elements of communication. *The American Journal of Clinical Hypnosis,23*(1), 23–33.

Zeig, J. (Ed.) (1985). *Ericksonian psychotherapy. Vol. I. Structures.* New York: Brunner Mazel.

Zornetzer, S. (1978). Neurotransmitter modulation and memory: A new neuropharmacological phrenology? In M. Lipton, A. di Mascio, and K. Killam (Eds.), *Psychopharmacology: A generation of progress.* New York: Raven Press.

INDEX

*State-Dependent Memory, Learning, and Behavior

280

Comfort
creating 185-186
evoking physiological 107-109
inducing paradoxically 186-188
pregnancy fears and 181
protecting 121-122
utilizing 161-163
"Common Everyday Trance" 211
Complex
Freud's use of 233
Jung's association experiments
and 233-234
Concentration
Abbe Faria's use of 250-251
(Table 7), 254
Conditioning
SDMLB 212-213 (Table 2)
Confusion 129-132
Conscious (consciousness) (mind)
coexistence with unconscious
74-75
"divided" 207
opposite messages to 170-171
questions and 175-177, 201-202
"set" 127-128
talking to 140-141
Contact lenses 192-194
Context(s)
altered 214-215 (Table 3)
bound 213, 225
cues and 15-17
experimental work and 54
frames of reference as 236
free 225
hypnosis and 214-215 (Table 3)
hypnotic rapport and 48
memory and 52-54, 212-213
(Table 2)
natural 224
physical and semantic 212-213
(Table 2), 214-215 (Table 3),

222-227, 237
real-life 236
recall and 214-215, 224
SDMLB 212-213 (Table 2)
social and cultural 212-213
(Table 2), 214-215 (Table 3),
222-227
therapeutic 232, 237
Control (controlling)
hypnotic 1-65
knee jerk 14-15
nonhypnotic 2-4
voluntary 2-4
Conversation 140-141
Convulsions
historical hypnosis and 249,
250-251 (Table 7), 252
Couples
biological rhythms and 217
Creative unconscious 158-160
Criminal applications of hypnosis
63
Critique of Pure Reason 230
Cues
altered 213, 214-215 (Table 3)
behavioral 22-24, 186-188
cognitive and somatic 213
context and 15-17
distinctive (*See also* Acquisition
conditions) 213, 215
endogenous state-dependency
221
evoking statebound information
236
hypnosis and 214-215 (Table 3),
236, 237, 240-241 (Table 4)
internal 237
matching 215
minimal 24-25, 49-50, 186-188
neurobiology of memory &
learning 240-241 (Table 4)

297